LINCOLN'S WRATH

FIERCE MOBS, BRILLIANT SCOUNDRELS AND A PRESIDENT'S MISSION TO DESTROY THE PRESS

Jeffrey Manber and Neil Dahlstrom

SOURCEBOOKS, INC.®
NAPERVILLE, ILLINOIS

Published by Sourcebooks, Inc.
P.O. Box 4410, Naperville, Illinois 60567–4410
(630) 961–3900
FAX: (630) 961–2168
www.sourcebooks.com

Library of Congress Cataloging-in-Publication Data

Manber, Jeffrey.
   Lincoln's wrath / Jeffrey Manber and Neil Dahlstrom.
      p. cm.
   Includes bibliographical references and index.
   ISBN-13: 978-1-4022-0398-5
   ISBN-10: 1-4022-0398-5
   1. United States--History--Civil War, 1861-1865--Censorship. 2.
Lincoln, Abraham, 1809-1865--Relations with journalists. 3. Hodgson,
John, fl. 1843-1863. 4. Jeffersonian (West Chester, Pa. : 1855) 5.
Freedom of the press--United States--History--19th century. I.
Dahlstrom, Neil, 1976- II. Title.

E609.M36 2005
342.7308'53--dc22

2005027261

Printed and bound in the United States of America.
BVG 10 9 8 7 6 5 4 3 2 1

Such is the all but superstitious devotion of the people to the liberty of the press that these pernicious journals have, with the exception of a single instance in St. Louis, never been interfered with.

—Edward Everett, 1861

FREEDOM OF THE PRESS—There has been no interference with the usual publications of the press during 1862, beyond the orders to abstain from publishing information of intended military movements.

—American Annual Cyclopaedia of the Year 1862

ACKNOWLEDGMENTS

This book is the culmination of more than fifteen years of research, and included the assistance of many historians, archivists, librarians and scholars in both the United States and England. During that time, the process of doing research changed dramatically. When we started, much of our time was consumed photocopying crumbling pages of newspapers. By the end, we were taking advantage of tremendous digitization programs at the Library of Congress, Historical Society of Pennsylvania, and the Making of America project at the University of Michigan for access to original diaries, manuscripts, and newspapers.

Our thanks to Matt Hendon who read early versions of the manuscript and helped sort through countless issues of the *Jeffersonian*, helping us piece together the Hodgson story.

Always helpful were Diane Rofini and Pam Powell at the Chester County Historical Society, Laurie Rofini at the Chester County Archives and Records Services, Joan Lamphear at the Burlington County Historical Society, Elizabeth Fuller at the Rosenbach Museum and Library, and the archivists at the University of Delaware Special Collections. Historian Douglas Harper, who told part of the Hodgson story in his definitive book *West Chester to 1865: That Elegant & Notorious Place*, was a champion of the project from our first correspondence and wonderfully thrilled that the full story of the Hodgsons and the *Jeffersonian* was finally being told.

Lee Arnold, Jack Gumbrecht, and the staff of the Historical Society of Pennsylvania greatly assisted us as we worked to uncover the correspondence, speeches, and editorials of men seemingly long forgotten by historians.

The Albany Public Library, New York Public Library, and British Library in London proved invaluable as we traced the movements of some of the most agile newspapermen of the nineteenth century, and traced public opinion of the Civil War from the United States and abroad.

It should be noted that to a surprising degree, many of the antiwar newspapers of the Civil War are located only in the historical society of the publishing town. It is often overlooked how tenuous are the links to our past. Assuring the preservation of full collections of those newspapers that may not have supported the Lincoln administration is as critical as preserving those more popular.

Without John Willig of Literary Services, Inc., who immediately recognized the timeliness of the story, and his son Josh who championed the project, we would not have had the privilege of seeing this book in print.

We would also like to thank the entire team at Soucebooks, who have been incredibly open in respecting our thoughts on all aspects of the book. Peter Lynch provided superb editorial direction and guidance, helping us to refine our story in ways that had previously eluded us. Michelle Schoob was diligent in her efforts to ensure the integrity of both content and design. Ewurama Ewusi-Mensah located obscure images, and Genene Murphy led us through the always-interesting area of public relations.

Special thanks go to our wives, Dana and Karen. Without your support this book would not have been possible.

CONTENTS

INTRODUCTION

The story in the following pages is a classic Washington whodunit: a story of mystery, of greed, of power gone amuck. That it took place during the Civil War and involves a man named Abraham Lincoln only adds to the intrigue.

The facts are simple to relate.

At the start of the Civil War, pro-Southern newspaper editors and writers like John Hodgson of West Chester, Pennsylvania, publicly criticized the early actions of the Lincoln administration. These editors believed that the Southern states had every right to invoke secession. States' rights were paramount to national government, just as Thomas Jefferson had long ago preached, so if South Carolina wanted out of the Union, let it go. There were dozens of antiwar newspapers throughout the Northern states that brazenly took on the new president and his war policy. There was little fear, of course, as freedom of speech is a basic right under our Constitution.

But Lincoln, as the men would soon learn, was playing by a new set of rules. On August 19, 1861, John Hodgson's newspaper office was broken into and all the equipment was destroyed. Assessing the damage, it seemed clear that this outspoken editor would never be able to publish his beloved *Jeffersonian* again.

Who ordered the newspaper destroyed?

If there were eyewitnesses that evening, no one was talking. After all, Hodgson's *Jeffersonian* was an eyesore to the town of West Chester. Each week Hodgson's editorials threw barbed criticisms at the Civil War and at Lincoln personally. He wrote colorfully against those who swarmed around the president, calling them sycophants and pimps. His editorials were works of spiteful art, sparing no politician his sarcasms and insights.

As we researched Hodgson for this book, it was difficult for us to have sympathy for him and his *Jeffersonian* newspaper. The editor displayed all the crass racism too common among many of the pro-Southern supporters, and his writings displayed a fear for any change from the status quo of a nation divided by slavery. Yet we have also grown to admire this man, who picked up the pieces of his destroyed newspaper and prepared to resume publishing, risking the mob violence sweeping the Northern states.

Then an extraordinary event took place. On Friday afternoon, August 23, 1861, as Hodgson worked to rebuild his paper, the *Jeffersonian* was closed again. But this time it was not by an angry mob. Instead, the newspaper was shut down by two federal marshals acting on orders, they said, from the president of the United States.

At this point, we discovered, the mystery moved to an entirely different level, involving break-ins, cover-ups, and political abuse reaching all the way to the top offices in Washington.

Did Abraham Lincoln really order his operatives to shut down this anti-war newspaper? And, if not Lincoln, were those in power really concerned about what John Hodgson was saying?

This is the true story of a forgotten battle of the Civil War, one that pitted antiwar Northerners against the power of the mighty Lincoln administration. It is the recounting of the "Summer of Rage," of 1861, when the Republicans around Lincoln systemically shut down all dissenting voices. Editors and writers of antiwar newspapers were subjected to myriad punishments. Some were tarred and feathered, some were thrown into federal prisons and held without trial for months at a time. Others were forced to change their opinions and publish only glowing praise of government actions.

On one level this is the story of an angry, emotional, colorful, and stubborn bigot who was also a passionate believer in the freedom of the press. He took on an American icon named Lincoln, who at the time was not yet the icon we think of today, and who to many was merely a tyrant.

It is also a window into the Lincoln administration's policies on civil rights, and what was destroyed in the name of preserving the Union. And it is a surprising new look at the great Lincoln as a politician extremely sophisticated at the use of the media. We have come to believe that Lincoln was our first "media" president, adroitly manipulating the press and public opinion.

For ten years we have read these antiwar newspapers and pored through the personal diaries and letters of a forgotten generation of editors, writers, and publishers. We have come to feel their fear of taking on an administration in the midst of the Civil War, and their anger that the Constitution was being trampled.

The elasticity of the Constitution in a time of unparalleled threats is the very issue confronting us again today. How far can we go in criticizing a president during a national crisis? How far can the president go to preserve the United States, and what does it mean to give up rights in the name of security?

Interestingly, after all these years, we as authors disagree as to whether the draconian actions of Lincoln and his administration in muzzling dissenting voices were justified. Perhaps it is right that two historians cannot agree, for the role of the Constitution in a crisis is a basic American dilemma. Is the Constitution only to be obeyed during times of national peace? Hodgson thought not, and perhaps we are a stronger nation today because of the personal courage of these Civil War-era editors.

Prior to its outbreak, John Hodgson thought a lot about the consequences the coming Civil War would have on our country. Yet, though he was spitting mad at Lincoln's willingness to shut down any loyal opposition, Hodgson still wore the optimism so common among Americans in times of crisis. Days after the first shots were fired opening the great Civil War, this antiwar patriot sat at his writing desk and penned that "we have hoped and prayed that this terrible thing might pass, and that not a single star should be soiled by a drop of blood; but the die is cast.

"God grant that out of the midst of all this gloom a more loyal, faithful, glorious Union of the whole brotherhood of States may rise in majesty, power, and harmony."

Part One

FIRE IN THE NORTH

In the opening months of the Civil War, the battlefront between the Blue and Gray troops swiftly extended from land deep in Virginia to the Union's maritime blockade of the Carolinas. Another sort of battle also was in full swing; that of the Union's efforts to suppress any dissenting voice within the remaining loyal states.

On Wednesday, August 28, 1861, readers in New York were provided a rare overview of the extent of the Lincoln administration's efforts to shut down the peace movement. They certainly knew of mob action in their own city, but often only rumors swirled regarding censorship and mob violence elsewhere. Above all else, everyone wanted to know who was behind this unprecedented assault on our cherished civil liberties—a local gang of thugs or the men working in the new administration in Washington.

New York Herald
August 28, 1861
An Accounting

Northern papers destroyed by mob

Jeffersonian, West Chester, PA   *Standard,* Concord, NH
Sentinel, Easton, PA   *Democrat,* Bangor, ME
Farmer, Bridgeport, CT   *Clinton Journal,* KS
Democrat, Canton, OH

Northern secession papers suppressed by civil authority

Catholic Herald, Philadelphia, PA   *Christian Observer,* Philadelphia, PA

Northern secession papers died

Herald, Leavenworth, NJ   *American,* Trenton, NJ

Northern secession papers denied transportation in the mails

Journal of Commerce, NY   *Day Book,* NY
News, NY   *Freeman's Journal,* NY

Secession papers changed to Union

Eagle, Brooklyn, NY   *Democrat,* Haverhill, MA
Republican, St. Louis, MO

Secession papers yet in existence in the North
New York

Argus, Albany   *Republican,* Saratoga
News, NY   *Democrat,* Ithaca
Journal of Commerce, NY   *Gazette,* Hudson
Day Book, NY   *Union,* Watertown

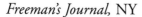

Freeman's Journal, NY
Prattsville News, Prattsville
Budget, Troy
Observer, Utica
Watchman, Greenport, LI
Courier, Syracuse
Advertiser, Lockport
Union, Troy
Herald, Sandy Hill

Gazette, Geneva
American Union, Ellicotville
Herald, Yonkers
Franklin Gazette
Democrat, Niagara
Democrat, Schenectady
Gazette, Malone
Sentinel, Mayville

New Jersey

Register, Patterson
Journal, Newark
Republican, Farmer
Journal, Belvidere

Democrat, Hunterdon
Herald, Newton
Gazette, Plainfield

Pennsylvania

Valley Spirit, Chambersburg
Patriot, Harrisburg
Catholic Herald, Philadelphia
Examiner, Washington
Star, Easton
Democrat, Allentown

Democrat, Coshocton
Republican, Pittsburgh
Union, Wilkesbarre
Herald, Honesdale
Republikaner (German), Allentown
Christian Observer, Philadelphia

Connecticut

Times, Hartford
Mercury, Middletown
Advertiser, Bridgeport

Register, New Haven
Sentinel, Middletown

Iowa

Bugle, Council Bluffs
Herald, Dubuque

State Journal, Iowa City
Citizen

New Hampshire

Patriot, Concord   *Gazette*

Wisconsin

Democrat, Kenosha   *See Bote (German)*, Milwaukee

Maine

Argus, Portland   *Watchman*

Ohio

Enquirer, Cincinnati   *Democrat*, Galian
Crisis, Columbus   *Empire*, Dayton

Minnesota

State, Winona

Rhode Island

Post, Providence

Illinois

Union, Cass county   *Times*, Bloomington
Democrat, Alton   *Signal*, Joliet

Indiana

Gazette, Evansville   *Sentinel*, Indianapolis
Journal, Terre Haute

Vermont

Spirit of the Age, Woodstock

Kansas

Bulletin, Atchison

Chapter One

THE NEWSPAPER PRESIDENT

I need not tell you that I have the highest confidence in Mr. Greeley [of the New York Tribune]. He is a great power. Having him firmly behind me will be as helpful to me as an army of one hundred thousand men.[1]

—Abraham Lincoln

As sure as there is a God in Heaven, we will have fearful times in our country should the North elect Lincoln. His election will not only be an intentional insult to the South, but will be regarded as a declaration of war.[2]

—John Hodgson
Publisher, the *Jeffersonian*, West Chester, Pennsylvania

Monday, August 19, 1861, was a quiet and unassuming night in the Philadelphia suburb of West Chester, Pennsylvania—an ordinary night in an extraordinary time. The passions unleashed by a war that pitted neighbors against one another had caused tensions to run raw, but tonight it was the heavy humidity and recent rains that were creating discomfort.

Most of the town was nestled inside the brick and timber homes that fronted the side streets and dotted the alleyways of this typical Pennsylvania town. It was the perfect cover. Darkness had consumed the intersections of commerce, the moonlight created shadows of low buildings that disappeared into the darkness. Through the shadows, as the clock on the towering courthouse nearby read almost midnight, a faceless group of men slid unnoticeably into the borough.

Military battles of the nineteenth century were often well defined, both in their origin and location. The rules of conduct were well understood by both parties and so defined were the boundaries that many women and politicians from Washington enjoyed watching the first battle of Bull Run, just outside of Manassas, Virginia, safe from harm and protected by centuries of tradition and etiquette. Yet just a month or so later, a different sort of battle was taking place, one involving the blurred boundaries more closely associated with modern warfare.

For the intent of these unknown loyal Union men was to destroy the printing office of a legally publishing newspaper that had for years passionately argued politics between its eight pages. Amidst the high emotions of the day, its sole crime was that it stood squarely against the administration of Abraham Lincoln and its prosecution of the war. The *Jeffersonian* supported the radical wing of the Democratic Party, giving its readers a regular stream of reasons to support the breakaway Confederacy over the Lincoln Republicans. For its opinions, the paper apparently was destined to be crushed, its publication stopped, and the fear of God put into the heart of not only the local family that owned the paper, the Hodgsons, but so too all the subscribers who still opposed the administration's conduct of the war.

Imagine the total destruction of a local newspaper in any small town in America today. The impact on small-town publishers across the country; the fear that would fall over local subscribers to the paper; the chilling effect on shop owners who advertised and even those who patronized the newspaper's advertisers. No matter the illegality, it would certainly cause a chill for any opponents of the administration.

On this hot and oppressive evening, the actions of this mob achieved their most immediate objective. Within several hours in the dead of night, the *Jeffersonian's* vital subscription lists were destroyed, the printing type thrown out of the window, and the huge printing press broken as best as possible by the sheer strength of the men. As such, it appeared a simple act of thuggery. But the actions on this evening also set in motion one of the most calculated attacks on American liberty since the exploding cannon and dull thud of Revolutionary muskets ceased.

Given the lack of witnesses, given the military precision with which the attack took place, it would be reasonable to believe, or to worry, that this action was not the work of a bunch of drunken hoodlums seeking some thrills. One is left, therefore, wondering what group of powerful officials endorsed the action, paid the men, and assured its success in shutting down the vocal Democratic newspaper. And if a conspiracy was afoot, how high into the Republican Party was such violence condoned? To the Philadelphia party organization, or on a state level in Pennsylvania, or right into the executive mansion in Washington, DC?

It is not as outrageous as it may initially seem to believe that the destruction of dissenting voices was in accordance with the wishes of the president. Abraham Lincoln had already made it clear in the opening months of the Civil War that his first priority was the preservation of the Union—at any cost.

A critical component of the complex Lincoln personae is overlooked in discussions of the Civil War. With his election, voters handed the reins of the government to a man who in many ways was our first media politician. Lincoln was a man who understood the press and continually manipulated its chief editors to support his policies. He was the politician who helped create the modern American journalist, which continues to hold incredible influence over public opinion. He was a man who capitalized on the media's powers and its rewards and suffered from its inherent failings. An understanding of this unique politician must include an understanding of his unique perception of the power of the nineteenth-century media. Lincoln grasped its emerging power, stating later in the war that "no man, whether he be private citizen or president of the United States, can successfully carry on a controversy with a great newspaper, and escape destruction, unless he owns a newspaper equally great, with a circulation in the same neighborhood."[3] This statement goes far to explain many of the decisions Lincoln made as president, holding close some newspaper publishers and avoiding others he considered unimportant to his presidency.

During this period, despite the relationships between politicians and newspapermen, the ability of a newspaper to expose hypocrisy or express an opposing view was as vital as it is today. Argument can be made that it was more vital, as there was no other outlet for news coverage. The country, in many ways, ran on the latest headlines from New York, Chicago, St. Louis, and the country's other large cities.

Yet, newspapers of the era were mainly political organs. Support came from subscribers, of course, but equally vital was government advertising given to a favored newspaper representing the party in power. It was a symbiotic relationship between editor and politician, and no cabinet was more intertwined with the newspapers of the day than that of Lincoln's.

Abraham Lincoln had not come late to understanding the power of newspapers to sway public opinion. Lincoln, whether or not he knew of the specific events unfolding that hot summer night in West Chester, was far from innocent when it came to manipulating the press to achieve his own political agenda. Adroit use of the media of the day to achieve his political objectives was something that separated this Illinois politician, far before his rendezvous with history, from many of his political challengers.

The times forced Lincoln to rely on newspapers as no president ever had. He also gave the media access as never before. The fact that the media was given special mention—and protection—by the founders in the very first amendment of the Constitution set the stage for the incestuous relationship between politicians and the press. Lincoln's cabinet was composed of the greatest politicians of the day and each member prospered from robust, mutually beneficial business and political relationships with some of the country's greatest editors. Like never before or since, most of the cabinet owed their political success and their fortunes to publishing.

Of course, other politicians had manipulated newspapers before Lincoln, understanding the power and dangers of the press. Alexander Hamilton well knew the power of the newspaper, founding the *New York Evening Post* in 1800 to push his political agenda. George Washington also understood newspapers, considering them "such easy vehicles of knowledge, more happily calculated than any other, to preserve the liberty, stimulate the industry, and meliorate the morals of an enlightened and free people." But Washington also realized the dangers, writing in 1792 that "if the government and the officers of it are to be the constant theme for newspaper abuse…it will be impossible, I conceive, for any man living to manage the helm or to keep the machine together."[4]

Lincoln, though, controlled the medium like no one before him, immersing himself in the politics of the newspaper business from the earliest stages of his career. In 1832, he introduced himself through the columns of the *Sangamo Journal,* telling readers that every man has ambition, though "how far I shall succeed in gratifying this ambition is yet to be developed."[5] In the coming decades, he learned the power of the press in reaching far beyond the limitations of a stump speech or athenaeum lecture hall.

In early 1856, Lincoln appeared at an editor's banquet in Decatur, Illinois, where he gave a typically modest but calculating speech. He started with an apology for appearing before so many editors, himself the only man present who was not an editor, followed by a self-deprecating story that brought raucous laughter. He had already gained a widespread reputation in Illinois for his humor and for his homely appearance, both of which he used for dramatic affect. The editors probably knew afterward that they had a candidate who could attract voters.[6]

Two years later, in April 1858, four Chicago editors propped up Lincoln as the next senator of Illinois. At the state convention in Springfield in June, they offered a resolution that "Abraham Lincoln is the first and only choice of the Republicans of Illinois for the United States Senate, as the successor of Stephen A. Douglas." Lincoln was prepared for the occasion, and that night delivered his now famous "house divided" speech. When he was finished, Lincoln handed the speech to Horace White of the *Chicago Tribune* with instructions to take it to the office of the *Illinois State Journal* for publication. Lincoln soon arrived himself and proofed the copy, reinserting the famous phrase, "A house divided against itself cannot stand," and the sentences that followed, counter to the prodding of the editors who thought it weak. Soon the speech was being printed throughout Illinois, including in pamphlet form, before at last seeing publication in Horace Greeley's *New York Tribune.*[7]

During his legendary debates with Senator Stephen A. Douglas in 1858, Lincoln further developed his contacts with the editors who now clamored to reprint his speeches in full. Lincoln eventually lost the election to Douglas, but had intentions of salvaging his campaign message in printed form for the masses. Throughout 1859, Lincoln worked to find a publisher for a collected volume of the debates. The lawyer-turned-politician had collected the reprints from various newspapers and made his own edits, as editors had the tendency to make their own changes. To make the publication legitimate, Lincoln offered Douglas the chance to also edit his own speeches prior to publication, though Lincoln refused to let anyone else have control of the volume he had amassed until after publication. Lincoln sought to have it printed in Springfield so the scrapbook collection would never leave his control, and not a single word could be changed without his consent.[8]

There was also a darker side to Lincoln's use of the press. In May 1859, Lincoln secretly financed a German-language newspaper in Springfield, the *Illinois Staats-Anzeiger*. Brokered by banker Jacob Bunn, Lincoln paid four hundred dollars for the press, type, and equipment and hired Theodore Canisius as publisher. Lincoln went with Canisius despite a warning from a state senator, and one of his future presidential campaign managers, Norman Judd. Less than two weeks prior to the deal, Judd told Lincoln "what you know that Canisus [sic] is a leach. He sucked more blood from you at Springfield" than had the entire state republican committee. Judd would know—he was its chairman.[9] Lincoln, as usual, kept to his original plan and secured the desired German voice. And Canisius even printed some of Lincoln's speeches in English.[10]

At the time, four hundred dollars was a princely sum for a man to spend on a foreign language newspaper, especially given he had just lost his bid for the Senate seat. Why did he purchase the paper? One explanation may be he wanted a vehicle to carry his speeches to German-speaking voters. The German immigrants were an important voting base in the far west, which was then Illinois and Missouri, as well as the German Jews of New York. They were attracted to the Republican Party because of their progressive views on society, and unlike other immigrant groups, notably the Irish Catholic, they did not consider freed blacks a threat to their job security.

Was it purchased to prepare for another Senate race, as is the oft-cited historical explanation? Or is it more likely to shore up his support among a group of immigrants who might be expected to support one of the other candidates for the Republican nomination, such as the famous Governor Seward of New York? Seward had been labeled by one observer as the "great hero of the foreign-born."[11] What better way to take on the Senate from New York than by having silent control of a key segment of the Senate's voting base? The timing of the purchase is also interesting as it strongly suggests that despite his defeat for the Senate seat, the Illinois politician was already planning a presidential run. The German community was often far more liberal on the question of slavery, and Lincoln may have felt that he had a good chance to take these voters for his own not-yet-announced presidential campaign. Whatever the answer, the purchase of the German paper shows Lincoln to be far more serious about his future political career, and the role of the press in it, than he let on.[12]

Even within the relaxed ethical confines of the time, the secret ownership of a newspaper was unusual. Most politicians were more open regarding their use of a local paper for self-serving purposes—it was expected and common. Lincoln seems to have had misgivings given the pains he took to conceal it from the voters. No public mention was made of the politician's support. No advertisements announced the paper's support for Lincoln or thanked him for his patronage. It was a relationship far more subtle than was common for the time. Perhaps it was the guilt of the conflict of interest that convinced him to sell the paper in 1860, or maybe the ambitious politician felt some embarrassment in being associated with an immigrant paper. Clearly his ownership was strictly politics—it had helped him reach some of the seven hundred thousand German immigrants living in the United States. Conveniently, Lincoln sold the paper one month after his election to the presidency, after which it was taken over by Gustav Koerner, another German whom Lincoln had known since 1842.[13] More likely, winning the presidency made continued ownership irrelevant.

Lincoln's rise to national power came about because of sophisticated use of the media, not passive luck. In early 1860, Philadelphia's most important paper, John Forney's *The Press,* did not even consider Lincoln a viable presidential contender. *The Press* had abandoned the Democratic Party and been reborn a Republican organ. Already it was an integral piece of the emerging Republican machine. Lincoln's name appeared nowhere in *The Press*'s published list of forty-five potential candidates for the nation's highest office. By the future president's absence, Forney showed he did not consider him a player in the national arena.[14]

Clearly a lot of work needed to be done, and undertaken by his team was a deliberate and very modern-looking marketing campaign. Highlights during February 1860 include the publication of a biography in a Pennsylvania newspaper, the speech at Cooper Union that introduced him to the critical New York media, and one of the earliest uses of the still-new invention of photography as a political campaign tool. Each reached a particular market and a particular voter class at an opportune time, and each made a dramatic impact on Lincoln's credibility heading into the Republican convention in mid-1860.

From the earliest moments of Lincoln's quest for the presidency, he was clearly not an unassuming player in the political media games of the day. He was deliberate, calculating, and forward thinking, perhaps at times even deceptive. Once the decision was made to run for the presidency, the courting of East Coast newspapers soon aggressively followed. The reality is a far cry from the image of a simple rail-splitter from Illinois who found himself suddenly in the national limelight. According to one of the lawyers who rode the Illinois judicial circuit with Lincoln, "He was wise as a serpent in the trial of a cause, but I have had too many scars from his blows to certify that he was harmless as a dove...Any man who took Lincoln for a simple-minded man would very soon wake up with his back in a ditch."[15]

When he made the decision in 1860 to seek the presidency, Lincoln and his friends stepped up their use of the press. In 1855, Edward Lewis moved from West Chester to Bloomington, Illinois, and was later introduced to Lincoln by his boyhood friend, Jesse Fell, one of Lincoln's campaign managers (and founder of the *Bloomington Pantograph*). Since he was mostly unknown on the East Coast, Lincoln sought to obtain a more national following as the Republican convention approached in May of 1860. Lewis and Fell worked with Lincoln to write a short biographical sketch for publication in eastern newspapers. Lincoln not only agreed to the sketch, but wrote the copy himself.

The *Chester County Times* in West Chester, Pennsylvania, had the privilege of being the first to print the modest biography on February 11, three months before the Republican National Convention in Chicago and only two weeks before Lincoln gave his famous speech at Cooper Union in New York.[16]

"If any description of me is thought desirable," Lincoln described himself to Pennsylvanians, "it may be said, I am, in height, six feet, four inches, nearly; lean in flesh, weighing on average one hundred and eighty pounds; dark complexion, with coarse black hair, and grey eyes—no other marks or brands recollected." The caricature-like biographical sketch of the prairie lawyer probably encouraged more curiosity than consideration, but it was only the first shot fired in a sophisticated campaign to bring Lincoln's name to the mass of voters in the eastern states.[17]

Two weeks after his biography hit the press in Pennsylvania, Lincoln appeared before one thousand five hundred people at the Cooper Union in Manhattan. The most important speech of his political career to date, Lincoln afterward headed to the office of the *New York Tribune* on the invitation of Horace Greeley, where despite the clock heading toward midnight, Lincoln pored over the proofs, making careful corrections. Four New York papers printed the speech the next day and a dedicated pamphlet with full text was soon available. At least one thousand seven hundred copies were being circulated in newspapers the next morning.[18]

Earlier that morning Lincoln slipped into the studio of Matthew Brady, on the corner of Broadway and Bleecker, and had his photograph taken. It was not Lincoln's first time before a camera, but like the speech he gave later that night, it was the most important. In due time, that photograph would be reproduced in hundreds of papers—*Harper's Weekly,* Frank Leslie's *Illustrated Newspaper,* and others. Currier & Ives would print lithographs, and dozens of other variations soon appeared throughout the country.[19]

Abraham Lincoln had at last been introduced to the voters.

Lincoln's rise to the highest office in the land, amidst heated sectional conflict, seemed appropriate for a country still enduring growing pains. No man would have been celebrated by the entire nation in 1860, but Lincoln was especially hated. Southerners despised his anti-Jeffersonian views, which Lincoln anchored on the merits of a stronger Union, predicting his subordination of the rights of states on the key issue of slavery. Northerners thought him the lesser of many evils. National politicians struggled to hide their jealousy for a man who was a newcomer on the national stage.

By the start of the Republican National Convention in May of 1860, Lincoln had positioned himself among the serious contenders. His opponents were among the most experienced, ambitious, and some would say villainous, men ever assembled to battle for their party's nomination. Lincoln had been considered by some a strong vice presidential nominee, and a few newspapers even ventured to name him as a viable contender for the presidency. Lincoln was considered a viable candidate not because he was necessarily the best, but because the others would tear each other apart, giving Lincoln the chance to become the one survivor to grab the nomination.[20]

Unlike his challengers, who relied more heavily on the tried-and-true method of confining their campaigning to back-room dealing with little public outreach, Lincoln had engineered a savvy campaign. Campaign biographies had been printed in eastern papers, his speech at Cooper Union was being read by hundreds of thousands of voters, and that portrait taken by Mathew Brady only hours before his Cooper Union speech was now being retouched and published in newspapers, broadsides, lithographs, and other formats. But in order to send the vote to the people, he had yet to be nominated by his party.[21]

The famous Chicago convention became a raucous free-for-all, and with all of the maneuverings of editors over the prior year, it at last became clear which candidate each supported. All the powerful newspaper publishers supporting the Republicans were coming together. William Cullen Bryant of the *New York Evening Post*, the man who had brought Lincoln to Cooper Union, was writing editorials on the corruption of Thurlow Weed; Joseph Medill, the

Washington correspondent of the *Chicago Tribune*, threw his support behind Lincoln; Horace Greeley was seemingly against Seward at all costs. On the other side was Henry Raymond of the *New-York Times*, as part of the Seward-Weed machine, among many others. All seemed to revolve in one way or another around the candidacy of the senator from New York, the honorable William Seward. Thurlow Weed's man had the most to gain, and the most to lose.

Behind the scenes, the Greeley-Weed feud was the battle to decide the nomination. At times, Seward, Lincoln, and the other candidates seemed merely pawns in their game. It was Greeley and Weed who were on the floor, corralling votes and promising favors, while the candidates sat at home waiting for news of any kind.

Weed's man was the five-foot-four-inch tall, beak-nosed, gray-haired William Seward, the undisputed leader of the Republican Party. Born in 1801, he was accepted to the New York bar shortly after college, was a state senator before the age of thirty, and in 1838 was elected to the first of two terms as governor. A Whig, he formed his earliest ties with *Albany Evening Journal* founder Thurlow Weed while governor, but was surprisingly defeated in 1842. He returned to private practice until going to the United States Senate on the coattails of his strong antislavery views. While there, he opposed the Missouri Compromise and eventually became an early convert of the new Republican Party while becoming more conciliatory toward slavery proponents, a move likely to court potential supporters for the Republican convention and subsequent election.

Seward and Lincoln first met in New England in 1848 during the presidential campaign, and even shared a hotel room on one occasion. Seward had done it all by the eve of the Civil War and was considered by most to be the only Republican nominee, if for nothing more than the sheer power and financing behind him. His greatest weakness was probably in his power, specifically the dominance of Weed, who had gained the resentment of most of New York's lesser editors. A track record of abolitionism also made him unattractive to those seeking a compromise with the South; so, too, his affinity for the many immigrants who poured into New York of German and Irish origin.[22] Whether an enlightened view or political necessity, it hardly mattered. The governor also suffered greatly in the run for the presidency because of his support for allowing public money to be used for Catholic education.[23] Lincoln was more of a clean slate, having only served ineffectually as a congressman some years before and known principally for losing to Douglas in a bid for the Senate.

To everyone's surprise, Horace Greeley, the well-known publisher of the *New York Tribune,* threw his weight behind the candidacy of sixty-seven-year-old Edward Bates of Missouri. The son of a Virginia planter, Bates saw limited service in the War of 1812 before practicing law in St. Louis. He served one term in Congress beginning in 1826, but lost his seat primarily due to his opposition of Andrew Jackson. A Whig, Bates was from a critical border state, an attractive and conciliatory proposition entering 1861 when the president-elect needed to assure the loyalty of those in the most wavering of states.

The Republican Party confronted a large slate, but many of the candidates would serve only as points of negotiation. Horace Greeley's sudden political interest in Lincoln after his Cooper Union speech, for example, was an attempt to divert support from Seward and Weed. Greeley had not brought Lincoln to New York, but quickly took Lincoln's success and made it as his own by giving Lincoln the pages of the *New York Tribune* for his speech's first printing. Greeley feared the election of Seward, backed by the Albany, New York, publisher, could well destroy his own growing New York publishing empire. Despite his efforts on Lincoln's behalf in New York, Greeley arrived in Chicago backing Edward Bates, a move stunning to all political observers as Bates had little following prior to being adopted by the

New York publisher. But Greeley was on the lookout for a more promising candidate.

The rivalry between Greeley and Weed followed them to the convention. Weed was responsible for the passage of a street railway bill in New York, passed to raise upwards of half a million dollars to finance Seward's campaign. Weed also controlled the New York delegation in Chicago, and blocked Greeley from representing the state of New York. Greeley did finally get to Chicago, but as a delegate from Oregon.[24]

The Lincoln camp was led by Judge David Davis, who early on received a telegram from his candidate: "I authorize no bargains and will be bound by none." Davis was heard to huff, "Lincoln ain't here, and don't know what we have to meet."[25]

Seward, as was the custom, waited in his upstate New York home for the results. Ready were the celebratory bands and cheering neighbors. With no speeches from the candidates, the politicking was left to their managers and the editors who supported them: they were often one and the same. Weed was offering to put big money behind Seward's campaign while Davis offered Simon Cameron of Pennsylvania a cabinet post on Lincoln's behalf. The bartering continued deep into the night.

On Thursday evening, Ward Hill Lamon and Jesse Fell ordered a local printer to create a large number of extra tickets and distributed them among Lincoln supporters, urging them to arrive early on Friday morning. When many of the Seward supporters arrived with legitimate tickets, they were turned away: the hall was already filled.[26]

On the first ballot, Seward received 173½ votes, Lincoln 102, Simon Cameron 50½, Salmon Chase 49, and Edward Bates 48 votes.

On the second ballot, the swing began. Seward picked up eleven more votes. Lincoln secured seventy-nine more, forty-eight of those votes coming from Pennsylvania. When the call was read, Lincoln was only one and a half votes shy of nomination. Meanwhile, Joseph Medill, the editor of the *Chicago Tribune* who had come out for Lincoln's presidency in February, put himself near the Ohio delegation. After the call, he whispered to their chairman, David Cartter, that if they could throw Lincoln over the top, Salmon Chase could have anything he wanted. Cartter stood up and passed four votes to Lincoln, putting him over the required 233 votes.[27]

Because it was improper for candidates to campaign and appear on their own behalf, Lincoln, who was sitting in Springfield, received the news of his nomination by telegraph.[28]

It is said that Seward, in the heat of the moment, declined an immediate offer of the vice presidency. Thurlow Weed wept as his life-long ambition crumbled. Both blamed the Pennsylvania delegation, including Governor Andrew Curtin, for the surprise downfall. Others involved included Greeley, who was seen whispering among the key delegations, and so too Lincoln's campaign team, who in the famous story disregarded Lincoln's admonitions and promised cabinet seats where necessary. They would sort that out later on.[29]

In one of the more celebrated political upsets, Lincoln's team of editors and supporters swiped the nomination from Seward. Now it was time to create an iconic image of the middle-class lawyer from Illinois. George Templeton Strong of Philadelphia provided an eyewitness account of the propaganda machine revving up for the candidacy of Lincoln right after the convention. Writing in his diary, the lawyer derides the emerging folklore about Abraham Lincoln. "Lincoln will be strong in the western states," Strong wrote, "but he is unknown here.

The *Tribune* and other papers commend him to popular favor as having had but six months' schooling in his whole life; and because he cut a great many rails, and worked on a flatboat in early youth; all which is somehow presumptive evidence of his statesmanship. The watchword of the campaign is already indicated. It is to be 'Honest Abe'"[30]

Having secured the nomination of his party, in part by masterfully using the press before his nomination, Lincoln the candidate immediately employed time-tested strategies during the presidential campaign, which he would win in November 1860. Besides his own attempts to proof all speeches before publication and add to the public support of so many editors nationwide, Lincoln also relied heavily on the secretive correspondence of secretary John Hay to spread his campaign message through several papers in New York, Missouri, and other northern states. Prior to joining Lincoln's staff, Hay was a correspondent for the *Missouri Democrat*. After joining Lincoln, he began writing secretly under the pen name "Encarte" for several newspapers in an effort to spread Lincoln's message. Hay's activities continued even after the campaign.[31]

Each faction of the party, whether strongly antislavery or more moderate, sought to determine the makeup of the cabinet as the Southern states began their withdrawal. But, as typical throughout his political career, Lincoln seemed most comfortable not with fellow politicians, but with editors and publishers vital to his political agenda. This can be understood given that many of the politicians closest to the president had their own political agendas; within a few years two members of his own cabinet were again angling to take the Republican nomination as in 1860.

Some of the newspaper men who became close to Lincoln were longtime friends, some acquaintances, and some new devotees looking to cash in on the spoils. He relied on daily dispatches from New York, Philadelphia, and Chicago to learn what was going on at the front and within the government, and to a surprising degree took the advice of the private letters of editors for patronage recommendations and for the pulse of the country. Edward Everett, the noted public speaker, referred to newspapers as "for good or evil, the most powerful influence that acts on the public mind." The newspapers, backed by competing editors, could whip the public into a frenzy. Their support for the war was absolutely critical, and Lincoln knew that.[32] Lincoln would spend countless hours reading dispatches in the telegraph office and ask the multitude of reporters that hung outside of his office for the latest news. Lincoln received three Washington papers every morning, the *Daily Morning Chronicle,* the *National Republican,* and the *Evening Star.* His personal secretaries, John Nicolay and John Hay, fingered through more than a dozen every morning to report items of interest to the president.[33]

Like their president, the public also responded in a very modern way with a hunger for the latest news. For the nineteenth-century news junkie, the capitol developed its own version of twenty-four-hour, seven-days-a-week access. The Baltimore dailies were sold by hundreds of newsboys every morning by six o'clock; these included the *American, Sun,* and *Clipper.* The major Washington newspapers, the *National Intelligencer* and *Chronicle,* were peddled an hour later at seven. The Philadelphia train arrived at eleven, bringing *The Press* and the *Inquirer.* At three in the afternoon, the Washington afternoon papers were on the streets, followed every thirty minutes by later editions if warranted. The arrival of the New York train at five in the evening brought the day's *Herald, Tribune,* and *New-York Times,* which were "howled about the streets, depots, landing camps and hospitals till night; this closes the day's news."[34]

Some of the publishing icons—whether the Blair family of Maryland and Missouri, Horace Greeley of the *New York Tribune,* Thurlow "Boss" Weed of New York's *Albany Evening Journal,* John

Forney of Philadelphia's *The Press* and DC's *Washington Chronicle,* or a young Democrat like twenty-nine-year-old Thomas Kinsella of the *Brooklyn Eagle*—had more influence on a community than their elected representatives, and reaped their profits from lucrative government contracts. And though there seemed to be enough for everyone, no one could find contentment.[35]

After winning the presidential election in November, the real politicking began as Republicans sought to climb into Lincoln's good graces, some following up on promises made to them at the convention. What followed has become something of an American legend, as the chief politicians of the day fought to include themselves but not their competitors in the new administration.

In casting about to fill a cabinet that would at best keep the Union together and more realistically prevent further defections from the Union, Lincoln understood that the appointments of those who had also fought for the Republican nomination could not be avoided. They were indeed politically qualified, despite their motives or their agendas. By the time of his inauguration in March 1861, Lincoln had assembled his powerful and independently minded cabinet of advisors: Secretary of State William Seward, Secretary of Treasury Salmon Chase, Attorney General Edward Bates, Secretary of War Simon Cameron, Secretary of the Navy Gideon Welles, Postmaster General Montgomery Blair, and Secretary of Interior Caleb Smith.

Never before had a president assembled a cabinet composed of his strongest political competitors. Those who lost at the convention, Seward, Cameron, Chase, and Bates, were now the top choices to fill Lincoln's cabinet. The inescapable tension that plagued Lincoln early in the war was predictable but unavoidable. Lincoln himself thought that much of his presidency had been given away during the convention. "They have gambled me all around, bought and sold me a hundred times," Lincoln wrote of the promises made by his campaign managers to secure his nomination. Many of his cabinet members were the result of those favors.[36]

Months after his selections, Lincoln's choices were still being debated by both Republicans and Democrats. Lincoln's position was unenviable, as several of the men who would join his cabinet— specifically Seward, Chase, Bates, and Cameron—were on paper better qualified for the job than he was. Each was politically strong, had loyal followings, and would bring their own power structure into the White House. Each also had strong commercial relations with major Republican newspapers. In the coming years, it would be difficult to determine whether decisions were made for public or personal interest.

The team of politician William Seward and publisher Thurlow Weed was the president's greatest challenge. The efforts of many an editor, Horace Greeley and William Cullen Bryant top among them, to block Seward's presidential bid was well known. For these editors, the issues were not often ideological; after all, both Governor Seward and Greeley were determined to end slavery and both agreed on many trade and economical issues. Rather, it was often based on personal rivalries springing from conflicts in their publishing endeavors.

Despite his loss to the Illinois politician, Seward thought Lincoln not up to the task before him, and, imagining himself as a new prime minister of the Union, pushed the president hard for decisive action in the early months, while he prepared for the chief executive's imminent failure. Seward famously saw himself as a modern day chief of staff, operational officer, and chief politician of the ruling party, all rolled into one. And everyone knew it. Seward later would tell the British minister in Washington, Lord Lyons, that he could ring a bell on his desk to order the arrest of anyone in the United States.[37]

Seward's partner Weed was the boss of the Republican Party in New York. Weed was also the publisher of the influential *Albany*

Evening Journal. The two men could be said to have long represented "big business," including the manufacturers of New England and the banks of New York. The relationship was so close that Seward told the cabinet members that "Seward is Weed and Weed is Seward. What he says, I endorse. We are one."[38]

Even during this busy period, Lincoln's hands-on approach with the press could be seen. During the cat and mouse game of pulling together his cabinet, a small story appeared in the Blair family's *Missouri Democrat,* (which was, despite the name, a Republican organ, having followed the Blairs' migration from the old to the new party). The article stated with civility that "we have the permission of both Mr. Lincoln and Mr. Bates to say that the latter will be offered and accept a place in the new cabinet, subject of course, to the action of the Senate," and, in a further bit of tease, the column added that Lincoln was still unsure which cabinet position to offer the St. Louis lawyer, whether secretary of state or attorney general.[39]

Lincoln, possibly through his secretary John Hay, was the author of this political piece, putting pressure on Seward's backers.[40]

Indecision and the bickering of cabinet members—still bitter that they were serving under the Illinois lawyer—occupied the initial months of the Lincoln presidency. The prospects of appointing men like Seward and Cameron, whose careers were indebted to powerful editors, was indeed a dangerous but lucrative business, with far reaching implications. Not only were Lincoln's cabinet members indebted to editors, in most cases they were powerful editors themselves at one time during their rise to national office. Both Simon Cameron of Pennsylvania and Ohio governor Salmon Chase are two such critical examples. Cameron had a reputation for unethical business practices, and oftentimes the politician seemed blissfully immune to the raging policy issues of the day. For him, public office was a means to a personal fortune, and one such means to that path was an active role in newspaper interests. Cameron's media interests were wide and deep. By the time he was twenty-two, Cameron had already become the editor of two Pennsylvania papers, the *Bucks County Messenger* and the *Doylestown Democrat*. Within a year, in 1822, he moved to Washington where he worked as a journeyman printer for the *National Intelligencer*, married, and then returned to Pennsylvania where he entered into a partnership with the *Pennsylvania Intelligencer*, the Democratic organ in the state capital of Harrisburg. After two years as the state printer of Pennsylvania, Cameron was involved in a number of business interests, including the operation of several railroad companies, the founding of a bank, and, beginning in 1845, the first of two nonconsecutive terms in the United States Senate, the second an appointment to a vacated seat in 1857.

Cameron was the leader of the Republican Party in Pennsylvania despite the baggage he brought with him. He also brought the most powerful newspaper in the state, the *Evening Bulletin*, with him.

A Dartmouth College graduate, Salmon Chase moved to Washington, DC, in 1826 to study law. His rise was sharp and fast in both legal and political circles. Moving to Cincinnati and quickly earning a reputation for his work on high profile antislavery cases, Chase represented the Free-Soil Party in the United States Senate in 1849, returning to Ohio to be twice elected its governor. A fierce opponent of both the Fugitive Slave Act and the Kansas-Nebraska Act, Chase was a founder of what became the Republican Party. In 1860, Ohio sent him back to the Senate, but coming into the convention Chase was the next logical candidate for president behind Seward. Lincoln's eventual secretary of the treasury, Gideon Welles, thought Chase had a "good deal of intellect" and knew "the path where duty points, and in his calmer moments, resolves to pursue it," but was more often selfish, vain, and seduced by power, traits which "impair his moral courage."[41]

The newspapers were a far more powerful voice on the limited number of citizens who voted.

"Mr. Lincoln was nominated to the presidency over the heads of several of those who now compose his cabinet," James Gordon Bennett's *New York Herald* voiced publicly. "Their apparent chances of being elevated to power were greater than his; their claims upon their party had been more definite and acknowledged; and their long continued public careers had endowed them with a weight of external authority and influence, to which his was inferior." The *Herald,* a staunch Lincoln supporter, admitted that the president, of course, recognized this, and "naturally entered, therefore, upon his presidential duties with extreme deference for the opinions of the distinguished leaders of republicanism, from among whom he chose his advisors. Time has taught him," it continued, "that many of these gentlemen are actuated by conflicting motives of selfishness and ambition and that their collective wisdom is marred by suspicions, rivalries, and intrigues."[42]

Another strong Lincoln supporter, Treasurer of the United States Lucius E. Chittenden, wrote in a biography published after the war that the cabinet was perfectly unique; a unique experiment in American democracy, bringing together the major players from the nominating convention. Dangerous business in the most stable of political times; extraordinarily precarious at the outset of a civil war.[43]

According to the *Missouri Unionist:* "I never since I was born imagined that such a lot of poltroons and apes could be gathered together from the four corners of the Globe as Old Abe had succeeded in bringing together in his cabinet."

Not everyone was as radically skeptical, but there were times that Lincoln surely was.[44]

On the mid-August morning after the mob attacked the *Jeffersonian* in West Chester, Lincoln's cabinet met and quite possibly sealed the fate of those newspapers opposed to the raging war. Only speculation exists about the exact details of the cabinet meeting, though ensuing events suggest that a profound decision was made by the administration.

Were the mobs extensions of political arrests already enacted by Secretary of State William Seward and Secretary of War Simon Cameron? Or just an emotional reaction to the growing realization that this would not be a snap victory for the North?

The Lincoln administration was in a precarious situation. Civil war had been inaugurated, troops had been mobilized, and the Republican-controlled Congress had just ended its first session. Fort Sumter, a Union fort, had been surrendered in April, and in mid-July the Union army suffered an embarrassing defeat on the outskirts of Washington, DC, at the battle of First Bull Run. Lincoln had shown himself to be calculating—what his cabinet early misjudged as indecisiveness. By August, Lincoln showed signs that he was coming into his own. He had immersed himself in diplomacy and the art of war, and consulted with anyone who would talk to him on such matters. The deliberateness that would mark his entire presidency began to show itself not as weakness, but strength.

Republican newspapers reported on the August 20 cabinet meeting afterward with few details, but there was ample speculation. Telegraphic dispatches from Washington, first appearing in papers most loyal to the administration, revealed that "the severe newspaper strictures upon the members of the cabinet are regarded here as attacks upon the country, and those who make them are now suspected of being in the interests of the Secessionists. This subject has attracted attention at Washington."[45] A frustrated and worried cabinet seemed to be preparing to strike back against its most dangerous opponent at home—openly hostile newspapers who were harshly critical of the administration and its policies.

Legally, any decision by the administration to support the mobs or even to ignore the activity and do nothing was an unparalleled act—the United States government endorsing the elimination of the opposition press. Not since the 1798 Sedition Act, which made it a crime to publish "false, scandalous, and malicious writing" against the government, had the press been so vilified. The Sedition Act soon died an inglorious death after heated public outcry and political opposition. The fate of the Union reintroduced the debate of a free press.[46]

In the aftermath of Fort Sumter, a consensus seemed to be developing from the president on down that antiwar newspapers were indeed legitimate and critical targets that might prevent the effort to save the Union. On Friday, August 23, the *Philadelphia Inquirer* reported to its sixty thousand subscribers on "A New Order of Things," which it considered to be "equally founded on sound policy."

> The Constitution provides for the freedom of speech and of the press. But it also provides for the privileges of the writ of habeas corpus. It has been found that the safety of the republic required the suspension of that writ. The administration is now satisfied that the safety of the Republic requires that those papers in the North which do not yield a hearty support to the government, and to all the measures of the administration, and which, by their sympathy with the South, nourish at the North a hostile feeling against the government, shall be warned to desist, and if they persist, shall be suppressed. Attorney General Bates has been consulted on the subject, and says that the government would be perfectly justified in doing so.[47]

Note that the anger was directed toward not only those who remained neutral, but also those who failed to "yield a hearty support" for the administration. But was it justified? If such a decision were made and endorsed by the attorney general, it was merely a formality to the summer wave of mob justice that was spreading through Northern towns in August of 1861. Was it founded on sound policy or on the thin skin of Secretary of State Seward, who was plotting to emerge as the savior of the Union and leader of the Republican Party? And where did President Lincoln stand on this most extraordinary activity?

With little fanfare, one of the administration's strategies at home was to launch a campaign to shut down those newspapers opposed to the war and to jail editors and writers with strong antiwar views. A critical point must be made here. The newspapers that suffered were not the only ones often opposed to the war. Republican papers often stood against administration policy, especially in the opening days of the conflict.

But Republican editors, the temperamental Horace Greeley included, were to be won over by Lincoln, while the fate of most Democrats was more brutal. Under the cloud of the conflict there would be ample opportunity for elimination. Lincoln well understood the momentous decision, but he made the call that the fate of the country transcended the rights of citizens to speak and publish their own political views.

Clearly, Lincoln showed his mastery of the political environment, using his patience and the sophistication to win over editors of critical newspapers, whether they were pro-slavery or captivated by another politician. Those he had no use for would fall under the heavy hand of the cabinet. But was Lincoln personally responsible for the heavy hand leveraged against those newspapers opposed to the war?

This much was clear: Lincoln certainly endorsed the unprecedented actions taken in his name by his media-savvy political team against

Democratic newspapers and greedily accepted by the political appointees surrounding the president. Lincoln's assembling of the largest concentration of often power-hungry politicians who controlled their own media was a fact not lost on the public. A contemporary account of that time by John W. Urban explained the young administration's poor handling of General George McClellan with the wry observation that "the movements of the army were, to a great extent, dictated and controlled by men at Washington and New York who understood journalism better than military science."[48]

Could the events on that muggy night in August by a mob hired to crush a popular newspaper been set in motion by a sophisticated president well versed in the power of newspapers to sway votes? Lincoln once remarked that a newspaper man such as Horace Greeley was worth one hundred thousand men. If this were true, how many fewer soldiers would be needed to defeat the South if all dissenting editors were silenced? That was the equation of interest to our first media president.

Chapter Two

THAT TORY HODGSON

We are further told that in times of great public danger the people ought to sustain the hands of their rulers by confiding in their integrity and disinterestedness of action. You cannot increase and strengthen virtue, and courage, in a people by teaching them that in times of great public calamity and danger to the State, they must rely for the safety on the power and good will of their rulers.[1]

—John Hodgson, December 28, 1861

Civil War-era Washington, DC, was littered with reminders of the fragility of the American experiment. The Washington monument, built in celebration of the country's first president and most famous general, had sat untouched for years, less than half-built, its base surrounded by livestock and acres of open pasture. Funding difficulties had kept construction at a standstill. When Lincoln met with his cabinet on the second floor of the White House, the unobstructed view of the monument was a constant, disheartening reminder of the work before them.

The dome of the capital building, the future idyllic symbol of liberty, lay sinking into the ground next to the building it was built to adorn. Lincoln demanded that construction continue, though for now there was only a network of scaffolding standing in its place. The Senate chambers would soon double as sleeping quarters for Union soldiers, young men far from home who had answered the call of their president. "The scene was quite novel," wrote Lincoln's personal secretary, John Hay. "The contrast was very painful between the grey-haired dignity that filled the Senate chamber…and the present throng of bright-looking New England rusticity…scattered over the desks and chairs and galleries."[2]

The three brutal days of fighting at Gettysburg in the summer of 1863 were in some ways the culmination of the battle that was taking place in Pennsylvania, Maryland, and other Union lifelines by the spring of 1861. Pennsylvania and Maryland were critical to the Union. Both harbored fanatical southern sympathizers, but more importantly, both harbored influential Unionists—congressman, state legislators, and editors—who supported peace and wanted to prevent a dismantling of the Constitution.

The Philadelphia suburb of West Chester, Pennsylvania, boasted a population of only five thousand souls, but its one Democratic editor spoke with the fire of fifty thousand by himself. He was introduced to the candidacy of Abraham Lincoln by one of his West Chester rivals, the *Chester County Times,* in early 1860. John Hodgson, editor of the *Jeffersonian,* had since kept a worried eye on the awkward prairie lawyer who spoke with precision and conviction on the indignities of slavery and the strength of the federal government. The bold and defiant editor, the mouthpiece of the radical wing of the Democratic Party in Chester County, berated Republican efforts to manage the relationship with the South. He was the type of editor who made the Lincoln administration nervous,

a man with influence and an inability to compromise when it came
to either the Constitution or states' rights.

Despite strong Democratic Party opposition in West Chester, the
biography of Lincoln and the ensuing presidential campaign did
influence the formerly strong Whig district, which the Republicans
had replaced in Chester County. There, a well-organized Republican
ticket had been assembled and a fierce struggle for control had begun.
After the surprising win for Lincoln in Chicago, dashing the
presidential hopes of Edward Bates, Simon Cameron, and others,
local Republican voices emotionally and whole-heartedly threw their
support behind the future president.

For Democrats, the 1860 campaign was far more complex. The
party split at their presidential convention in Baltimore. While the
moderate majority threw their support to Stephen Douglas, the
legendary senatorial debating foe of Lincoln, the more radical among
them stubbornly supported John Breckinridge. But the confusion did
not deter John Hodgson. Hodgson only got louder as the election
became more hopeless for the Democrats.[3]

Only days before the November election, Hodgson attempted,
one last time, to rally the Democratic faithful. Convinced of the
travesty about to befall the country he fought so tirelessly to defend,
the editor printed a frustrated "prediction that, in the event of
Lincoln's election to the presidency, dissolution of the Union will
follow. We are no alarmist," Hodgson reassured the subscribers of the
Jeffersonian, "but we can read the 'signs of the times,' and the
'handwriting on the wall.' His election would not only be an
intentional insult to the South, but will be regarded as a declaration
of war…We have said that the election of Lincoln will be the death-
knell to our Republic. We say so because we believe it."[4]

The columns of the *Jeffersonian*, though speaking to a small public
in comparison to the *New-York Times* or other large market papers,

would be consistently accurate in its predictions as the presidential election came and went. Hodgson's words were as sharp as those coming out of the nation's largest newspapers, yet his pleas were drowned out by the four republican newspapers in West Chester. Chester County cast 7,732 votes for Lincoln and 5,022 for radical Democrat John Breckinridge. In West Chester, the vote followed the same course, with Lincoln more than doubling the vote total of the nearest contender. Nationally, the two Democratic candidates, Breckinridge and Douglas, mustered more popular votes than Lincoln in all, but the rail-splitter swept the electoral college in every Northern state but New Jersey.[5] Lincoln's 40 percent of the popular vote remains the lowest percentage of any presidential victor. Certainly, it did not portend well for the ability to heal a divided country.[6]

The day after the secession plans of four Southern states were voted upon in January 1861, Hodgson prophetically tackled yet another delicate and little-discussed question. "Now in view of the...Lincoln war against the South, soon to be commenced, the question arises— who will be the volunteers? Who will march South," he asked, "and with the coveted aid of Negroes, shoot and butcher our fellow country-men? Whichever party will be willing we know one that will not. The Democratic party will not. Not a single Democrat can so volunteer."[7]

Hodgson was openly raising a point few others wished to consider in public. The incoming president was bluntly being told that no Democrat would openly take up arms against the South and "with the aid of Negroes, shoot our fellow countrymen." Calling those in the South fellow countrymen struck a passionate chord with many, especially the majority who voted Democrat. Southerners were not foreigners, strangers, or even opposed to the United States. It was an emotional view that forced Lincoln to consider his Republicans a minority even within the United States. Of course, many a Democrat did volunteer in the name of the Union, but should Hodgson's racist view prevail, then both the war and the Union itself was already lost. Hodgson was firing away with every argument he could muster to stop Lincoln in his tracks, and reveled in pointed attacks made by his Democratic colleagues. His continued attacks on blacks also showed his patriotic blindness, as almost six hundred of West Chester's 4,757 citizens were black.[8]

Few Northerners in early 1861 had yet to believe that the looming war would either free the slaves or even be fought over that issue. Most believed war would still be averted. It may well have been the goal and hope of leading Republicans, men like Secretary of the Treasury Salmon Chase, publishers like Horace Greeley, and the small but powerful band of antislavery politicians in Congress, but they were far ahead of not only the public, but also probably the president. More typical was the peace feeler put out by Secretary Seward early after the election. Using the cover of Thurlow Weed's *Albany Evening Journal,* a series of compromises were put forth, only to be knocked down by the incoming president. Weed, acting no doubt on behalf of the future secretary of state, proposed that federal laws be enacted to protect slavery in the Southern states. It was, in reality, a proposed return to the old Missouri Compromise, allowing slavery in certain states. This was an idea Seward had rallied against his whole career. Implementation of such a plan, editorialized Weed, would keep the Southern states from seceding.

The idea of a compromise with the South fell on deaf ears with the president-elect. So, too, Seward's desire to "make any sacrifice to save the Union."[9] The *New-York Times,* another part of the Seward-Weed machine, also weighed in, suggesting compromise in the interests of maintaining good business relations with Southern trading partners. Lincoln was not amused and Seward was forced to disavow Weed's comments. He chose to do so through Greeley's *New York Tribune.*

Hodgson's raising of the slavery issue threatened to undermine the support of Unionists throughout the loyal states, the very sort of families that would soon be asked to send their sons and husbands to fight the war.

Hodgson was a complicated and paradoxical figure. Racist, yes. Against the proponents of a strong federal government, also yes. But a firm and dedicated believer in the Union and the need to keep the country together nonetheless. And in this regard, he was at times far more loyal than men like Horace Greeley, who steered every which way.

Hodgson was incensed at the early inaction of the newly elected Republican. With the war at last upon them, it appeared that some of Hodgson's predictions had come to fruition. Instead of working to heal the nation's wounds and solicit the return of the Southern states in an amicable manner becoming of the office, Hodgson portrayed Lincoln as "Nero fiddling while Rome was burning," which was "not an inept illustration of Mr. Lincoln smoking his segar, drinking his lager beer, and cracking his familiar jokes up in Springfield, while the country is on the verge of ruin." Hodgson asked a fundamental question: What was Lincoln doing to placate Southerners during the more than four months between election day and his inauguration? The then lame-duck, James Buchanan of Pennsylvania, was incapable and unwilling to solve the national crisis and for Hodgson, the months before Lincoln's inauguration were a license for the Southern states to break away and the bloody war to commence.[10]

At one point Hodgson had asked himself what the South should do if the Republicans—and Lincoln—won the election. Predicting that Lincoln's election would justify the South withdrawing from the Union, this passionate defender of states' rights quickly added: "I do not bind myself, personally to this particular course. I think Southerners should meet in conference, as some plan may be devised to save us from the disunion that all deprecate." Hodgson knew that legislators throughout the North were doing just that.[11]

Still, his frank opinions were drawing both more and more supporters and political enemies—a dangerous combination as the war loomed closer.

John Hodgson was the son of English immigrants, smooth-faced and still handsome in his mid-fifties. The one known photograph of Hodgson reveals a deep and complex countenance, his features uncharacteristic for a man passing middle age. The lustrous, wavy brown hair of his youth had grayed, but his brow was as sharp as ever; his eyes still possessive of a subtle but overwhelming sensitivity.

Much of Hodgson's life mirrors that of many of the immigrants of the early nineteenth century. Nine-year-old John Hodgson arrived in Pennsylvania in 1818 with his father, William, his mother Anne, a brother, and three sisters. Two more brothers and a fourth sister were soon born in the United States, the family finally settling in what would become the foothold of the Methodist district in West Chester. Hodgson's father, a "zealot Methodist Episcopal preacher," was one of the central figures responsible for the growth of both the religion and the district that would develop on the edge of town. Reverend Hodgson organized regular services and weekly prayer meetings at the church on the northeast corner of Market and Darlington streets. The Reverend's wife sold candy from a tiny store in the front of their home on West Gay Street.[12]

Probably without the benefit of much formal education, John went to work early. He joined the *Village Record* in West Chester, where he apprenticed until the age of seventeen under the outspoken Charles Miner, an eccentric former state legislator, author, editor, and successful politician. Miner lived in a large house on South High

Street where, as his master raised several very educated daughters, young Hodgson probably learned a thing or two about books and the fairer sex. Years later, Miner would go to Congress and see firsthand the thriving slave trade in Washington. The experience led him to redouble his efforts to end the horrors of slavery.[13]

When his apprenticeship was complete, Hodgson moved to Doylestown and joined the staff of his brother-in-law's *Bucks County Intelligencer* as a compositor, further cultivating an appreciation for the power and influence of the written word. Also while in Doylestown, the enterprising young Hodgson met and married Elizabeth Hall, the pretty daughter of Samuel Hall, one of the town's most prominent citizens. Together they would have five children: William, Elizabeth, Anne, Charles, and John.

After a stint with the *Intelligencer,* Hodgson attempted to move on his own and rejuvenate the *Norristown Herald.* After a few years of failure, he left the endeavor behind and moved his family to western Virginia. Seemingly plagued by failure, he moved again shortly after. In Philadelphia, at a time of deep soul-searching and difficult realizations of his own talents and skills, the pressures of a growing family forced Hodgson to abandon his so-far-unsuccessful attempts in the publishing world altogether. He tried his hands in dry goods. But merchant life, he was soon to discover, lacked the drama and excitement of the newspaper scene.

Around 1843, Hodgson's life was jolted with the untimely and devastating death of his wife. The devoutly religious John Hodgson was raised as a journalist and now, during the most critical period of his life, made a most important decision. Without work and with very little money, the depressed and defeated father packed up his five children and moved back home to the familiar setting of West Chester.

Eager to leave behind the failures of several false starts and the memories of his wife, Hodgson wasted little time getting out the first issue of his newly established *West Chester Herald,* which debuted on September 3, 1843. The *Herald* would have a short life, however; Hodgson merged the paper with the *Jeffersonian* in October.

The *Jeffersonian,* formerly an advocate of the Whig party, had survived three name changes in five years, having most recently converted its allegiances wholly to the Democratic Party. After a brief period of publication, the *Jeffersonian,* "owing to a combination of unforeseen and untoward circumstances…" had been suspended. Its editor, though, Asher Wright, expected "to be enabled to resume before any great period shall lapse; when I shall be prepared to unfold a tissue of wrong and persecution that will bear its own comment and show how harshly I have been dealt with."[14] Apparently the paper, unable to find the right combination of politics and patronage, nor the right combination of editorial staffing, had come under heavy fire. Wright, looking for more firepower, and Hodgson, looking for greater stability and an audience, decided to combine their efforts. Under its bulky banner, the *Jeffersonian and Democratic Herald,* Hodgson and Wright published in partnership until early 1845, after which time Hodgson gained full possession and editorial control over the endeavor. From that critical moment, Hodgson began to wrestle control of the local Democratic machine, and to lay siege upon those who opposed its platforms.

In fact, of all of his undertakings, John Hodgson was perhaps best at making enemies. He passionately believed in his principals and never wavered. In that regard, he was ill-equipped for the turbulence of the war that now engulfed the nation; an unprecedented period when new political parties and personal alliances were created with a frequency not seen since. For Hodgson, now eighteen years since the first issue of the *Jeffersonian* was printed in partnership with Wright, political posturing gave way to overwhelming frankness and sincerity, and as such, he was often his own worst enemy.

By mid-1861, Hodgson was expounding weekly upon his readers what he considered to be the true reasons for the war that was threatening to split the Union that he loved so dearly. He lashed out at many of the radical abolitionists in the Republican-controlled Congress.

> It is very evident from the developments of Pomroy, Lane, Lovejoy, Potter, Browning, Hickman, and other abolition demagogues in Congress, when carefully considered in connection with the known sentiments of Lincoln and Seward, and the daring and high-handed outrages upon the Constitution perpetrated by the president, that the purpose of the present war is not to restore harmony and peace and consequent union between the two sections of the country, but to subjugate the South and "wipe out" slavery.
>
> In brief, its purpose is to benefit the Negro at the expense of the white man. Such is the object which Lincoln and his abolition backers and counselors have in view. To effect this object...thousands of and tens, perhaps hundreds of thousands of Northern lives are to be destroyed, and millions of dollars of weighty and crushing debt, with its never-ending taxation, are to be fastened upon Northern citizens.[15]

Hodgson's worries about the efforts to eliminate slavery may seem surprising, given that slavery had ended in Pennsylvania in 1780. (Freed blacks were not given the right to vote and rarely could hold meaningful positions of employment though.) Yet, it might be explained by his fervent, almost religious interpretation of the Constitution and the principals of the country as a loose collection of cooperating states. As a contributor once remarked in the *Jeffersonian,*

"I am not the friend of slavery. [But] as a citizen of Pennsylvania I would doubt my right to interfere directly or indirectly in the domestic institutions of a sister state."[16]

The pro-slavery position might also have come from his father. The Reverend William Hodgson had been active in the 1830s in the Pennsylvania branch of the American Colonization Society, whose goal was to see the end of slavery in America by sending all blacks, both those held in slavery and those free, back to Africa. In this regard, it shared the view of Thomas Jefferson himself that blacks could never be safe or truly free in America. Though of course never realizing its stated objectives, the Society did achieve the dubious milestone of establishing the nation of Liberia in Africa as a colony for former slaves.[17]

Indeed, Hodgson's embrace of slavery may well have been driven by his religious beliefs. It was noted that he was deeply alarmed by the freethinking tendencies of the religious liberals who made up much of the abolitionist society. He believed that blacks were not suited for living in American society and was willing to express that racism bluntly, being absolutely convinced of his Christian convictions. It is hardly an excuse, but further embarrassing to state that Hodgson's state of Pennsylvania was viewed by many, even by the great black statesman Frederick Douglass, as being the most racist of the northern states. One historian went so far as to state, "Most white Philadelphians regarded Negroes as members of an inferior race that might be treated contemptuously, with impunity."[18] Reasons are complex, but the racism was probably due to the fear of so many of the Irish immigrants settling in Philadelphia who often viewed the free blacks of Pennsylvania as a threat to their livelihoods. It is equally as difficult to determine whether Hodgson's views on slavery were entirely personal or exaggerated for political effect.

Hodgson did make a concerted attempt in early 1861 to support the Union effort, even if that meant suppressing some of his own opinions, but that lasted only a short time. It was not just the views on slavery upon which the paper was finding itself increasingly voicing views contrary to many of the local citizens in Chester County, but views on impending issues such as federal taxes, tariffs, and other measures restricting personal liberties that consumed Hodgson.

Now run by John Hodgson and his oldest son William (the paper had been sold a few years earlier to his two sons, but only William played an active role), the *Jeffersonian's* editors, contributors, and readers stood firmly against many of the new ways offered by Lincoln and the uncontrollable band of rogue politicians who were infiltrating the Executive Mansion and Congress. William tried to take a more conciliatory approach to politics, and although his name graced the front page of the *Jeffersonian* as its proprietor, he could not curb his father's insatiable temper nor prevent it from spilling into the paper's columns.

John Hodgson, and to a lesser extent William, was diametrically opposed to the centralization of the federal government. It was the same battle fought sixty years earlier by great men like Thomas Jefferson and James Madison against Federalists like Alexander Hamilton. They opposed the issue of federally imposed taxes, most especially to pay for war. All in all, they were against change for the sake of change and the intrusion of federal government, which was what they were seeing as the decisive and underlying purpose of Lincoln's war. For many of the *Jeffersonian's* readers, bigotry and racism was the only life they had ever known, and the issues of the day—states' rights, slavery, immigration, federal taxes, the protective tariff, and other federal initiatives—threatened the downfall of the great American society. It was the American society Hodgson loved more than he loved anything else in his life; one built on laissez-faire principals, where a free-market is the absolute ruler of economics. It allowed a young, dreamy-eyed immigrant to work his way through life, to provide comfort and greater opportunities for his children. It was Hodgson's own life story, but one that was shared by thousands fighting on his side. When the war opened, Hodgson, worth a comfortable six thousand dollars, had eleven people living under his roof: a sister; his son William, whose twenty-three-year-old wife had died in 1857; several other small children; four apprentices at the *Jeffersonian;* and a live-in domestic.[19]

Hodgson defended the principles, but consciously he also needed to justify his own existence. The *Jeffersonian* had passionately upheld the traditions of strong and independent statehood for almost twenty years while at the same time devoting itself to the purpose of unity between those states. But now, in a time of turbulence and shifting moral and political thought, the opposition voice had gained indomitable strength, and times were changing. A primary force behind that change was the young Republican Party, a group, as Hodgson would say, of political throwaways, who learned quickly to collectively manipulate the land of the free just as well as their Democratic counterparts. With the great War of the Rebellion, as Southerners were calling it, now seemingly inevitable, only time would tell how the Republican way of thinking might flourish. John Hodgson had put himself on a crash course with the Lincoln administration and the very men he most despised.

In late February 1861, almost a year to the day after his biography was printed in West Chester, president-elect Abraham Lincoln was smuggled into Washington amidst swirling rumors of assassination and kidnapping plots. Secret service agent Alan Pinkerton devised a change of course that would blacken Lincoln's highly anticipated arrival in Washington. A grossly embellished story first filed with the *New-York Times* and picked up by rival papers reported that the president wore a "Scotch plaid cap and very long military cloak, so that he was entirely unrecognizable." Newspapers of all parties mocked the move, and in a *Vanity Fair* cartoon, the kilt was traded for a dress the president had borrowed from his wife. By the time Abraham Lincoln arrived in Washington, he was the laughing stock of the entire country, and the so-called loyal Republican press was its regrettable source.[20]

Hodgson, who was never impressed by Lincoln, offered a more sobering portrait of him in the final week of February:

> The election of Abe Lincoln to the presidency will, we doubt not, go down in history as the great mistake of this age and of the American people. Some of the deplorable fruits it has already produced are before the world. The states discordant and almost belligerent, the Union virtually dissolved, commerce, manufactures, and agriculture seriously depressed, and thousands and tens of thousands of mechanics and laborers without employment.[21]

Lincoln never had a chance to appease John Hodgson or the thousands like him in the North who abhorred even the idea of preventing secession through bloodshed.

Lincoln spent less than a month in Washington before his inauguration, which took place on Monday, March 4, 1861. The ceremony was held under partly cloudy skies and a chilled temperature in the mid-fifties. Looking down upon the anxious crowd, he spoke candidly, dedicating most of his words to the constitutionality of secession and his assurance not to interfere with slavery as it existed, a last attempt to conciliate the Southern states. To Lincoln, any issue, including slavery, was secondary to preserving the Union. Lincoln acknowledged Southern anger, but confirmed the illegality of a state to remove itself from the Union, and tried to pacify fears and concerns. "Apprehension," he said in a gross understatement, "seems to exist among the people of the Southern states that by the accession of a Republican administration their property (including slaves) and their peace and personal security are to be endangered." Seven states— South Carolina, Mississippi, Florida, Alabama, Georgia, Louisiana, and Texas—had by now left the Union.

"I take the official oath today with no mental reservations," Lincoln continued, "and with no purpose to construe the Constitution or laws by any hypocritical rules." However, "if, by the mere force of numbers, a majority should deprive a minority of any clearly written constitutional right, it might, in a moral point of view, justify revolution—[it] certainly would if such right were a vital one."[22]

Lincoln's interpretation of the Constitution exactly mirrored the view of Southerners. Plurality had no moral right in trampling the civil liberties of a minority. And what is more vital than preserving one's way of life? Here was the voice of a politician seeking to obtain his overriding objective; stopping the rebellion. In these words he sought to speak to his opponents through their own constitutional concerns.

The two sides were finally, at long last, speaking the same language. But it was too late. Hodgson was right; Lincoln, for whatever reason, had lost the opportunity to become part of the debate.

The address produced a host of emotions. According to L. E. Chittenden, "The inaugural address called forth opinions as diverse as the issues which disturbed the county. Even Democrats were torn. Douglas Democrats supported the tone of the speech. The secessionists denounced it as 'mischievous,' and insisted it was the 'death-blow of hope.' Some Republicans were unsure, Secretary of State Seward among them; disliking Lincoln's pledge not to interfere with slavery."[23]

Hodgson described a ceremony that was "a lame, unsatisfactory, and discreditable production, inferior of every respect to anything that has ever emanated from any former president."[24]

The day following his inauguration, Lincoln was alerted to a tenuous situation that was developing off the coast of Charleston, South Carolina. Major Robert Anderson of the United States Army was running short on supplies at Fort Sumter, the strongest of three forts in Charleston Harbor. A previous attempt by President James Buchanan to send supplies had been met by Southern cannon fire from the other two forts located in the harbor. Anderson told Lincoln that supplies were needed by April 15 or the fort would need to be evacuated.

Having been counseled by his chief commander, General Winfield Scott, that it would take at least twenty thousand men to hold the fort, Lincoln assembled his cabinet. Seward pressed for compromise, and would even go as far as to unofficially accept Southern commissioners, then give them assurance that the president would soon evacuate the fort. On April 1, Seward assumed further responsibility for the situation by offering Lincoln "Some Thoughts for the President's Consideration." Seward was disappointed that "we are at the end of a month's administration, and yet without a policy, either domestic or foreign." Furthermore, as Lincoln had not offered a resolution to the Fort Sumter crisis, Seward suggested that such responsibility could be given to a cabinet member, meaning himself. "Once adopted," Seward suggested, "debates on it must end, and all agree and abide." Lincoln could not have agreed more, but not in the manner that Seward envisioned. "I remark that if this must be done, I must do it…" Lincoln wrote in response.[25]

News traveled fast, a phenomenon only recently made possible by the telegraph. Now a president's every communication, meeting— seemingly every thought—was front-page news. Lincoln, who was at the same time signing off on appointments and patronage contracts at the request of visitors and supporters (including providing a federal job to his old law partner), attempted to send provisions to Major Anderson, but was rebuffed. Confederate General P. G. T. Beauregard demanded surrender and evacuation on April 11. When Anderson responded that a response from Washington would take time, Beauregard, Anderson's former pupil and teaching aide, responded more decisively. Anderson was afforded one hour to reinforce his position. The first cannon boomed in the early hours of April 12.

For the first time in American history, citizens were receiving up-to-date coverage of transpiring events. Newspapers in Iowa reported the events in Charleston Harbor as easily as the *New-York Times* or Philadelphia's *The Press*. In West Chester, John Hodgson followed the course of most newspapers, Democratic or Republican, and gave surprisingly benign and reflective reports of the unfolding crisis in his April 13 issue, possibly during a time of introspection that was forced upon him that Friday night.

On the evening of the twelfth, he took a short stroll to the nearby Mansion House for a quick dinner in the basement oyster bar. The Republican district was growing combative in response to Hodgson's coverage of the evolving Fort Sumter incident, and he soon received the message in a most personal manner. For Hodgson and West Chester, the war began that night in a drunken brawl in a downtown oyster bar; a sign, if one was needed, that this war would not be a gentlemen's conflict reserved for carefully chosen battles among traditional combatants.

We know the events of this battle because a rival paper went to extraordinary lengths to embarrass Hodgson. A man identified only as Mose, a former correspondent of the *Jeffersonian,* took the time to write and distribute the news of that night. According to a handsomely produced broadside soon printed and distributed throughout town, the battle of "Hodgson vs. Springer, otherwise, Secessionist against Republican!" was the perfect metaphor for the evolving crisis at Fort Sumter. The broadside laid bare the facts in dramatic fashion:

WAR BEGUN!
HOSTILITIES COMMENCED!!
IN AN OYSTER CELLAR

"Secessionist fires first shot—Republican answers beautifully." The author of the broadside wrote that the battle was brought on by an onslaught of "oysters and pale ale," during which Hodgson, identified as "Major," spoke "gloriously on the prowess of the Southern rebels— goes it strong on secession." Consequently, "on mature reflection, and an honest conviction of the rectitude of his conduct, and evidently with well-selected epithets," Charles Springer of the "Upholstery," called the Major "a liar, scoundrel, traitor, and coward."

Hodgson, unable as always to ignore a verbal assault, answered the challenge.

> Major takes no exception to the first three expressive appellatives, inasmuch as they embrace a triangular syllogistical, self-evident proposition (vide the Weakly columns of the *Jeffersonian* and the flaunting unfurled Palmetto Flag over his office), but on the last mentioned title the Major's bump of combativeness swells prodigiously, and instanter he joins issue with Charley on the cowardice question.

In John Hodgson's world, being a coward was by far the worst of personal fallibilities, even compared to accusations of traitor or scoundrel.

The observer continued:

> He'd let Charley know that he was Major Hodgson, a soldier—a calf of Johnny Bull, and no coward.
>
> Charley rejoins, "by my troth, a calf unweaned, I admit—a soldier!!! a thief!! an assassin!!! a pest to society; for your treason you deserve to be made the wad of a field piece, and shot through a thorn hedge, and lodged in a crab apple tree."

Not one to lose a verbal confrontation, Hodgson, the furious editor:

> plant[ed] his crumpled digits full on Charley's calabash, which, with the aid of the aforesaid ale, knocked him off his pins over a chair. Although of the time apparently the victor, the Major beats a disorderly retreat, marking time to the "Rogues" March.

As Hodgson attempted to leave the scene:

> Charley, true to his name, springs at him and plants a blizzard on the jugular of the redoubtable Major, throwing him on his beam ends, and after a convulsive effort to right himself, he sinks stern foremost, "down to the dust from whence he sprung, unwept, unhonored, and unsung."

The perfectly planted punch on Charley's "calabash" notwith-standing, Hodgson apparently lost the fight to Charley Springer. In the prose of the broadside, "The Major was Upholstered."

Hodgson's debating and sparring opponent was, like the writer of the broadside (and possibly the same person), a former correspondent for the *Jeffersonian!* Friends and colleagues had again become bitter enemies. It was a reality all too familiar to Hodgson.

Hodgson responded to the events at Fort Sumter after his fight, but was strangely silent about the attack on his person. He may have been temporarily shaken by the encounter, and it is even possible that the altercation was a minor one exaggerated by his enemies in the slanderous broadside. In his next issue, Hodgson showed his desire to defend the Union, calling for the safe return of the soldiers from Fort Sumter and an end to the fight. But still, he could not resist a pointed attack on a more distant enemy—the Lincoln administration. "There can be no doubt, now," he wrote, "about the policy of the administration. It is coercion, and nothing else."[26]

But the emotional publisher stayed close to his true intentions. On April 20, Hodgson's next issue, the *Jeffersonian* returned to its old combativeness, leading with a word-for-word printing of the First Amendment: "Congress shall make no law respecting an establishment of religion, or prohibiting the free exercise thereof; or abridging the freedom of speech, or of the press; or the right of the people peaceably to assemble, and to petition the government for a redress of grievances." He followed it with a short editorial on the war euphoria being displayed in Northerner papers and a piece on the "bloodthirsty" sermons of clergymen throughout the North. He also questioned who was running the government, concluding that it was not "we the people" as many thought. "The mistake was discovered, however, last winter," he wrote, "[when] Congress said, no, gentle-men, you, the people, are not the sovereigns; you are not to be trusted.

We are your masters; Mr. Lincoln will show you that you have a government, independent of 'we the people.'"[27] Two columns over, with "War News" reporting the latest particulars on Fort Sumter in between, Hodgson printed a proclamation by the president calling for seventy-five thousand militia and convening a special session of Congress on July 4.

In a further sign of things to come, the "mob spirit was rife in Philadelphia," reported Hodgson, as "vagrants and half-grown boys…paraded the streets and attacked every man they suspected of being a Democrat, and mobbed houses, stores, and offices, breaking windows, &c." At one point, they descended on the *Palmetto Flag,* a newspaper recently launched in Philadelphia to defend the institution of slavery, and forced the editor to display the American flag before moving on. [28]

The mayor showed a tolerance far greater than his fellow Republicans in Washington. Standing in front of the angry mob, Mayor Henry waved the American flag and shouted, "Fellow-citizens, while I conjure you to stand by the flag of the Union, do not forget the private rights of the individuals." Despite this, the *Palmetto Flag* never published another issue.[29]

Democratic papers considered Fort Sumter to be "the great folly of Lincoln's administration." But it was still early. And as news filtered through the North and the new Confederacy, Hodgson was also licking his wounds while the mood of the Union was transformed overnight. The people were angry, upset, scared, and puzzled, and so too were political leaders. Who among them thought blood would spill over this issue? Tolerance gave way to intolerance. Huge crowds gathered and men rushed to sign up.[30]

In New York, the great James Gordon Bennett, proprietor of the *New York Herald,* confronted an angry mob outside of his office at Fulton and Nassau Streets. He had to push his way through the crowds to gain access to his offices, unfurling an American flag once inside to disperse the mob. From that day on, the *Herald's* office always had loaded rifles on hand.[31]

And patriotism, as it so often does, brought together many political enemies. Abraham Lincoln's great political rival, Stephen A. Douglas, best represented those feelings in an encounter with John Forney, the Philadelphia editor soon to play a major part in the administration's newspaper policies. Running into Douglas on the steps of the capitol, Forney asked, "What is to be done now? My dear friend, what are we to do?" Answered Democratic champion Douglas, "We must fight for our country and forget all the differences. There can be but two parties—the party of patriots and the party of traitors." Forney would later write that only Douglas's premature death in June prevented Lincoln from bringing the former Democratic foe into his administration. It was this sort of patriotism above politics that became the fashion of the day for most citizens.[32]

Patriotism swept through the air and Douglas's comment was but one example. Democrats such as General Benjamin Butler, Ulysses S. Grant, and George McClellan threw their support to the Union. Read one account at the time, "A patriotic fever swept the land. In losing Sumter we have gained a united people."[33]

But not every Democrat felt the need to unite behind Lincoln. A small minority kept true to their political principals regardless of the looming threat, and as the war moved farther away from the Fort Sumter incident, the parties would continue to polarize like never before.

Wrote Democratic editor Frank Howard in the *Daily Exchange* of Baltimore, "The war that government has wantonly begun we regard as a wicked and desperate crusade, not only against the homes and rights of our Southern brethren, but against the fundamental American principal of self-government."[34]

In the new climate of the Northern streets, these sorts of comments stirred the anger of the mobs. Men like John Hodgson and his blunt comments were suddenly no longer welcome given the harsh realities of a war pitting brother against brother.

In West Chester, tongues were wagging about their outspoken Democrat. A letter written soon after the Union surrender of Fort Sumter typifies the thoughts that must have been common. West Chester resident Charles Shippan wrote privately to his mother that "Hodson [sic] & one or two others have been talking pretty strong here within a few days for secession; Now as war has begun if they don't come out of the Union or at least keep quiet they will be—hung I was going to say—mobbed I will. The *Jeffersonian* building will not stand long unless Jno. Hodgson dries up."[35]

Chapter Three

PUBLISHING AND POLITICS

*We are told also that when this public danger shall have passed away
the Constitution will be restored to its pristine vigor, and the people will
be allowed to resume their accustomed liberty. When was this ever so?
When were the invaded and restricted rights of the people ever restored
to their exact position except by the sword?*[1]

—John Hodgson, December 28, 1861

J ohn Hodgson was but one of the idiosyncratic and opinionated
editors who ran the newspapers of the Civil War era—an era
when the founding editors of some of today's greatest papers were
just beginning to establish their empires. The *New York Tribune's*
enigmatic and finely dressed Horace Greeley and the thin,
deceptive-looking James Gordon Bennett, founder of the *New York
Herald,* are perfect examples. Many of the twenty-first century's
most circulated papers were still in their infancy at the outbreak of
the Civil War, fighting themselves for survival in the country's
largest cities.

Though the challenges were monumental, the rewards were never more lucrative, both politically and financially, for the successful editor. Newspaper editors were not mere word slingers, their columns also meant to amuse and entertain, a necessity to keep subscriptions up. The most successful journalists were also national political drivers. It was once remarked that Greeley "would be the greatest journalist in America if he did not aim to be one of the leading politicians in America."[2]

Greeley's impact on so much of American life was recognized but dismissed by the traditionalist John Hodgson. He described Greeley as "the man who through his infidel-abolition *Tribune* gives currently to Free-Loverism, women's rights-ism, Socialism, and all the infidel isms of the day."[3] Greeley must have appreciated that description, for the words were, as usual with Hodgson, blunt and bordering on rude, but accurate in summing up the highly energetic and socially conscious editor.

Powerful New York, Chicago, Philadelphia, and Baltimore editors influenced elections as much as the politicians themselves influenced elections: during this period, candidates rarely campaigned on their own behalf. Abraham Lincoln did not even attend the Republican National Convention that nominated him to be the party's candidate. Instead he read telegraphic updates in Springfield. Campaigning was left to colleagues, politicians, and editors, the latter able to speak to thousands in the time the former could speak to hundreds. Once their candidates were elected, editors were well rewarded. They were in daily contact with the White House and the Congress, and spoke directly to the voters on their behalf. It was rare to find a successful politician without finding a successful editor standing next to him.

Plainly, newspapers were extensions of political parties, their editors holding power both in the back room of the political hall and among like-minded subscribers. They moved comfortably from publishing to political positions. Greeley's protégé, Henry Raymond, was a shining model. In 1848 he left Greeley's *Tribune* and was elected to the New York state legislature. In 1851 he was elected speaker while founding the *New-York Times*. Three years later, in 1854, he became the state's lieutenant governor. His role in Albany lead him to become friends with Thurlow Weed, who saw Raymond as far more reliable than the emotional Greeley—a better route to the lucrative New York City market. Soon after, a bill was passed requiring the banks to advertise their weekly transactions. The lucrative new advertising contract went not to the *Tribune,* but to a new paper, Raymond's *New-York Times*. Raymond and his newspaper became yet another tool under the Seward-Weed political machine.[4]

Such privilege bred fierce competition, especially in New York's close-knit circle of competitors. If a paper's closest competitor held a senior post in Washington while also running a newspaper in Pennsylvania or New York, they not only had the inside track on an important story, but also held unmatchable influence on the intricate daily dealings of the party. Such prized information made its holder highly valuable himself. Financially, those on the inside were first to the scoop, and that sold papers.

Government patronage for newspapers first began in earnest under Andrew Jackson, a period that catalyzed the metamorphosis of newspapers into powerful campaign weapons. Government subsidies, offered separately by the House of Representatives, the Senate, the Supreme Court, and the executive office, spent hundreds of thousands of dollars on printing contracts to private individuals and their papers. These contracts included not only advertisements in the papers, but special printings of bills, speeches, and laws. During the twenty-sixth Congress, from 1839–1841, the executive branch alone spent just under $175 thousand on printing. These jobs were awarded only to political allies.[5] Greeley estimated that Seward holding the governorship of New York was worth more than $20 thousand to Thurlow Weed's *Albany Evening Journal* in advertising, plus the powerful perk of patronage.

The trend of awarding patronage jobs to loyal editors also began under Jackson. In 1830, more than fifty editors received such appointments. The job of postmaster, the man who controlled the distribution of mail and most importantly, newspapers, became one of the most sought after. Combined with state and local patronage awards, loyalty became a fierce commodity. And it finally all became too much, leading to a congressional investigation into abuses of patronage—including the behavior of Lincoln loyalist John Forney—which resulted in the creation of the still-operating Government Printing Office in 1860. That office included the appointment of one public printer.[6]

When Abraham Lincoln took office, outright printing contracts based on party loyalties were illegal—in theory. However, political appointments and government advertising in choice papers more than made up for the policy change. Lincoln was adept at many things, flattery being one of the most useful. Besides that, he took care of editors who supported, or who he wanted to support, his position. This fact was lost on no one, from scheming New York giant Thurlow Weed to the fiercest Democratic editors.

"Republican editors," wrote the *Brooklyn Eagle's* eloquent editor, Thomas Kinsella, in August 1861, "have been well taken care of by the present administration. A whole host of appointees to foreign missions were taken from the *Tribune* office. The *Evening Post* is still more fortunate; Mr. Thayer, one of its editors is counsel general at Alexandria. Mr. Bigelow, another, has been appointed consul at Paris, and Mr. Henderson, a third, has the lucrative position of navy agent." Added to the list could have been Theodore Canisius of Lincoln's *Illinois Staats-Anzeiger,* appointed consult to Vienna, and Frederick Hassaurek of Ohio, appointed as minister to Ecuador, and others.[7]

"But that *Albany Journal*," wrote Kinsella, referring to Thurlow Weed's paper that was now the political organ of Secretary Seward, "is more lucky still." One can only assume that Kinsella used the word "lucky" with a heavy dose of sarcasm. Two of his editors received lucrative postmaster positions, in Albany and Rochester, and another was appointed assistant secretary of state. Another was working as a clerk for Philadelphia editor John Forney, who himself was serving as secretary of the Senate as appointed by Lincoln (at an annual salary of two thousand five hundred dollars). Other appointments for Weed's staff were just as lucrative.[8]

Kinsella had only scratched the surface. At least twenty editors received appointments from Lincoln within a month of his inauguration. The ministers to Rome, Portugal and Turkey, commissioner of patents, and at least eight postmaster positions were awarded as favors upon newspaper editors. Murat Halstead of the *Cincinnati Gazette* printed all of the names and their positions, what he called a "disgrace to journalism." Clearly, it was a prosperous business indeed.

This has no connection to Lincoln's overall strategy for saving the Union, other than an obsession with controlling public opinion. And those editors and publishers left on the outside were in a weakened position—never more so than in the opening months of the Civil War.[9] Lincoln knew better than most how to silently yet effectively manipulate public opinion through the use of patronage. Nothing illustrates this better than the Frémont saga.

John Charles Frémont, or the "Pathfinder," as he was known, did much to popularize the western frontier in the early part of the century. Politically ambitious, he ran as the first candidate for the Republican Party four years before Lincoln. His family connections were superb. He was the son-in-law of a powerful senator, Thomas Hart Benton, though the senator refused to support Frémont's candidacy due to its antislavery position.

Frémont was still politically ambitious in 1861 and he sided with the more radical wing of the Republican party—those in Congress who wanted the immediate emancipation of the slaves. In the fall, General Frémont issued an order freeing all slaves in the occupied territory under his control, including Missouri. Lincoln, fighting to keep the border states in the Union, could not tolerate the situation, and he removed the popular Frémont from command. But adroit manipulator of public opinion that he was, Lincoln went further to cement support from Western voters.[10]

Lincoln quietly gave jobs to key editors in the region. The *Chicago Tribune,* a strong supporter of Frémont, published story after story in favor of the emancipation, even stating at one point that the "abolition" proclamation from Frémont had done no harm in the border state. This meant that Lincoln was on the wrong side of the slavery issue. Then, suddenly, such criticism stopped. In its place was a story "frigid" in its tone, much like the dispatches of later despotic governments. One article warned that more mistakes from the general would leave the public prepared for his removal. Why the sudden change in editorial tone? What happened to the support for Frémont?

The Democratic *Chicago Times*—a bitter competitor of the *Chicago Tribune*—surprisingly went public, accusing Lincoln of using the Chicago post office to keep Illinois editors who criticized Lincoln's handling of John Charles Frémont in line. "How sweet are the drippings of the Chicago post office! And Abraham Lincoln dispenses those drippings!"[11]

Overall, if a publisher lost in a policy battle or an election, they would need to fill other public positions and find new outlets for government contracts. For the newspapers of the Civil War period, government printing contracts often offered double the pay of commercial customers, and at a far greater volume. In addition, government contracts were guaranteed and were often obtained without the necessity of a competitive bid. The rewards for blind political loyalty were well worth the effort.

How did Democratic editors differ from their Republican competitors during the early days of the Lincoln administration? It was a two-front war. First, of course, was the survival of the United States. The fundamental difference between Democrats and Republicans was that the former considered the Union to be a voluntary contract, the latter considered statehood a binding, permanent state of existence. Second, Democratic editors were fighting for their own survival. If history proves anything, it is that war favors the winners and those in power. Democratic editors held no favor in a White House filled with men owing their fame and fortunes to Republican newspapers, and instead clung to what many saw as the suddenly out of fashion principles of the Constitution.

Though lucrative for publishers in large markets, newspaper publishing was not lucrative for all. The patronage system was a politician's primary source of leverage, which is why the relationship between politicians and editors worked so well—each had something the other needed. Most of the country's two thousand five hundred papers were rural publications with several thousand subscribers. Of those periodicals, eighty percent were considered by the government census "political in their character." That estimate was probably low.[12]

Editors like John Hodgson sold enough copies to survive financially, supplementing their income by printing special broadsides, speeches, ballots, and other specialty items. And although a dynamic field, the fundamental processes of running a paper had changed little for hundreds of years, though those traditions were rapidly disappearing. While New York papers could afford the faster and more efficient presses being introduced in the 1860s, country papers could not and the divide was widening. The dramatic growth of Republican papers and the editors who built them were a death knell to small rural publications that still held true to the Democratic cause.

A typical daily newspaper was priced at two cents per issue, though some New York papers had been working to raise their rates to three cents. The *New-York Times* charged two cents for each of its daily editions, one for the morning and one in the evening. A subscription through the mails cost five dollars annually. Smaller papers, such as the *Jeffersonian* in West Chester, Pennsylvania, printed only twice a week. Its annual subscription rate, at two dollars a year, had not changed since 1845. The *New-York Times* (semi-weekly) cost three dollars a year; two copies to one address cost five dollars. The weekly issue of the *New-York Times* sold for two dollars a year. The railroad was now allowing same-day delivery to Washington, DC, and other cities, so New York papers were infiltrating new markets at an unstoppable pace.

One of the most startling publishing developments that took place at the onset of the war was the printing of a Sunday edition. This was another matter of contention to traditionalists who believed that publishing on the Lord's day was an immoral development. The *New York Herald* had been the lone publisher of a Sunday edition in New York before the war, but now it was becoming commonplace. Even so, as with most new media developments, many of the publishers assumed that a seven-day-a-week schedule was a temporary phenomenon of the war, to be disbanded once peace was achieved. As the *New-York Times*'s Henry Raymond informed his readers: "The *Times* will be published tomorrow morning as usual, and will be issued on Sundays as on other days, during the continuation of the war excitement."[13]

Disapproving of the Sunday edition, smaller editors were reacting to more than their religious concerns. Publishing on Sunday represented one more competitive issue stabbing at their commercial prospects. The world was changing and small town papers were having trouble competing. They found it difficult enough to print once or twice a week, so a Sunday edition was simply impossible to produce. But the public hungered for war news seven days a week, and enterprising journalists were ready to deliver. It only widened the gap behind the large and small presses.

Editors at smaller papers, like Hodgson, were fortunate if they could even own their own presses. It took Hodgson almost two decades in the business before he could afford to purchase and run his own press; before that time, he was sharing with other local presses.

In 1855, Hodgson was able to proudly announce that his paper had taken this major step. The April 7, 1855, issue of the *Jeffersonian & Democratic Herald,* as it was then called, proudly headlined an article on "Borough Improvements." The feature: "Our New Power Press." The news was considered of great importance. "Our new CYLINDER POWER PRESS is in operation and this sheet is run off upon it."

His enthusiasm beaming through the pages of his paper, Hodgson glowingly reported that the press "is erected in our old establishment in the basement adjoining the Mansion House, where we shall now be able to turn out work comparable with that of any press here or elsewhere." Boasted Hodgson, "Our prices, as is seen by our advertisement, are the same as other presses of the borough. We hope our friends will give us a call. We are now no longer a slave or humble servant, dependent upon others, as we have been."

Hodgson complained, with his usual lack of diplomacy, that he had been the victim of "exorbitant prices for press work and treated as though it were a favor at that."

Now Hodgson had the ability to print his own paper, not to mention "hand-bills, cards, &c. We consider the addition of our POWER PRESS as one of the improvement of the borough, as it certainly is of our means of doing business, as well as a great saving of expense to us." Concluded the proud publisher, "New machinery works hard at first, and a little time is necessary to get fairly into 'the way of it.' We calculate, however, to learn every hand in our office seeks the proper mode of working our new press the first week."

"Bring on the work," he printed proudly.[14]

There was plenty of work to go around. Readers were also demanding greater content, with the plethora of political and military news providing enough for several issues a day. But still, low subscription rates did not generate money, and so for their two cents a reader received four to six pages of news and advertisements. During the Civil War, editors typically devoted editorial space to stories that fell into a few main categories. One was the opinion editorial, with headlines such as "Party vs. the Country," and the *Chicago Tribune's* August 16 article asking for a "more vigorous prosecution of the war with treason and rebellion," entitled "The Popular Demand."[15] Reprints of speeches in Congress by leading politicians and orators, men like former vice president Edward Everett and 1860 presidential hopeful Senator John C. Breckinridge, and of course, the president and his cabinet members, were widely read.

By the summer of 1861, a new type of article had appeared: reports of newspaper suppression and censorship, public or political malevolence, and individual attacks against those responsible. Most of the newspaper articles at the onset of the war carried no byline. Correspondents who were unknown to the readership wrote stories, and editors wanted it that way. Writers who did sign their work used false names or initials to protect themselves from physical retribution for their usual scathing attacks. This would change later, as Union generals demanded greater accountability from war-front coverage. Unwittingly, the era of the star reporter was born from the military concerns of battlefield coverage.

In addition, papers traded stories with "exchange" papers—papers of similar affiliations from which they would simply reprint articles. The exchange system was an integral way to provide relevant information countrywide without having to employ an army of correspondents. And it was one more reason why the suppression of a newspaper in Pennsylvania would have dire effects on a newspaper in Ohio: it was one less source of information.

Stories ranged from the strictly factual, such as notices of anyone of importance entering the city, often including boarding arrangements, to the outwardly sensational. Writing of the sectional conflict, the Philadelphia *Christian Observer* printed such a story. "Reunion is an utter impossibility," it deduced in August 1861. "The gross, brutal, fiendish, demoniac outrages perpetrated by the chicken stealers sent here to ravage the country, pillage the houses and burn them, outrage the women, and shoot down for amusement peaceable citizens, and even children, on the streets, have greatly exasperated the people."[16]

John Forney laced *The Press* with personal concern for the well-being of his chief benefactor and the first family. Papers also served a role equal to a twentieth-century tabloid to feed the public's infatuation with those in power. "No respectable journal would thus pander to public curiosity," wrote Forney, though most all publishers did. And ironically, Forney was among the best.[17] Editors used their columns to publicly debate the merit of such frivolous reporting. "It is doubtful whether any newspaper has ever exhibited more decided bad taste than, in its details of Mrs. Lincoln's visit to Long Branch, has been shown by the *New York Herald*," *The Press* clucked unfavorably.

Jenkins of the *Herald* follows Mrs. Lincoln, in two mortal columns of small type, and, all the time, making melancholy efforts to be smart and facetious—such as calling one Master Lincoln "prince William," and bestowing the nickname of "Tadpole" on another.

Unassuming and quiet as Mrs. Lincoln is, it is a pity, the myrmidons of the *Herald* follow her about, inventing items of gossip about her when they cannot find them.[18]

For the casual reader, it was difficult to determine what papers were to be considered the most reliable, and what information could be dismissed as petty bickering. As outright political organs, their stories were tainted with partisanship and party propaganda. Editors blatantly attacked each other, and oftentimes news would be secondary to the slanderous attacks by editors on other editors.

Such a relationship was inevitable "whereas every man, and almost every woman and child, in the United States, is a politician, keenly alive to the influence of public events of personal actions, of party principles, which make them turn to the newspapers for information, and to several newspapers, to learn all sides of a question." If John Forney was correct, and every American was a politician, then it was only a matter of time before the country's greatest source of information was directly tied to the profession.

The Press slightly overestimated that there "must be over three thousand" newspapers in the United States, but correctly surmised that "almost every country town has at least one newspaper."[19] The overwhelming number of papers offered plenty of column space for the most famous to the most local politician. West Chester was a prime example, with four papers operating within only blocks of one another, all headquartered in a village of fewer than five thousand people. Vicksburg, Mississippi, a town of four thousand five hundred, had six papers. William Howard Russell, the dry British correspondent who covered the war for the *London Times* until he too ran afoul of the administration, commented that the American public regarded the "chiefs of the most notorious journals very much as people in Italian cities of past time might have talked of the most infamous band of assassins."[20]

Papers separated themselves from the competition by the size and neatness of type, the column and page layout, and of course, by their front-page mottoes and designs. Illustrations were rare, except for an occasional woodcut or engraving. But these were cosmetic selling points. Hence the shock value of candidate Lincoln's novel use of a photograph to support his speeches. A paper's greatest assets were its writers, editors, and contributors. A paper's political positions, representing specific platforms and candidates, truly set competing papers apart. If they backed a popular political view, then they had more subscribers and advertisers would follow. It was a vicious but profitable circle.

Workers made little money, on average less than twenty dollars a week in New York.[21] Besides the inadequate pay, the days were long and filled with "drudgery." A staff member of the *New York Tribune* provided a glimpse of his daily duties.

> Shall I say it—there is drudgery connected with my work, a good deal of drudgery, a very little real hearty work, which leaves one better than it finds him. Drudgery in reading newspapers and scissoring them for things of no earthly interest to myself but of supposed interest to others; drudgery in looking over the telegraph & saying what shall be in this type & what in that; drudgery in fixing up other people's bad English & no special apparent utility in either

of these branches of labor; an occasional pleasure in turning a paragraph relative to the news, or "Ed. Head," as we
call it, but oftenest drudgery therein also; and a climax of
drudgery in hanging around the "forms," deciding what
shall go in, out of several things.[22]

A critical point is that even during the turbulent times of the war,
journalism was a financially lucrative business for a select few. Only a
small number of large newspaper owners were able to gross more than
twenty-five thousand dollars a year, or could support a staff of more
than two hundred employees like the *New York Tribune.* In July 1861,
the *New York Courier* and *Enquirer* sold to the *New York World* for one
hundred thousand dollars, which was atypical.[23] But with the financial
prospects of larger papers on the rise, the incestuous relationship
between politicians and publishers only grew stronger. Newspapers
proved a double-edged sword for those in elected office: power
through shaping public opinion and power through the wealth of government contracts.

The real profit of such a position was in political influence and the
spin-off income that followed. Nonetheless, smaller newspapers still
struggled to survive financially. A newspaper rented column space for
advertisements, personal ads for property, and other miscellaneous
items that might bring additional revenue. "A public newspaper,"
Hodgson's *Jeffersonian & Democratic Herald* reported in 1855, "so far
as advertisements are concerned, is, to a considerable extent, similar to
a stage coach or railroad car—a kind of common carrier. The
proprietors may be, and frequently are, very much annoyed, but good-
naturedly put up with it."[24]

The first issue of the *New York Herald,* in 1835, more succinctly
predicted the future of the industry:

What is to prevent a daily newspaper from being made the greatest organ of social life? Books have had their day—the theaters have had their day—the temple of religion has had its day. A newspaper can be made to take the lead of all these in the great movements of human thought and of human civilization. A newspaper can send more souls to Heaven, and save more from Hell, than all the churches or chapels in New York—besides making money at the same time.[25]

Advertising space was often sold to purveyors of "quack nostrums and patent medicines." In West Chester, Hodgson had particular distaste for these, though he needed the sales to pay his bills. "The authors," of such advertisements, "as a class, are generally impudent and exacting," he warned his readers, "and if they do not swindle the printer, they are sure to make a hole in the pockets as well as the constitutions of the poor dupes that are caught by the forged certificates, and the flaming falsehoods of important cures that are professed to have been made." Having been warned by the publisher, the reader would still find such tasteful ads in the *Jeffersonian* as the one advertising for "New Remedies for Spermatorrhoes" and other "diseases of the Sexual Organs."[26]

Nor were editors adverse to self-promotion. Papers fought violently for a small market, especially in remote country towns where patronage was at a minimum. With "the advertising season…about commencing," Hodgson announced, "we would say, that the JEFFERSONIAN offers inducements unequalled by any other paper in the district, having a wide and extensive circulation in Chester and Delaware, beside the adjoining counties. Merchants and advertisers should remember this."[27]

A Hodgson article from the same issue was more direct. "WE WANT MONEY," he titled a short piece.

> There is a large amount due us for subscription and advertising, which ought to be settled without further delay. Our expenses are necessarily heavy, and we stand much in need of what is justly our due. Will not those who know themselves indebted make an effort to square up, or at least pay a part of what is due? We dislike this mode, in fact any mode, of dunning, but necessity pinches.[28]

A nationwide financial panic made money scarce in the late 1850s, and Hodgson's direct approach to his finances had kept him in business for almost twenty years. The lessons of several failed attempts had paid off. Henry Raymond of the *New-York Times* admitted that "the pressure of the war has made itself severely felt upon the advertising patronage of newspapers everywhere—and nowhere more than in this city. Hitherto the policy of the leading city journals has been to receive from sales just enough to pay for white paper and ink, leaving all other expenses—typesetting, correspondence, telegraphic news, reporting and editorials—to be paid for by advertisers." This relationship worked well while advertising was good, he admitted, but in tough times like the present, "Most of the papers are consequently more or less crippled.[29]

The *Times* noted that papers like the *Herald* were putting advertising in large type, a beginning, no doubt, of even greater intrusion of advertisements in the newspapers out of financial necessity. In addition, Raymond concluded that the price of newspaper stock had never been lower, yet the cost of using the telegraph to cover the war had never been higher. Despite the competition, economics of the business forced editors to work together. Several New York papers banded together, forming the Associated Press to decrease the staggering cost of using the telegraph. Still somehow, at least from Raymond's reference point, it was still good business.[30]

The Civil War also created the war correspondent, yet another cost that added to the business of running a paper. Correspondents in the capital before the war were usually on temporary assignment to cover important congressional battles, and even that was rare. The cost of keeping a full-time reporter in Washington was too exorbitant for one paper, and journalists that did work on assignment usually wrote for several different papers.

The exchange system was instead a more practical and necessary means of reporting. Papers of the same party stuck together. As such, a Democratic paper in Pennsylvania would reprint a story carried the week before in a Democratic paper in Missouri. The practice eliminated the need for a correspondent corps, and provided papers with national news. It was a wonder, however, how long this practice would be required, as the advent of the telegraph system made the delivery of news an hourly instead of a weekly job. The cooperation of like-minded newspapers was an absolute journalistic rule of the nineteenth century. There were few exceptions. L. E. Chittenden remarked on how, when campaigning for Lincoln in the fall of 1860, their handlers kept them isolated from any newspapers aligned with the Democratic Party. There was no effort whatsoever to win over any of what we would today call the undecided voter.[31]

The telegraph made field reporting a reality during the war. It was such an accurate reality that the federal government, specifically William Seward, began to censor the news by seizing control of all telegraph wires out of Washington in April 1861. This was, in fact, the first step in the administration's unprecedented muzzling of the news. Begun logistically to prevent the Southern enemy from understanding troop movements and Union intentions, it would soon become the first step to controlling all news, of whatever sort, not sympathetic to the administration.[32]

Still, the telegraph, in use since 1844, was not always reliable. Inclement weather and competition by droves of reporters fighting for the use of only a few lines from Washington made their reliability difficult. The telegraph office was conveniently located across the street from the White House, and was frequented by Lincoln and Secretary of State Seward for the most recent war news.

A few blocks behind the brick building that housed the State Department and next to the famous Willard Hotel, home to the many men who wandered the lobby looking for political favors (hence the term "lobbyists"), was a long row of houses that would come to be called Newspaper Row. At least sixty newspapers would have offices on this strip by war's end, many already laying claim in 1861. Washington's pre-war population, at almost sixty thousand people, would soon triple, the correspondents of those sixty newspapers included.[33]

The Press gave an account of New York reporters working in Washington who, "with a few honorable exceptions, use their proprietors for the ventilation of their private griefs [sic] against public men" who "often find themselves in embarrassing and conflicting positions, by reason of the mendacity of those who represent them in Washington City."[34]

It was a popular view of the publishing industry in the early months of the Civil War. Led by men of egos, newspapers were political organs on the verge of becoming respected sources of information. The nation was changing. The pace of news was quickening. Yet advertising was drying up and with the election of Abraham Lincoln, patronage was a game for Republicans only.

For Democratic editors during the war, there was little talk of prosperity in any form. Republican editors knew times were tough, but understood that they needed to only weather the storm for a short while. Democratic editors, on the other hand, were drowning in the floodwaters, hoping to see the end of the war.

As the political storm of 1861 swept through the North, peace papers were beginning to suffer devastating setbacks in terms of advertising. Storeowners understood not to advertise with the antiwar papers, and local politicians well understood not to take their announcements to papers supporting the Democratic Party. It was political suicide, and everyone knew it. The winners were the strongest Republican papers, backed by men like Thurlow Weed, Horace Greeley, and John Forney.

Though candid discussions of the political boycott by advertisers is difficult to come by, the *Brooklyn Eagle* did touch on this subject in a backhanded sort of way, recognizing that the Democratic newspaper, "The *Trenton True American,* edited by Judge Naar, who had a brother, an ex-Mayor of Trenton, at the late battle, has been deprived of the corporation advertising because it was not sufficiently furious for the war. It is a dignified and able journal, calm and conservative and exceedingly moderate."

The editor explains the pecuniary effect of the deprivation, that "in 1860 the total receipts for advertising for the city was $49.96." Up to this point, the paper had done annual "work to the extent of $28.12" for the city government in Trenton, almost half the previous year. After crediting the city for one year, the *True American* was unable to continue its generosity. From there on, bills were payable in "city orders, available at the collection of taxes."

The *True American* added that on them "the moral effect of the efforts of the black Republicans to abuse and defame us, is all we could desire. It has given us an importance in the journalism of the state we had never aspired to; it has increased our circulation, and has served to rally around us many of our party friends, who had, for some time, in consequence of unfortunate domestic dissensions, looked coldly upon us."[35]

The paper truly reflected the inevitable tug between the newspaper business and its responsibility to truthfully inform the public. The city was cutting off revenue to the *True American,* but their value to those who shared their antiwar views, if the account is to be believed, was rising. And why not believe it? This would take place all over the Union; the closing down of papers and squeezing them economically caused many to rally to the Democratic cause. Often an increase in subscriptions occurred; an unforeseen change of fortune, but it was also a price that no editor wanted to pay.

The war only made competition more cutthroat. For the radical newspapers, those backing the end of slavery and a strong federal government, it was the beginning of a golden era. For those, like Hodgson, who believed in something suddenly old-fashioned, such as states' rights, the mob attacks and the mighty fury of men like Seward, Cameron, and Blair suggested that a two-class system of American journalism now existed.

Economics was one factor. So too remained the struggle for freedom. Abraham Lincoln's role was so far unclear, but national events would again force his hand, for better or worse, and he would soon weigh in on the constitutional crisis befalling a nation at war with itself.

Chapter Four

THE FIRST
BATTLEGROUND

The only way to preserve the government is to preserve the Constitution;
to observe its limitations and obey the prohibitions.[1]

—John Hodgson, December 28, 1861

Lincoln did act after Fort Sumter. Not to calm the people, but rather to forcefully suppress any further thoughts of secession. The early days of the war were panic stricken. Lincoln proved indecisive, and his cabinet members, especially William Seward, were making preparations for the president's failure. But Lincoln soon showed his backbone. On April 15, the president issued a proclamation calling up seventy-five thousand militia for three-month enlistments. He also convened a special session of Congress, which would begin on the fourth of July. But neither the troops nor the legislators would arrive soon enough to help the president wade through his next crisis. The unfolding events in Baltimore and the Lincoln administration's actions would have long-lasting repercussions for newspaper editors throughout the North.

On April 18, just three days after the official surrender of Fort Sumter, a regiment of fresh Union recruits, the Sixth Massachusetts, arrived at Bolton Station in Baltimore on their way from Pennsylvania to Washington. The historically divided city, which the *Baltimore American* predicted would be "the battlefield of the Southern revolution," was in a frenzied state. The following day, as the thirty-five-car train made its way along Pratt Street, a crowd of several hundred angry citizens hurled bricks and bottles at the passing cars, finally dumping enough sand and cobblestone onto the tracks to prevent its further movement. To avoid a fiasco, the front seven cars, which were past the point of the barricade, were unhitched, and the rear cars reversed on the tracks and pulled one by one by teams of horses to President's Station from where they had just come. Separated from the rest of the force, about two hundred men marched through the city with a large and unwelcome escort of angry Southern sympathizers.[2]

On the corner of South and Pratt streets, several residents were attacked and killed. On Stiles Street, two soldiers were killed and their muskets confiscated by angry citizens. By the time the city's police force arrived, at least four soldiers and several civilians were dead and many more wounded.[3] Later that day in Washington, the "streets were full of the bruit of the Baltimore mob."[4]

The entire Union watched the proceedings with apprehension. Tensions had been disturbingly fragile in Maryland, the only state physically North of Washington with a completely Southern mentality. The Baltimore riot, an early breach of public support for the war, caused the military occupation of the city. As a direct result, the president's wartime measures began in earnest. Whatever doubts regarding the president's determination to keep the Union whole were now swept away. He could not permit Washington to be surrounded by enemy states; it would have ensured victory right then and there for the Confederacy. He needed to move quickly—and he did.

The next day, Maryland's governor called the state legislature into special session. Governor Hicks chose not Annapolis but Frederick in an effort to comfort federal authorities, as the city was believed far more pro-Union than Annapolis. In Washington, Lincoln was watching very carefully, lest the legislature call a special state conference to vote on secession.

Surprisingly, secession never came to a vote. Instead, in what might today be called a public relations nightmare, there was strong condemnation over treating Maryland as a "conquered province." Furthermore, reflecting continuing concerns, the war was declared unconstitutional and the delegates expressed their sympathy with the South. It seems, in retrospect, to have been the worst possible path for both parties. Lincoln remained fearful of secession by Maryland, and yet Maryland remained in the Union while denouncing everything about it.

Confronted with the threat of Maryland's legislature calling a second state convention that might lead to secession, Lincoln moved decisively. The president directed General Winfield Scott to be prepared for a vote on Maryland's secession, and should a move be made in this direction "to adopt the most prompt, and efficient means to counteract, even, if necessary, to the bombardment of their cities." Their cities. The president was speaking of a loyal state, not one that had left the Union, though his opinions towards Maryland were clear.

With Congress still a week away from convening, and with no precedent behind him, Lincoln reacted. On April 27, Lincoln, under the discretion of General Scott, suspended the privilege of the writ of habeas corpus from Philadelphia to Washington. The writ of habeas corpus guarantees the right of a citizen to be charged with a specific crime if arrested, a basic constitutional guarantee. With this single stroke, the commander in chief officially took matters into his own hands. Also in a single stroke, he claimed responsibility for all that followed.

Only two weeks later, on May 16, Major General George Cadwalader, in charge of the Union forces that had occupied Baltimore, received an order from General Scott. "Herewith you will receive a power to arrest persons under certain circumstances and to hold them prisoners though they should be demanded by writs of habeas corpus."[5] It was a bold and critical move.

Baltimore continued as a focus of Lincoln's efforts. The legislature met again, this time in a far uglier mood. They were in communication with Jefferson Davis and lashed out against the suspension of the writ of habeas corpus. Though the May session also ended without a vote on secession, Lincoln was not prepared to give the legislature another opportunity to secede. Bombarding the cities was unnecessary, as no secession vote had taken place, but now was the time to forcefully assure that Maryland's troublesome political leadership would be muzzled.

The chief justice of the Supreme Court, appalled at the extreme use of executive power, soon weighed in on the question. On May 27, 1861, eighty-four-year-old Chief Justice Roger Taney ruled that the military arrest of Maryland resident John Merryman, accused of burning bridges after the Baltimore riots and later recruiting Confederate officers, violated the privilege of the writ of habeas corpus. His defiance of the president's act caused a constitutional windfall that clearly defined wartime policy. Taney, after being rebuked by Cadwalader upon the issuance of several writs, wrote that the president "cannot suspend the privilege of the writ of habeas corpus, nor authorize any military officer to do so. Only Congress has that power."[6]

Taney may have seen the work of William Seward behind Lincoln's actions. Taney so hated Seward that after Seward attacked the chief justice in an 1858 speech to Congress, Taney stated privately that if Seward were ever elected president, he would refuse to administer the oath of office to him.[7]

Ultimately, Taney ordered that the case proceedings be sent to the Circuit Court of the United States for the District of Maryland, and for a copy to be sent directly under seal to the president. "It will then remain for that high officer," wrote Taney, "in fulfillment of his constitutional obligation to take care that the laws be faithfully executed to determine what measures he will take to cause the civil process of the United States to be respected and enforced."[8]

But Lincoln would not be pressured by the Chief Justice, and he ignored the ruling. Clearly he was prepared to take whatever steps were necessary to quell public expressions of support and sympathy for the Confederacy. The president, who just weeks before was harshly criticized by both Democrats and Republicans for inaction, now seemed determined to keep the border states as part of the Union, no matter how.

Baltimore became one of the first political battlefronts of the Civil War. Its loyalty, a well-established fact of life, was to be held at any cost. Its location, just forty miles below the Mason-Dixon line, the imaginary line that divided North from South, made the city a no-man's land of sorts. Less than sixty miles from Washington, it was also a short journey by train via the Baltimore and Ohio Railroad. Baltimore had become a mishmash of cultures, a dynamic and divided city that had maintained an uneasy cultural hegemony of both North and South, but clung devotedly to its Southern sympathies.

Baltimore was the home of every Democratic National Convention between 1832 and 1852. After delegates walked out of the 1860 Democratic convention in South Carolina, a second one was held in Baltimore. After several days of talking in Baltimore, a splintered group of Virginians led another delegate walkout, and a third convention was held in the city. The divided party, unable to come to terms, now offered two candidates: Southern radical John C. Breckinridge, and Abraham Lincoln's nemesis, Stephen A. Douglas.

In the same city, the Constitutional Union party, the country's third political party, its platform advocating the preservation of the Union at any cost, nominated John Bell of Tennessee and former vice president Edward Everett of Massachusetts.

In the presidential election, Maryland cast more 42,497 votes for Breckinridge and 41,177 for Bell. Stephen Douglas, who ran as a second candidate from the fractured Democratic Party, pulled almost six thousand votes, while his long-time adversary Abraham Lincoln mustered less than half that number in the state.[9]

The vote showed approval of a Democratic candidate sympathetic to the South and a Constitutional Unionist from the South. With the votes totaled, almost ninety thousand were cast in favor of anti-Republican candidates. The Republican, Lincoln, received two thousand three hundred votes. However, he was the only Republican candidate. Like the division of the Democratic Party in Pennsylvania led by editor John Forney, the fractured Democratic Party in Maryland divided its vote as well. The electoral vote put Abraham Lincoln into office.[10]

Baltimore reacted predictably.

After the clash of brick-throwing citizens and newly enlisted Union soldiers in April 1861, President Lincoln was thrust into the unenviable position of pacifying the most immediately critical Northern state, not to mention the most belligerent one.

One of the men overseeing it all, Major General John Adams Dix, knew the importance of the city to the war. "The loss of Baltimore would have been the loss of Maryland; the loss of Maryland would have been the loss of the national capital, and perhaps, if not probably, the loss of the Union cause."[11]

No less than eight newspapers in the city, pushing for Southern rights, fueled Baltimore's hostility. The *South,* the *Daily Exchange,* the

Daily Republican, and at least five other "secession" journals were being produced that opposed the war in all of its forms. At least one paper, the *South,* was created "in anticipation of the very troubles that are now upon us—and in the hope…to stay and avert them." But as not to confuse its readers to its loyalties, the *South* editors told their readers in its debut issue that its staff "recognize[d] the fact that the people of Baltimore and of the state of Maryland are at this moment in open and armed rebellion against the government of the United States. We would have preferred, had we our choice, that what has been done should have been done by authority of law, and in pursuance of an Ordinance of Secession, emanating from the sovereign power of the state. We hope," the article continued, "that under the passage of such an ordinance we will soon sunder forever our present relations with the federal government and the Northern states and unite our fortunes, where all our sympathies and interests combine with those of our sister states that have already withdrawn from the Union."

Still they were not done, but went on to invite dissension and mock those that disagreed.

> In the meantime, the fact that we are in a state of revolution simply makes no difference in our eyes as to the justice of our cause. It is a righteous and a holy cause and we are ready to stand by it to the last. If it is rebellion we are content to be rebels—if treason, traitors—we care not under what name—we are contending for the inviolability of the soil of Maryland and her emancipation from federal thralldom and section domination.[12]

The bantering for the Confederacy came from a large part of Baltimore's population, and the dissension had been brewing for some time. Such talk, though, created panic in the new administration just a few miles away in Washington. In an attempt to curb the disloyal sentiments, the Lincoln administration moved to early action to sweep it aside by targeting the disloyalty.

Baltimore's city government was elected in late 1860 under the auspices of an independent reform party. The corruption of city officials was so flagrant that in 1859 the state legislature had unseated all ten members of the Baltimore delegation. In response, a special session of the legislature was called to elect new city officials. To prevent further corruption, they removed several important mayoral powers, including the appointment and control of a city police force. Instead, the legislature appointed a Board of Police Commissioners, composed of leading men of the city. Charles Howard, William H. Gatchell, Charles D. Hinks, and John W. Davis were charged, with the mayor, George Brown, to protect the city. Their force of 398 men roamed the streets armed with revolvers.[13]

Charles Howard, the president of the commissioners, was the grandson of three-time governor John Eager Howard, the hero of Cowpens and the third highest-ranking American officer during the Revolutionary War—behind the American decorated Frenchman Lafayette and his close friend George Washington. Charles Howard, long distinguished for his community service, was a Maryland judge and philanthropist.[14]

The loyalty of the police commissioners was tested, with Howard and the others acting swiftly during the April 19 riot, all in all preventing what could have easily become a much bloodier catastrophe between citizens and soldiers. But despite their efforts at this critical time, such measures on behalf of the city would not override personal politics and the possibility of what might come. Lincoln showed he would not take any chances, even with men who had to date proven their loyalties.

Soon the city was under military law. On May 13, General Benjamin Butler, whom Lincoln put in charge of the newly created

Annapolis Department, sneaked trains into Baltimore where they spent the night fortifying Federal Hill, overlooking the city. The United States Army, not the police force, now controlled the city. Butler wired the commander of Fort McHenry: "I have taken possession of Baltimore. My troops are on Federal Hill, which I can hold with the aid of my artillery. If I am attacked tonight, please open upon Monument Square with your mortars." The next morning he issued a proclamation to the citizens of Baltimore stating his intentions to keep peace in the city.[15]

The recently installed Reform Party, which had helped prevent secession in the state legislature, was also under suspicion for disloyalty. On June 27, Marshall George Kane, one of their leading members and the leader of one hundred thirty policemen during the April riot, was arrested. Around 4 a.m. on July 1, a month after at least one of his sons fled South, Charles Howard, president of the Baltimore City Police Commissioners, was torn from his house on Cathedral Street. Simultaneously, the three other members of the Board of Police Commissioners, John Davis, Charles Hicks, and William Gatchell, were pulled from their homes and arrested by soldiers. They were sent to nearby Fort McHenry where they waited, without trial, and without being charged with a crime.[16]

With the events at Fort Sumter and then in Baltimore behind him, and with assurances that there was more dissension to come, Lincoln was anxious for the upcoming session of Congress, which ran from July 4 to August 6. Citizens did not feel safe. War fever was rampant, tensions were high, and enthusiasm was as threatening as opposition. Editors watched Congress closely, as the future direction of the country now lay in the hands of elected officials in Washington.

Congress worried John Hodgson. It was the first Republican congress in American history. With well-known radical elements leading many strategic committees, Hodgson could not predict the impact that body would have on the administration's prosecution of the war, and more importantly, the restrictions they might put on individual liberties, specifically the right to a free press.

On July 4, Lincoln addressed a special joint session of congress. Besides asking for money to pay for the war, he directly tackled the case of the Baltimore police, and extrapolated the precedent it had set for future security within the Northern states. For one, Lincoln refused to recognize the right of states to leave the Union. Furthermore, he traced his own authority back to the general election, noting that:

> ballots are the rightful and peaceful successors of bullets; and that when ballots have fairly and constitutionally decided there can be no successful appeal back to bullets; that there can be no successful appeal; except to ballots themselves, at succeeding elections. Such will be a great lesson of peace; teaching men that what they cannot take by an election, neither can they take it by a war—teaching all, the folly of being the beginners of a war.[17]

Lincoln addressed his own reservations about the future, recognizing that "no popular government can long survive a marked precedent that those who carry an election can only save the government from immediate destruction by giving up the main point upon which the people gave the election. The people themselves, and not their servants, can safely reverse their own deliberate decisions." But for the time being, he was willing to take that risk.[18]

Lincoln asked the Congress, rhetorically, "Must a government, of necessity, be too strong for the liberties of its own people, or too weak to maintain its own existence?" His answer was that "no choice was left but to call out the war power of the government; and so to resist force, employed for its destruction by force, for its preservation." Questions of the "legality and propriety" of his suspension of the writ of habeas corpus were unfounded, he pressed. The Constitution clearly stated that the privilege of the writ of habeas corpus as defined in the Constitution was not a law, but a provision "that such privilege may be suspended when, in cases of rebellion, or invasion, the public safety does require it." Baltimore and the future of the Union depended on the suspension, and so it was done, and now offered to the Congress, the attorney general, and the judiciary to determine if the justification warranted the act. Chief Justice Taney had already rebuked the president, stating that the power to suspend the writ of habeas corpus was reserved for Congress: the Republican Congress was more accommodating.[19]

The first few days of the first session of the Thirty-seventh Congress were chaotic after Lincoln's address. Republicans held majorities in both the House and the Senate. Republicans had taken 32 of 38 seats in the Senate, and 106 of 176 in the House. Seats from Oregon, Nebraska, and Pennsylvania were in dispute, as were representatives from the western part of Virginia. On July 8, the House of Representatives voted to exclude all business not related to the military and naval operations of the government from their discussions. On July 10, ten senators from Southern states were expelled.[20]

Sandwiched between arguments for an increase in pay for soldiers, the creation of a national day of thanksgiving, and pension allocations for the widows of congressmen, the session quickly became an exercise in constitutional elasticity. Lincoln was himself not a strict constitutionalist, but instead referred frequently to the Declaration of Independence as the nation's unalterable code of behavior. "I have never had a feeling politically that did not spring from the sentiments embodied in the Declaration of Independence," he told an audience at Independence Hall in February.[21]

The first major land battle of the Civil War, at Manassas Junction in Virginia, was still two weeks away, and legislators were working with the confidence that war could and would still be avoided. Clement Vallandigham of Ohio, who would later be expelled to the Confederacy and would run against Lincoln in 1864 from Canada, pushed a series of resolves condemning Congress's lofty language, making such promises as "to vote for any amount of money and any number of men which may be necessary to insure a speedy and effectual suppression of such rebellion...."[22]

One of the many bills aimed at the arrest of traitors and confiscation of property was offered by radical Republican John Hickman of Pennsylvania, who sought to provide Lincoln with the legitimacy he requested for his actions in Baltimore. In other words, he was to create a legal umbrella to justify the draconian actions the president had already taken. Hickman was also baiting Lincoln to take bolder action to defend the home front.

As such, it was an unusually dangerous bill.

Hickman's confiscation bill, like similar bills offered by Lyman Trumbull, Dwight Loomis, Henry Wilson, Charles Sumner, Zachariah Chandler, and others, was aimed at the confiscation of rebel property, and more pressingly offered the first debate of whether slaves could be considered such property. But Hickman may have had another agenda that would not be debated in committee or on the floor. A vague confiscation bill giving power to district attorneys and United States marshals, acting on their own discretion, would provide Republicans with an opportunity to silence their most outspoken critics in the North: newspaper editors. A confiscation bill would also provide an opportunity to destroy old enemies, and Hickman had the power to do it: he was chairman of the House Judiciary Committee.[23]

Chapter Five

THE LOYAL OPPOSITION

"What is the frame of government under which we live? The answer must be: The Constitution of the United States."

—Abraham Lincoln
February 27, 1860, Cooper Union, New York

"We [have] given on our first page the message of President Lincoln to the special session of Congress…The president admitted that he has violated his official oath, and now asks Congress to legalize his acts in bringing about the present war."[1]

—John Hodgson, July 13, 1861

Congressman John Hickman was publicly mistrusted by John Hodgson, and with good reason. Thin and wiry, Hickman stood not more than five foot, ten inches tall and weighed one hundred fifty pounds soaking wet. He suffered from "bleeding at the lungs," but maintained a ferocity and energy that outdid even the most energetic men. When a new courthouse was built in West Chester, its cornerstone laid on July 4, 1846, Hickman suggested that the motto engraved on its edifice should read, "Justice is damned uncertain here."[2] When standing "as a cross-examiner, Hickman was courteous—excessively courteous—never used a bludgeon; but upon discovering a weak point in a witness, thrust quickly and deeply," read one contemporary account. "As a speaker he wasted no energy. He dissected his opponents' argument with surgical skill and disposed of a half hour's rhetorical talk with a blast of sarcasm," a trait both melodramatic and effective.[3]

By the coming of the Civil War, Hickman was no stranger to public office. A delegate to the 1844 Democratic convention that nominated James K. Polk for the presidency, Hickman ran for Congress that same year but was defeated by a Whig candidate. In 1850, while serving as Chester County's assistant district attorney, the physically fragile lawyer served as chairman for the Democratic Party's State Central Committee. Four years later, bypassing a local agreement between the Democratic and Whig parties by which they sent candidates to Washington in alternate elections, Chester County's Democratic Party presented John Hickman as its congressional candidate.

Hickman, like his then longtime friend John Hodgson, had been a true and loyal Democrat for most of his life. But by the time he ran for Congress in 1854, his second attempt at that office, Hickman was being swayed by the national debates over issues that included the protective tariff, the acceptance of new states into the Union, and most directly, the spread of slavery into those territories.

Employing the campaign techniques of the day, the congressional hopeful refused to speak publicly during his campaign, and by doing so avoided many of the hard pressing issues of the day. Personally, he held views that were not popular with his Chester County constituents. Politically, he kept them to himself.

Hodgson, though perhaps skeptical of his candidate's strategy, stuck by him, as of "Mr. Hickman's standing in the community it is altogether unnecessary for us to speak." Hodgson always went toward the best interests of his party, and Hickman's tenacity and towering intellect were unmatched weapons in the pitched campaign that was coming to a head.

Just a few days before the election, Hodgson insisted that Hickman would stick by the ideals under which his party nominated him—uncompromising opposition to Know-Nothingism, and steady support to the national and state administrations. "Mr. Hickman," he assured the readers of the *Jeffersonian*, "having accepted the nomination of the party under such auspices, requires no further endorsement as a Democrat. He is not the man to swerve from the strict line, and, unless we are greatly deceived, would scorn to accept the nomination of a party whose doctrines were at a variance with his own."[4]

Hodgson offered unconditional support, but still Hickman was quiet.

Election night held more than one surprise. "Vast crowds hung about the hotels until late at night to learn the result," the *Village Record* reported. "As township after township was received the excitement grew still more intense.—The returns very significantly showed that there had been some strange voting in Chester county, and that the calculations of those heretofore wise in political matters were knocked into a cocked hat. No one knew where he was or what was to come next. Old party lines were broken up or disregarded and some districts disclosed the strangest political somersets."[5]

It was a sign of things to come.

When all was done, the Democrat received an eclectic mix of votes from all parties—Know-Nothings, Whigs, and Democrats. In West Chester, Hickman won by a sixty-two-vote margin, 298 to 236.

Overall, Chester County totals showed 6,794 in favor of the Democrat, with 4,195 votes cast for his opponent.

The aftermath was utter confusion. How did Hickman pull the required votes from opposing parties? Hickman was only one of seven Democratic victories for twenty-five congressional seats from Pennsylvania, a state in which one-third, or nearly one hundred twenty thousand votes, were controlled by the Know-Nothings. His slide away from the Democratic Party was becoming more transparent, and that swung voters. [6]

"John Hickman, Esq., has been elected to Congress from this district" reported the *Jeffersonian* victoriously. "He received the united support of the Democratic Party—and also of the Irish and Know-Nothings. His election is claimed as an anti-Nebraska victory. We cannot see on what grounds. He was nominated by the Democratic Party, but NOT ON THAT ISSUE." Hodgson was outwardly frustrated with the accusations, and was beginning to have reservations about Hickman's politics. "Having accepted the nomination of the party," the editor tried to convince himself and his readers, "he stands morally bound to advocate its principles, and we believe that he will not flinch from his duty. He may entertain views different to us on that subject; we do not know that he does; but if so it matters but little. That issue has been decided, and was legitimately out of the question in the election of congressmen."[7]

In 1856 Hickman won reelection. He campaigned hard for James Buchanan, but after his candidate was sworn in, things slowly began to turn sour between the two. Buchanan, a fellow Pennsylvanian, was followed by scandal and in the sway of a pro-Southern cabinet, and Hickman turned the other cheek. When the newly elected Hickman arrived in Washington to begin his second term in the United States Congress, his conscience motivated new moral leanings that continued to worry his Democratic constituents. Within a year, his political defection from the party was almost complete, and all of John Hodgson's fears, several years in the making, began to be realized.

In 1859, mid-way through his third term in the House of Representatives, Hickman addressed the Pennsylvanian legislature at the state capital in Harrisburg, using the occasion to warn of the dangerous times ahead. He blasted his former friends in the Democratic Party with hard-nailed accusations of corruption and greed, vowing to save Northern rights "by walls of fire and blood, if needs be."[8]

Hickman suffered several horrific personal blows while in Congress. In August of 1858, as he waited for the day's election returns, a tragedy occurred from which he would have difficulty recovering. It was one of the primary reasons that John Hickman was retiring in 1860, at least before his name was thrown about on the Republican presidential ticket.

"It was about two o'clock p.m.," a guest wrote in a letter to his daughter.

> I was sitting in the parlour. I heard a loud cry from the other side of the street & raising the window found it came from Mr. H's black girl who was coming across towards our front door. I met her at the steps, and the only articulate words I could understand from [her] were "Oh! Come Mr. Lewis, Mrs. Hickman is dying." I immediately called your mother who went over directly to Mr. H's & sent Enoch to bring the first physician he could find. Your mother on entering Mr. H's library found Mrs. H. sitting on a chair, the blood running from her mouth, & Mr. H. supporting her head. Your mother took Mr. H's place & supported Mrs. H. but she almost immediately sank down, gasped a few times, and expired.

Mrs. Hickman had not been ill, so the entire tragedy took the family by surprise. "It seems that after dining Mr. H. entered to his library to rest with instructions not to be disturbed till five o'clock," the letter continued in gruesome detail.

> Mrs. H. about the same time lay down in her own room intending to lie till four. Soon after lying down the rupture took place & she hurried to the library & knocked at the door. Mr. H. was roused by the knock & knowing something extraordinary must have occurred rose instantly and unlocked the door, when Mrs. H. staggered in saying that she was going, and was supported by her husband to a chair where your mother found her. It was probably not five minutes from the time the bleeding began till she was over.[9]

Another blow of a different sort took place in early 1860, when after making a criticism of the state of Virginia in a speech on the House floor, Hickman suffered further personal injury. "A personal confrontation occurred after the adjournment of the House today," reported the *New York Tribune*'s Washington correspondent.

> As Mr. Hickman was returning home through the capitol grounds he was overtaken by Mr. Edmondson of Virginia, who upon approaching him called out, and drew back his hand to strike. Mr. Clingman, who was accidentally passing, hastened up and seized his arm, when Mr. Edmondson struck at Hickman with his left hand, knocking off his hat, but doing him no injury. The whole affair was instantaneous, and seemed to surprise Mr. Hickman. Mr. Breckinridge, who came up, took him away, and the scene ended.

The attack was reported as the result of Hickman commenting that Virginia had been afraid of John Brown, the leader of the unsuccessful slave revolt in the state, "and twenty-one Confederates, and a cow."

The attack was an outgrowth of frustration over the Kansas-Nebraska Act, which gave incoming states the option to choose whether slavery would be allowed within its borders. Illinois senator Stephen Douglas pushed the idea of "popular sovereignty" hardest. After a speech by Douglas on the subject, Hickman was overheard commenting that "upon thy belly shalt thou go, and dirt shalt thou eat all the days of thy life."[10]

As chairman of the House Judiciary Committee, John Hickman had the power to kill or elevate bills for the House floor. Many, including several of the proposed confiscation acts offered early in the Thirty-seventh Congress, never made it out of his committee, which comprised John Bingham and George Pendleton of Ohio, Alexander Diven of New York, James Wilson of Iowa, William Kellogg of Illinois, Albert Porter of Indiana, Benjamin Thomas of Massachusetts, and Henry May of Maryland, the only border state representative of the group. In all it was a moderate group, like its counterpart in the Senate Judiciary Committee. Hickman needed help.[11]

In five years in Washington, John Hickman's transformation from a conservative Democrat to a radical Republican was well documented within the congressional halls. He had come out strongly against Southern attempts to spread slavery into the Western states. His frustrations with the administration of James Buchanan were apparent.

What worried him most now, above all else, was slavery. For his money it was the only question facing the country at this critical hour. Like John Hodgson, Hickman did not oppose slavery on moral grounds, but as a political and economic means. Slavery would be the single issue that would forever divide the nation, and there was no middle ground. It must be allowed to spread or be forever destroyed, he figured. Hickman had made attempts at conciliation with halfhearted support from Stephen Douglas, but his efforts did not last long.

Like the president, Hickman knew the importance of editorial support. His came in the form of the man who would become Lincoln's favorite editor, John Forney. Of all of the famous New York editors whose names are still familiar today, Greeley, Bennett, and Weed, it was Philadelphia editor John Forney who most flawlessly played the role of politician/journalist. Forney, who only recently had been caught up in a well-publicized government printing scandal, had circumvented the system by working from the inside, an enviable position that, despite the liberal patronage bestowed upon doting journalists, could not be equaled.

Colonel John Forney was an American of pure German stock, a product of American capitalism, and a political and journalistic tycoon. He stood almost five feet, nine inches tall, was handsome with a round nose, his face framed by muttonchops and a small beard on his lower lip, symmetrically groomed to perfection. He drank constantly and was rarely seen without a half-chewed cigar dangling from his lips.

Forney's career had bounced him from one newspaper to the next government job and back again. By 1860, several of the newspaper bosses in New York were competing for title to a monopoly over the Northern presses. Larger papers like the *New-York Times,* the *New York Tribune,* and the *Brooklyn Eagle* were fighting not only for subscribers, but also for political patronage. New York alone had 174 newspapers in 1860. The largest ones had financial resources and political connections that made competition by smaller papers laughable. But while the New York papers were devouring each other,

Forney had taken control of Pennsylvania and was on his way to greater spoils still.[12]

Forney had supported the Democratic Party through thick and thin, at least until after the election of James Buchanan in 1856. Still, he had decided to see it through. He thought Stephen A. Douglas could win the election in 1860, and the country could avoid the unavoidable war. But ambition soon got the best of him, and he wasted little time in transferring his allegiance to Douglas' long time nemesis, Abraham Lincoln. In fact, ambition had gotten to him years before, but opportunity was less frequent then, and not as exploitable as at the present.

He had been in the newspaper business since the age of sixteen and was proficient in the intricacies of the trade. Forney grew up in Lancaster, Pennsylvania, where he eventually purchased a local paper, the *Lancaster Journal.* During his tenure there, he grew intimate with another rising Lancaster boy, James Buchanan. After Buchanan's appointment as secretary of state under President Polk, Forney's friendship was rewarded with a lucrative position as surveyor of the port of Philadelphia. He had finally found his calling, learning to juggle his journalistic interests with the rewards of governmental patronage.

When the Democrats lost the presidency in 1848, Forney lost his position and moved to Washington to strengthen ties, working as an editor for the *Washington Daily Union.* But he was restless, as was his old friend from Lancaster. In 1851, Forney finally won the position he had come to Washington to gain: a congressional appointment as clerk of the House of Representatives. This appointment provided him with the best of both worlds—a means to political power and personal profit. From that point on, he worked diligently to obtain printing awards for the *Daily Union* from members of the House, a lucrative advantage to being nearby.

Taking a calculated risk, he resigned his position in the House to campaign for his old friend, James Buchanan, who went on to defeat the Republican Party's first ever presidential candidate, John Fremont, and former president Millard Fillmore, who was nominated by the waning Know-Nothing Party. With Buchanan in the Executive Mansion, the patronage would come ten-fold, and the curly-haired German whose poor financial condition forced him to quit school twenty years before was prepared to reap the benefits. In addition, Forney decided to press his fate and run for a Senate seat himself. It was a once-in-a-lifetime chance to be the master of his own destiny, a dangerous but attractive opportunity. Instead of reporting policy, he would make it.

But events went far from predicted. Forney lost his momentum, and so he looked to the newly elected Buchanan for help. It never arrived. In a climate where dissatisfaction toward government corruption gripped the country, Buchanan was unable or unwilling to secure the patronage due his counterpart. Unable to secure an appointment to the cabinet, Forney refused an appointment to the Liverpool consulate, believing the president would at least deliver for him the printing charge of the general post office. The post office printing would have secured his fortunes, requiring four to five steam presses working ten hours per day, year round, with at least twenty hands and just as many compositors and workmen. Charging for the resetting of stationary and other blanks ran at least fifteen dollars per change. All in all, the post office patronage earned at least double any other government-printing job.[13]

But by that time Buchanan's hands were tied. Defeated and frustrated, Forney returned to Philadelphia. But he wasted little time before beginning his newest project: a new democratic organ named *The Press*. Its existence as a democratic organ was short-lived, though, and Forney began to involve himself in the sea change sweeping the nation. The Democratic Party was growing militant. Most especially, their defense of Southern claims to slavery was becoming unbearable to him on a personal level. *The Press,* led by its proprietor, made an about-face and reinvented itself as an outspoken, anti-Buchanan propaganda sheet. Within a year it was the largest paper in Pennsylvania.[14]

Forney used his paper to put pressure on those he needed, and to destroy those who had let him down. Surviving a congressional investigation into the patronage given to editors by the federal government, the wily editor started over, this time from the other side of the aisle. His change of heart did not escape the notice of the *Jeffersonian,* which in the midst of the first session of the wartime Congress recognized that Forney "has been doing all kinds of dirty work for the black Republicans, and endorsing all the doings of the Lincoln administration."[15]

During the course of Forney's newfound faith in the Republican party, Hickman was experiencing a similar change in conscience. In short time, the "twin renegades," as Hodgson labeled them, would ruthlessly threaten even the dynasty built by William Seward and Thurlow Weed.[16]

Hickman's conversion produced the very worst situation in politics for Hodgson: a former friend now bitter political foe. Hickman at times seemed exasperated, and had become militant in his desire to persecute the war and most recently to rid the country of the great disgrace, slavery. Given Hickman's thirst for power, political clout, and new-found radicalism, it was not a recipe that bode well for the *Jeffersonian* or even, ironically, for Lincoln himself.

The relationship between the Thirty-seventh Congress and the administration was often strained. Even without Southern supporters, the Union spoke with many different voices. On one side were the moderates who often sought to find a means of compromise with the Southern states. On the other side were the radical members of the Republican party, powerful members of both Houses, who sought to push Lincoln into an immediate emancipation of the slaves as well as assuring a hard line would be taken regarding Southern leaders. They also at times sought to embarrass the president, as is true of many a Congress both before and since. It was a tumultuous time and the president struggled to maintain good relations with all. The result, of course, was often frustration and anger from those who wanted Lincoln to move faster against the South and those still seeking some sort of compromise.

On July 8, John Hickman offered his resignation from the House Judiciary Committee, but it was not accepted. Ironically, it occurred on the same day that the first confiscation act, one of eight offered over a two-week period, was proposed. His motivations are unknown, though it may have been a political maneuver to free his time, or to free him from conflicts with a series of critical wartime measures he himself would soon help introduce. Realistically, it was an empty gesture he knew would be refused. His work on legislation that he was sure would please his fellow Republican congressional radicals had already begun. These were the men who were frustrated at the slow pace of the war, the lack of Lincoln's support on efforts to free the slaves, and what many of the radicals saw as too weak a policy towards those supporting the rebellion.[17]

A week later he introduced one in the series of legislation aimed at the confiscation of property in the Northern states, which included: S. 25 to confiscate property used for insurrectionary purposes; S. 26 to confiscate property of persons in rebellion against the Constitution and the laws of the United States; S. 29 for the confiscation of property of persons in rebellion against the Constitution and laws of the United States; and S. 35 for the punishment of conspiracy and kindred offences against the United States and for the confiscation of property of the offenders.[18]

Hickman had come out enthusiastically for the war, leading the charge to finance it. When the president called for seventy-five thousand troops, Hickman demanded appropriations for "the largest number of troops necessary." When Lincoln's call for as many as five hundred thousand troops was scoffed at in the House, Hickman called for "twice five hundred thousand men."[19]

Hickman's stance was clear. He told the House, "We have met here, being entirely cognizant of the fact that certain men have come into this hall for the purpose of paralyzing the arm of legitimate power; but we have met here for the purpose of strengthening that arm. We have met here for the purpose of teaching those men that they cannot paralyze that arm, or diminish its power."[20]

On July 15, Hickman introduced a bill that both defined the criteria for a conspiracy and offered punishment for the offense. The bill, passed resoundingly that day by the House and a few days later unanimously by the Senate, gave district and circuit courts the power to try "persons who conspire to overthrow the government" or levy war upon it. Conviction would be punishable by a fine not exceeding $5,000, or imprisonment not exceeding six years.[21]

One investigation began before the Senate even read the bill. Representative Henry May of Maryland's Fourth District had only just left the House chambers, having been ill, when Representative John Potter of Ohio offered a resolution to investigate May for "holding criminal intercourse and correspondence with persons in armed rebellion against the government of the United States." The resolution passed, and the investigation was given over to the Committee on the Judiciary, chaired by Hickman, and on which May served.[22] May pleaded his innocence, having admitted that he had recently visited the Southern states as had been reported in several

Northern newspapers, but insisted he was not in collusion with the enemy. Within a few days, May was absolved of any wrongdoing, at least for the time being. More importantly, the Committee on the Judiciary relieved Lincoln of "any suspicion of a correspondence or attempted correspondence through Mr. May."[23] No person, not even the president, was beyond Hickman's reach.

Congress was moving swiftly, and sending a clear message to dissenters, starting within their own ranks. Hickman was among the small group of men frustrated with Lincoln's deliberate pace. The congressman's actions during this time were more than likely to give Lincoln the grounds to operate with impunity in Baltimore, throwing into jail more elected officials and any newspaper publishers whose sympathies lay with the South. And, if so, who requested this congressional action? A nervous Lincoln, a troubled Secretary Seward, Hickman himself, or perhaps, most likely, were public relations at work, assuring the government displayed a united front in these emotional times?

Hickman's efforts to define conspiracy and its penalty was the first in a series of steps consummated on August 6, the final day of Congress's first session. After its passage, the Senate began to discuss a bill to confiscate property used for insurrectionary purposes, or what would serve as a preemptive measure against those identified by Hickman's bill and pending trial, as well as a built-in evidence-gathering clause. The Senate easily passed the bill, but intensive debate continued in the House.

The issue was not so much confiscation, but a definition of property. Congressmen from the border states resisted a clause that identified slaves as property subject to confiscation, claiming that such action was unconstitutional. Thaddeus Stevens, a radical Republican pushing complete extermination of the Southern way of life, spoke on behalf of many Republicans when he denounced the argument and those that offered it: "Who pleads the Constitution against our proposed action? Who says the Constitution must come in, in bar of our action? It is the advocates of rebels, of rebels who have sought to overthrow the Constitution and trample it in the dust...I deny that they have any right to invoke this Constitution...I deny that they can be permitted to come here and tell us we must be loyal to the Constitution."[24]

The bill was voted down on its first and second readings. But Hickman was willing to give up something to provide the government protection against its own citizens. Massaging the section aimed at the confiscation of slaves, the language of which too specifically spoke toward emancipation, the bill passed by a margin of sixty to forty-eight votes.[25] On return to the Senate for the approval of new language, a twenty-four to eleven vote sent the concurrent bill to the president.[26]

On August 6, 1861, three weeks before the late August cabinet meetings in which the decision to target opposition newspapers was likely made, the president sent a message to Congress via his private secretary reporting the bills he signed that day. It was the last day of the first session of Congress that the presidential address of July fourth had kicked off, in which he rationalized the events in Baltimore and his subsequent actions, seeking congressional approval.

On August 6, 1861, President Lincoln signed S. 25, "An Act to Confiscate Property Used for Insurrectionary Purposes." According to the *New-York Times,* Lincoln was visibly unnerved by the lack of consensus in both the House and the Senate. President Lincoln, reported the paper, paused before signing the document. Congressman James Blaine remembered the same, noting that "it did not meet with his entire approval," Lincoln considering it premature.[27]

Recognizing that many of the chief executive's powers did not translate into a wartime atmosphere, Lincoln had spent the past month working with the Republican Congress on measures that granted the president wide executive authority. But he was still reluctant to seize the power the radical element of his own party was forcing upon him. In this case, one of the final measures of the session, one of the widest reaching, and soon, most widely abused, bill was enacted. Any persons engaged in supporting "the present or any future insurrection" by aiding and abetting the enemy in any form shall be open to the seizure of any property used for that aim.[28]

What it meant was that any Southern supporter in the North could face the loss of their property if it was used to help the Confederacy. Few would object if the bill was limited to say, a horse used to ferry cargo to the Confederates troops. But Union Democrats feared that the administration and men like Hickman would consider an anti-Lincoln newspaper to be a tool against the Union and hence, it could be confiscated. And not just the newspaper but the type, the press, the office, and all associated with it. In short, no matter the Constitution, John Hodgson and his allies could be wiped out financially.

The much-debated actions taken by this Congress would obviously have dire repercussions for newspaper editors in the North, and the fears of groups such as the Association of Democratic Editors in New York, as well as the rural papers such as John Hodgson's West Chester *Jeffersonian,* had much to fear. How the Confiscation Act would translate into their world was, as of yet, anyone's guess.

"We made history like magic," later gushed John Forney, and how right he was. He and Hickman must have continually pinched themselves at their good fortune. From political and business careers that were floundering, these two men were now trusted advisors to a new and uncertain president. Patronage and power were within their grasp and their social circles included the legendary men of the time.[29]

As Lincoln struggled to hold Northern and Southern factions together, John Hickman had pushed through a bill that gave President Lincoln broad power to quell Northern dissension. Unfortunately, the president did not have the power to control the struggle occurring within his own cabinet, let alone in distant areas where local officials might use the recent acts of Congress to make a name for themselves.

On the surface these actions were, of course, in response to the war. But for men like Hickman and Forney, Seward and Cameron, any tool to settle old scores and enforce financial gains was no doubt deeply appreciated. John Hodgson and other Democratic editors could only witness the frenzied rush of events from the Executive Mansion and Congress and pray that they could leverage the only weapon available to them: their readership.

Chapter Six

SUMMER OF RAGE

"There is no grievance that is a fit object of redress by mob law."[1]

—Abraham Lincoln, January 27, 1838

"The Democratic Party is now, as it always has been, the only true party of the Constitution and Union; and candid Republicans admit that if the country can be saved and the Union restored under the Constitution, it will be done by the Democrats."[2]

—John Hodgson, March 7, 1863

There is one peculiarity of a summer storm; it builds slowly as the dark clouds gather ominously on the horizon. Often, ample warning is provided. So, too, for Democrats during the summer of 1861. Many knew by now a different sort of storm was brewing and that there was little to do but wait.

On June 27, a week before the president opened the special joint session of Congress, a meeting of the Association of the Democratic Editors of the State of New York convened to discuss the rebellion and the future of their presses. It was more like a war council than a convention. The atmosphere was somber, but openly defiant in reaction to Lincoln's recent assumption of military powers, and the threat that action posed to the publishing industry. Lincoln's handling of events in Baltimore, the growing strength of Republican editors, and the military arrest of newspaper editors in the West had established an alarming precedent from which no one seemed safe.

The New York gathering of editors, one of many that would occur throughout the North, was presided over by Congressman Benjamin Wood, recent purchaser of the *New York Daily News,* an openly anti-Lincoln paper. G. J. Clark of the *Lockport Advertiser* acted as secretary.

Some of the papers represented at the meeting had stood behind peace advocate Stephen Douglas in the late presidential campaign, others for the radical John Breckinridge, a Kentuckian who served as James Buchanan's vice president. But, according to the *Jeffersonian,* "in the present crisis of the country passed [sic] presidential and other differences are buried in oblivion."[3]

Above the engulfing taste of tightly wrapped cigars, the sweet aroma of lingering smoke, and the hard bite of whiskey was an uneasy exchange of gossip, each participant careful not to let on to his uneasy fear for the future. Several primary issues were on the table: the constitutionality of civil war; fears of constitutional violations by President Lincoln; the expense of war; and finally, and most critical to their personal interests, concerns over the perpetuation of the freedom of the press. These fears arose despite the repeated assurances of the president to the contrary. Early in his administration and even before, the president argued that he stood squarely behind the rights of the press to freely publish their opinions. The president's recent actions in allowing a chill to settle over many traditional American freedoms, however, spoke louder than his words.

Another underlying issue was the unusual power base being established by New York publishers like Horace Greeley and Thurlow Weed, men who spoke directly to the president on matters of state. In a time of spoils, where good soldiers with the ability to sway public opinion would no doubt be rewarded, Greeley and Weed were not, as Democrats saw it, the only unrepentant victims unable to resist the temptations of power and influence. The idiosyncratic Greeley had wavered back and forth with his support of Lincoln before finally throwing his weight wholeheartedly behind the candidate at the Republican National Convention. His support was based on Lincoln's abolitionist tendencies, but the reward expected by the popular publisher was far more mundane, and the horse trading had already begun.

Other so-called supporters of the war were clawing their ways into the graces of the Lincoln administration for their own benefit. Lincoln's open door policy assured that they would continue to clamor into the halls of the Executive Mansion. Greeley and a few other exclusive publishers even had their own mailboxes in the president's office.[4]

The editors that gathered in June passed a series of resolutions that were widely printed in Democratic newspapers. The first resolution was diplomatic, the group desiring "the perpetuation of the Union of these states; but in the language of the lamented Stephen A. Douglas we believe that 'war is disunion,' and that if the Union be continued, it be upon the principal on which it was formed, viz: the voluntary consent of its members." Of course, the popular Democrat before passing away had offered his support to Lincoln without reservation, so this was a bit disserving.[5]

The final resolutions were more adversarial in reaction to current policy trends coming from Washington and the explosion of hatred and mistrust engulfing the country.

> Resolved: that the present alarming and deplorable condi-
> tion of our country has arisen mainly from the exercise of
> unconstitutional powers by the present chief magistrate,
> who has not hesitated to inaugurate a war, to enlist a large
> standing army, to increase the navy, to seize private papers,
> to deny citizens right to bear arms, and to suspend the writ
> of habeas corpus.

The men were eager to repeat the often-heard refrain that
Abraham Lincoln was guilty of not only starting the war, but had also
undertaken actions that were far beyond the powers given the
president and the executive branch under the Constitution.

It was no solace to the assembled men, but Lincoln, too, worried
he was violating the mandate provided by the Founding Fathers. But
saving the Union came first, decided the president.

The next resolution attacked the Republican Party in graphic terms:

> Resolved: that the Republican Party has proved that all its
> pretensions of devotion to freedom, free speech, and free
> discussions were simply cloaks to conceal their real enmity
> to liberty and the constitutional guarantee of citizens, and
> that the attempt to muzzle the Democratic Press by mobs
> and terrorism, to prevent citizens from expressing their
> honest opinions, calls for and deserves the earnest
> condemnation of every true friend of law, order and liberty.

Whether a public relation stunt or not, the assembled editors were
afraid. "By mobs and terrorism" were two administration weapons
most in the room had come to dread. Loss of their livelihood and the
muzzling of opinion were viewed as administration weeds that
sprouted throughout the Union.

Next came the call to resist the efforts of Lincoln to move the Union in a new direction:

> Resolved: that in view of the many manifest violations of the fundamental principals of the Constitution, it becomes the duty of the Democratic Press and of all friends of free institutions, to unite in resisting these alarming strides towards a despotic consolidated system of government: and that it be especially suggest to all friends of peace and constitutional liberty, irrespective of party, to agree upon a joint and mutual basis for action at the present crisis.[6]

The Democratic editors were themselves masters of public posturing and they sought gamely to position their party as the defender of the American way of life against all attempts to create a country that was un-American. These Democratic views would resonate even with patriotic supporters of Lincoln and would later hurt the Republicans in the ballot box as the administration seemed to many to begin to push too hard to silence Southern supporters.

The New York resolutions not only conveyed the basic fears of Democratic editors, but also initiated a united front, a call to publicly take on the commander in chief and anyone working through his administration to crush the "friends of free institutions." Several factors had been identified.

- First, the publishers and editors were concerned that Lincoln was trying to fashion a consolidated system of government.
- Second, from the perspective of the Democrats, this evolution was contrary to the concept of a united government of independent states, functioning in voluntary association to create a more perfect union.

- Third, it was their view that this association could be cast aside if so desired by the people in any given state.
- Fourth, that the Democrats were patriots; after all, none at that convention had fled south.
- And finally, the means for carrying out all of the above was that the very heart of the First Amendment would be sacrificed by Abraham Lincoln, the diabolical leader of this new power-hungry, sectional political party.

To these editors of Democratic political organs, the Republican Party was comprised of men like Weed and Cameron who were far more interested in the next huge government contract than the so-called principals that were openly being espoused by pious politicians sending tens of thousands of boys to war.

In early August, Baltimore *Daily Exchange* editor Frank Key Howard, shadowing the opposition coming out of West Chester and other places, wrote a piece headed "War on Northern Newspapers." He pressed the concern that even as far north as Connecticut there were a number of newspapers "which have provoked the wrath of the war party in that state, because of their efforts to secure an adjustment of our sectional difficulties by other means than fire and sword."

"Unsuccessful attempts," Howard bravely stated, "have been repeatedly made to crush them out, but intimidation, withdrawal of patronage etc, have proved vain."[7] Howard singled out his concern this time for the *Bridgeport Farmer,* a Connecticut paper holding close to its ideals despite continued warnings by the federal government and local citizens.

Soon there would be a long grocery list of papers that could be singled out, from Maine to Maryland to Missouri to Illinois. But let us stop for a moment and consider with an unprejudiced eye the crime of this Connecticut paper. Why were fellow Democratic editors concerned for the safety of the editor and the future of the paper? What was the crime for which Republican editors were so angry? According to accounts, the *Bridgeport Farmer* had been targeted for "speaking of President Lincoln as a despot, and for accusing him of using despotic powers, or in other words, powers not delegated to him by the Constitution of the United States."

Republicans were shocked at this sort of criticism, not because it was false, but because it was a time of war, and dissension should not be tolerated. Here was a newspaper calling the president of the United States a despot and, especially after its army had just been embarrassed on the field of battle, such rhetoric could not be tolerated. The mob, the *Farmer* was warned, would arrive soon.[8]

Editorials in Democratic newspapers argued that if there was illegality in their words, then why did they not "complain of it to the U. S. district attorney, who is a Republican, and one of the president's officials, and put the question to the test by a criminal prosecution?"[9]

The answer was ironically simple. Republican papers had been guilty of the same "crime" just one year before, when in anger over the policies of then-president Buchanan they unleashed a storm of criticisms against the president of the United States. Of course, Buchanan was a Democrat and as such was fair game for the Republican papers. With the roles reversed, why should it be different with a Republican in office?

The answer, they pressed over and again, was incontrovertible: the country was at war.

The *Bridgeport Farmer* saw trouble in late July and early August, and was, as warned, destroyed by mob on August 24. Heated dialogue over the motives and methods of those trying to destroy it seemed an unsubtle introduction to a firestorm that swept through Northern newspaper offices during the restless month of August.

Through June and July, the government made half-hearted attempts to utilize the judicial system to gain legitimacy for their war against administration opponents. Republican editors took it upon themselves to launch a massive verbal assault on Democratic papers in an attempt to stir fear and discontent in the minds of their subscribers. The Confiscation Act, passed in early August with Hickman's help, gave local officials a new weapon: presidential endorsement. A battle to win over the average American to a new era of suppression was now underway.

By August the summer storms were in full force. Secretary of State Seward had, for the time being, wrestled control of the newspaper question, and particularly the responsibility of civilian arrests, from the man who wanted to control them, Simon Cameron. With a willing Thurlow Weed looking over his shoulder, Seward was ready to act upon his supreme power. But now, with local authorities able to make arrests themselves, Democrats were asking who was in control.

From the outset of the war, Seward held legal control over civilian arrests, which he retained until it was transferred to the War Department in February 1862. Cameron fought throughout this time for ultimate authority under the justification that the entire country was at war. It also made sense because the State Department had no enforcement mechanism, and so civilian arrests were inefficient and unorganized. Many arrests were never recorded, nor were many of them even enacted on Seward's orders. Instead, local officials acted on his behalf.[10]

Seward clearly took on power far beyond that of a normal secretary of state in the battle to muzzle dissent. Sometime that summer, a group of Baltimore wives visited the president on behalf of their husbands who were being held in Fort Lafayette, begging for their freedom. The men were never charged with a crime and languished in the prison solely for supporting the Southern cause. Lincoln politely listened to their grievances, but answered that there was little he could do, as these were Seward's prisoners, not his. Not the sort of answer one would expect from the commander in chief and president of the United States. Nonetheless, Lincoln obviously supported the unusual actions of his secretary of state and soon, in fact, made sure he had congressional support as well.[11]

But Simon Cameron, the mistrusted and often unscrupulous secretary of war, also continued to order arrests without Seward's knowledge, accounting for some of the prisoners unaccounted for in the secretary of state's records. For those arrested, finding either a justification or a source was a monumental task. Editors did not know what to make of the system, even while being victimized. As shown in "The Accounting," published by Bennett's *New York Herald* on August 28, legally publishing Democratic newspapers began that summer to fall by the wayside in small towns and large cities alike, whether in New England or the far West. The pattern was depressingly similar. A Democratic newspaper that had been part of a local community was attacked by a mob, the office destroyed, the publisher threatened with his life. In some cases it was an economic attack, with advertising being withheld. In other cases the papers were denied access to the railroads, thus depriving them of much-needed out-of-town subscribers.

Whatever the course of action, it was greeted often with glee by the most passionate of administration supporters and with a growing sense by Democrats that this president, so versed in the ways of the media, was allowing those surrounding him to take advantage of the war to silence political opponents and newspaper competitors.

It was not an isolated occurrence as often reported. Nor was it limited to any one location or region. Nor was it the actions of a young administration only, as the assaults on antiwar newspapers continued throughout the war, though with a special vengeance right up to the mid-term congressional elections. For the first time in our country's history, an administration unleashed the full power of the government to shut down opposition newspapers.

The attacks conveniently began as the first wave of Union soldiers was coming home.

August 1861 was critical for the army and those men and women still at home. Union soldiers—farm boys, laborers, clerks, priests, fathers, and sons—had heeded Lincoln's call and rushed off to join the war via three-month enlistments into the world's greatest army. In August those enlistments expired. Many returned home to reenlist. Many returned home for good. All returned with a different perspective on the war and the world they lived in. After the confused horror of Bull Run, it was obvious that the war would be a drawn-out affair. The optimism of a quick and bloodless war, a misconception on both sides, no longer existed.

Now soldiers with a new perspective on Southern resilience found unprotected targets as they returned home. They had seen their friends and neighbors die a few short weeks before, the image of splintered shells piercing human flesh haunting their days and nights. Some were emotionally spent, and would pose no threat at home. Others were angry and vengeful.

Opposition newspapers had much to fear when they openly insulted the president that sent those soldiers to fight. The inevitable clash had the Hodgsons wondering if they had been made victims by a group of these disillusioned soldiers.

Republican editors, sensing an opportunity, helped stir the discontent, lumping together pro-Southern newspapers with antiwar newspapers. Peace Democrats were grouped with war Democrats, and anyone who dared speak against the Union cause was considered a traitor. George Pearce, Hodgson's weak-chinned, flat-nosed rival at the *Chester County Times,* plainly verbalized the point of view. "Whenever you meet with a man who begins to talk about peace, set the fellow down at once as a traitor."[12]

The war had come home, and no town was unaffected. Newspaper offices, regardless of their right to speak openly and unfettered, were now the targets of angry men and boys with knives and guns and torches. Local authorities stood to gain nothing by opposing these gangs of uniformed men protecting their country against "traitors," and so editors and compositors, men who often had no protection except words of compromise, defended their newspaper offices to the last.

It was a useless defense, and so some chose violent alternatives.

On August 8, two days after the passage of the Confiscation Act, soldiers of the first New Hampshire sacked the *Democratic Standard* in Concord, Maine. "While the city authorities endeavored to quell disturbance," a Baltimore paper reported, "the Palmers fired four shots, wounding two soldiers. The office was immediately gutted and the materials burned in the street."[13]

According to reports, at least six returning soldiers, their anger feeding from an unquenchable animosity, entered the office of the *Democratic Standard.* The far-off *Chicago Tribune,* a Republican paper run by Lincoln supporter Joseph Medill, reported that "it would have gone no further than personal chastisement…had not the Palmers defied a mob by making a very foolish display of guns and bludgeons at the windows."[14]

Frank Howard printed a detailed, and at times, embellished account as provided by its New York correspondent, all from the perspective of a Democratic newspaper. "Civil war has commenced in the old Granite State," it began, "and God only knows what ravages are yet in store for our people." According to the reporter, the office was ransacked, all of the property "taken into the streets by military men in uniform, and burnt to ashes in the presence of ten thousand people, women and children. The proprietors of the establishment, and the people generally, fought like heroes," he noted in defense.

> The troops were driven from the building three times by the proprietors alone. The people were unable to gain admittance at the stairway entrance to assist Mr. Palmer on account of the soldiers. The soldiers, finding they could not gain admittance at the doorway on the upper floor, which enters the office, without a great sacrifice of life, fell back, and commenced storming the building from the street with stones and bricks. Finding the crowd had increased and that one thousand volunteers were gathering fast, Mr. Palmer retreated from the premises, having received only a slight blow from a stone. He was attacked by the soldiers, but by the aid of his friends and his own perseverance, found his way through a crowd of ten thousand people, uninjured.[15]

Between the two differing accounts, the foolish defense offered by Medill and the heroic stance by Howard, several observations are undeniable. The mob activity "led to some important developments in the Northern conspiracy against the government," Medill's *Chicago Tribune* printed, "and is likely to bring still other facts to light, besides furnishing a wholesome warning, in its own fate, for the benefit of other like minded."[16]

The message was clear. Democratic opposition to the president's war would not be tolerated—no matter the legality—and Democrats who continued to oppose the war effort would be shown no quarter. There also seemed to be no predictability as to who would be attacked next.

On August 12, the *New York Daily News* printed a list of 154 "peace" papers. Three more newspapers (the *New York Ledger,* the *New York Day Book,* and the *Brooklyn Eagle)* picked up the list in the next few days before spilling into papers across the North. It seems to be the first time that a list was publicly compiled that listed in total those newspapers that were opposed to the Civil War.

Why was the list published? Why was it even assembled? It is quite possible that it was done for the same reason that the generals count the troops just before the battle. It may have been done for no other reason than for opposition papers to seek a vengeful comfort in the growing fears that must have been gripping Democratic editors.

The strategy, though, would backfire. Despite the threats and mob attacks, many of the newspapers still refused to change course, and their opposition to the war continued despite warnings of dire consequences. New Hampshire was neither the beginning nor the end. Papers in Missouri, Kansas, and Ohio had already seen trouble, their presses destroyed by angry mobs, and more would come.

As the list of peace papers was being circulated in New York, a mob closed in on the office of the *Democrat,* a newspaper printed in Bangor, Maine. The office was raided by a group of citizens, its equipment carried into the town square and burned. A local paper dispassionately reported that "the people have determined that a secession organ should not exist in our city."[17] There would be no arrest, no trial, and no defense. Mob justice, so far untamed by law enforcement, ruled supreme.

The editor of the *Democrat,* Marcellus Emory, provided his own stirring reaction in the columns of another paper. "Thus hath the freedom of the press been stricken down here in Maine," he wrote, "not from any patriotic impulse, but through the wicked instigation of a band of abandoned politicians who would willingly subvert all law and all order for the maintenance of a mere party dogma." Emory knew that the political institutions in the town, including the mayor, had deserted him and left him to the mercy of the Republican mobs.

Astonishingly, in a display of patriotism and a sense of right common to many of the victimized editors and proprietors, Emory still showed complete faith in the United States and its inherent sense of fairness to those opposed to the current administration.

> Though anarchy seems to be coming down upon our unhappy country like night, yet do I not despair. I still believe that there is yet virtue and intelligence enough in the people to maintain their liberties and protect a free press, which is their best guardian. By this act of mob violence, my all, the result of four years of unremitting toil, has been swept away; but I still have health, strength, and youth, and a heart also to struggle on in defense of the people's right.[18]

Faith in virtue and intelligence, though, was a difficult defense against an angry mob, and Emory was probably only trying to convince himself of the coming of better days.

How long could a proprietor and his staff subsist on such abstract and indefinable ideals in an openly hostile environment? That might prove to be the true test.

So far no editor had been killed by mob action, but not necessarily for lack of trying. The *Brooklyn Eagle* reprinted an accounting of an attack made by Bull Run veterans against a New Hampshire newspaper. The soldiers attacked the office, but the publishers themselves were armed and held out. Several of the attackers were shot, while the publishers escaped into the attic.

The publishers were finally rescued by city authorities and taken to the local jail for safety, the crowd following with cries of, "Lynch them! Lynch them!" The eyewitness believed that for the offending antiwar publishers, "their preservation from death was a very remarkable circumstance."[19]

No reporter was safe, not even the renowned *London Times* correspondent William Russell. He was welcomed upon his arrival in America with Lincoln's usual flattery for the press, "The *London Times* is one of the greatest powers in the world—in fact, I don't know anything which has much more power—except perhaps the Mississippi."[20]

Candid comments about the Union troops' poor handling of Bull Run, plus suspicions he was too far from the battlefield to correctly observe events, opened the reporter to the same dangers as Democrats writing against the administration. An August 14 letter from Russell's home office, whose editors were strongly anti-Union, sums up their feelings and concerns succinctly. "When your description of the Bull Run affair appeared everyone said 'Russell will be lynched'—and there was very serious apprehension for your safety. That anxiety however seems to be subsiding since people have seen the subject treated by the Americans themselves. What a press! Is it the result…of an utterly brutal state of morals? Are we to come down to that sort of thing here in England?"[21]

Russell finally left Washington and went to New York, where, incredibly, he reported privately to the *Times* that an unknown man had sought to bribe him to change his perceived anti-Union articles and even offered to buy the shares of the *London Times.* While there is little reason not to believe this veteran reporter, the identity of the man who offered the bribe remains a mystery.[22] The year after Bull Run the reporter was denied a military pass to travel with the Union army by the secretary of war. After Lincoln refused to help this man whom he had welcomed so warmly just the year before, Russell left America disgusted in April of 1862.

Not all agreed it made good sense to treat so poorly a reporter from a country as critical as Great Britain, whose continued neutrality in the war was vital to Lincoln and the Union. In September of 1861, C. F. Adams Junior wrote to his father, the ambassador in England, that "the folly of our press in assaulting so savagely an agency so formidable as Russell has troubled me."[23]

But the message was clear: Lincoln and his administration would take an active role in making it personally difficult for those reporters whose comments could not be trusted or controlled, whether for readers at home or those in critical European states. It was spin control beyond any previous White House.

On August 15, 1861, a week after the signing of the Confiscation Act, partially in response to the meeting held by Democratic editors in June and the recent escalation in tensions, the administration's battle against the antiwar newspapers broadened to include the courts. A grand jury was convened in New York under foreman Charles Gould to determine the legality of indicting Northern newspapers that openly opposed the war. According to the grand jury, "There are certain newspapers within this district which are in the frequent practice of encouraging the rebels now in arms against the federal government by expressing sympathy and agreement with them, the duty of acceding to their demands, and dissatisfaction with the employment of force to overcome them."

> These papers are the New York daily and weekly *Journal of Commerce,* the daily and weekly *News,* the daily and weekly *Day Book,* the *Freeman's Journal,* all published in the city of

New York, and the daily and weekly *Eagle,* published in the city of Brooklyn....

The grand jury are aware that free governments allow liberty of speech and of the press to their utmost limit, but there is, nevertheless, a limit....

The conduct of these disloyal presses is, of course, condemned and abhorred by all loyal men; but the grand jury will be glad to learn from the Court that it is also subject to indictment and condign punishment.[24]

The language was careful not to charge any of the newspapers with a crime, as the press, in theory, still had a right to publish freely. In reality, each paper identified was now a target and was publicly warned to change their editorial tone or face the consequences. Though the grand jury was really only questioning what might be done in this situation, the government quickly used the event to begin seizing the newspapers named and stopped their shipment through the mail.

On August 22, the newspapers named by the grand jury were suspended from the mail per order of the New York postmaster. As the papers arrived in Northern cities that day by train, the United States marshall for the Eastern District seized all copies. The legal justification was the War Department's General Order No. 67, which ordered that all correspondence and communications, verbal or written, that put the "public safety" at risk, should be confiscated. The punishment for creating such correspondence and communications, according to the order, was death.[25]

It is worth considering some of the points raised by the grand jury, especially the theory that the freedom of speech has well-defined limits. Even in the indictment, the worst offense that could be cited by these patriotic citizens was that a sample of the Democratic newspapers had published a list of newspapers opposed to the current war. There are no charges of working with the enemy, of publishing secret maps, of disclosing military information, or of printing incorrect information, all of which had at one time or another had taken place within the pages of Republican newspapers. Any of these actions would be serious grounds for disciplinary action.

The newspapers listed by the grand jury were deemed guilty of being in opposition to war. Granted, the war was not thousands of miles away but right in the hearts and minds of all Americans. As the grand jury asked, would not a soldier preaching peace to his fellow fighters be arrested despite the freedom of free speech guaranteed under the Constitution?

The response throughout the nation's history had been that the rules pertaining within civilian society are different from those enforced by the military. The military has its own courts and judges. Soldiers and military personnel are subject to a different set of regulations that the basic Bill of Rights affords to all under the Constitution.

In essence, therefore, the grand jury was saying that civil society no longer existed during this time of crisis, and that the rule of the military was now the rule of the entire country. President Lincoln had already shown this in his suspension of the writ of habeas corpus.

The crime of some of the largest newspapers in the nation, which already had been the topic of at least one issue of every squabbling newspaper in the North, was their opposition to the war. Despite the passage of the Confiscation Act and similar bills, Congress was still attempting to define such vague terms as "conspiracy" and "kindred offences." In the interim, mob justice would eliminate most opposition.

Democrats, as shown by the meeting in New York and others like it in the North, were showing that they would not be caught unprepared in the storm, their feet wet and their noses bloodied.

One of the emerging young journalists in New York decided to carefully tackle the points raised in the indictment and to expose the folly of the grand jury activities. Twenty-nine-year-old Thomas Kinsella was an example of the promise and hope of independent American journalism during the 1860s. Kinsella wrote that he was never an "extreme Democrat, and so I continued to steer the *Eagle* through turbulent times."[26] He felt he could depend on his keen writing and debating skills to both intellectually win over the Lincoln administration, which he thought ineffectual, and keep the paper publishing.

The Republican Party, he wrote in August of the upcoming state elections, "will lay down a platform of war and war only. Being a one idead [sic] party…now devoting its energies to remove all penalties for murder and convert the law into a shield for assassins, and anon devoting its energies to an antislavery agitation, it has never had a comprehensive policy embracing the whole country."[27]

His paper was idealistic, and operated without fear of violence or intimidation, no matter how strong the language. Kinsella's *Brooklyn Eagle* was the largest evening paper in the Union, so its hard-hitting columns in defense of the Democratic Party and a free press were widely read.

Kinsella's tone was defiant. His piece condemned the unprecedented New York grand jury investigation into several New York newspapers, his own *Eagle* included. It was the thought of an honest man speaking his mind about what was plainly a dirty political piece of propaganda unfurled against the Democrats and their supporters.

The young editor reminded his readers that it was Horace Greeley's "*New York Tribune* and other organs of the government" that had published the opinion that the government should submit to the Confederacy having lost the first major battle of the war at Bull Run.

"We never," he clarified, "uttered a word implying it to be a duty to follow such a course or 'accede' to the demands of the Confederates." Then, having clearly presented the observation that Republican newspapers were uttering far more treasonous statements than the Democratic papers, Kinsella pointed his pen at the overall folly of the recent grand jury. "It will be seen that the grand jury presents the daily *Eagle* and weekly *Eagle* as newspapers in the frequent practice of encouraging rebels," he began.

Kinsella then went to the heart of the matter, that "the fact is that the war organs of New York are in a rapid decline for lack of nutrition; they are, therefore anxious that their rivals should be crushed out, and hence endeavor to direct popular animosity against them."

"A list of the obnoxious papers was published, and among them was the daily and weekly *Eagle,*" Kinsella demurred.

> We observed the circumstances but did not consider it worthy of notice or remark. This list was the basis of the presentment of the grand jury, and this illustrious body accepted the partisan misrepresentation of the abolition organs as sufficient proof on which to base their conclusions without ever having, as we have reasons to believe, read a line in the *Eagle* or knowing whether the weekly, which they condemned, had an existence.
>
> So far as the principle of the free speech and a free press is at stake, we will vindicate and maintain it. It is a right which abolitionist, now in the ascendant, neither gave nor can take away.
>
> If this is treason they can make the most of it.[28]

Legally, Kinsella wondered what basis the grand jury had to meet in the first place. It was another example of the Republican administration manipulating the government at the public expense, using the courts as their personal instruments to achieve a political goal.

The *Brooklyn Eagle* was soon forced to adopt a more pro-administration slant in order to continue the business. In a unique first person perspective on just how subtly the threats sometimes were brought against the antiwar papers, Kinsella writes that "my predecessor brought the paper under the censor of the government that lead to his retirement." The incident took place in September of 1861 and according to Kinsella, "Finally, McClosky's withdrawal was demanded by the Postmaster General (Montgomery Blair) as a 'sine qua non' of having the papers standing restored." Continues this young editor who took over the chief editor position, "It was understood that McClosky's successor should be a 'union' man who would be acceptable to the leading Union men of Brooklyn." [29]

Kinsella also discussed the fears of the publisher that the paper would lose its power and hence circulation because of the grand jury actions. But the opposite happened; as during the "Summer of Rage," the circulation jumped from nine thousand to thirteen thousand in August.[30]

Regardless of Kinsella's objections, the desired effect was being achieved.

Papers were not always closed by faceless mobs. For the *Advertiser and Farmer* of Bridgeport, Connecticut, antiwar rhetoric, including passionate defenses of the Constitution, provoked Union soldiers. "The Constitution is the government," the edition dared to maintain, and "the president is but an agent to execute its provision…and when he departs from these, he violates his oath and is himself the greatest of rebels."

On August 24, in full view of more than five thousand onlookers, Union troops destroyed the office.[31]

But the mobs were not always unreasonable. William W. Harding's *Philadelphia Inquirer* offered the consolation that the Republican mobs did have a weak spot for a sweet-talking woman.

> In Easton, a mob ransacked the *Sentinel* office, then moved on to the *Argus* office, property of Col. Hunter, the ex-post-master, and it was broken into, and they voted then to give him twenty-four hours to amend his ways, or "reform," they then rushed on to attack the homes of several prominent Democrats, including that of Honorable Judge Porter. The order was given by the mob, "On to Porters"—one of the oldest and most exalted citizens of our Commonwealth.

But the mob was stopped cold, not by constitutional wisdom, but when "one of the accomplished daughters of the judge made her appearance at the window, and, in language most chaste and beautiful, assured the crowd of the love and reverence which the entire household bore for the Union and for its bright and glorious emblem!"[32]

Many were looking backward into American history to justify their beliefs both for and against stifling the freedoms of the press. "All who do not shout hosannas to Abe Lincoln and endorse his unconstitutional and unholy war upon the people of the South are denounced as Tories," wrote the editor of the *Circleville Watchman* in Cincinnati.

> The people behind Lincoln know perfectly well that it is not and never has been unlawful to discuss or to denounce

the measures of the government in times of peace or war. They know that not only in this country, but in England also, the people have been privileged for a hundred years past to avow their opinions and their own good pleasure about the policy of plans of their rulers…. When we were engaged in a desperate struggle with England, the papers of Massachusetts denounced our government and encouraged our enemies.[33]

Historical rights notwithstanding, the juggernaut against the Democratic newspapers continued. Now a seemingly coordinated assault incorporating the judiciary, the legislative, the executive, and all of their outlets seemed to be converging on the home front. Democratic editors braced for the worst.

Despite the fear of Democratic editors and the violence that had erupted against them, most Northerners looked the other way. It was deemed unpatriotic to take action against the boys in blue. The muted response from either the public or the media in the Union was noticed as far away as London, where the *London Daily News* openly marveled that the American public accepted the loss of press freedoms.

From the perspective of the British editor, it was of late an American tradition, as he believed that "very few were the journals which boldly and steadily upheld the principles of the Republic, and the rights of the citizens. This immensely aggravates the difficulty of the present hour. The American public have not been accustomed to tolerate an opposition press."[34]

No matter the subdued response from the public, the administration seemingly remained nervous about their unprecedented wave of activities and launched a sophisticated public relations campaign to prove the constitutional high ground for their activities. There may well have been concerns that it was the articulate responses of editors like Hodgson in Pennsylvania, Howard in Baltimore, and Kinsella in New York that were causing patriotic citizens to question the administration's war tactics. Clearly, a counter offensive was required.

On Monday, August 19, 1861, Edward Everett, a recent vice presidential candidate who would later take precedent over Lincoln at the dedication of a new cemetery in Gettysburg, published an article in the *New York Ledger* on the topic of "Northern Secession Journals." Everett's zealous call to arms would inspire a fanatical wave of citizen mobs across the North. It would also be the first attempt to rationalize such activity and came immediately after the August 1861 cabinet meeting blessed a federal effort to wipe out opposing newspapers. Opined Everett,

> There are presses, for the most part in the border states, though some of them are found in cities more remote from the scene of action which are daily pleading the cause of the enemy, misrepresenting and vilifying the government of the United States, exaggerating every article of unfavorable intelligence, and exerting themselves to the utmost to dishearten the friends and defenders of the Constitution and the Union.
>
> But such is the all but superstitious devotion of the people to the liberty of the press that these pernicious journals have, with the exception of a single instance in St. Louis, never been interfered with.
>
> It is in fact an absurdity in terms, under the venerable name of the liberty of the press, to permit the systematic and licentious abuse of a government which is tasked to the

utmost in defending the country from general disintegration and political chaos.[35]

First, Everett denied the existence of a problem. No newspapers, he argued, had been "tampered" with. Except for one way out in St. Louis. So there really, he contended, was no problem at all. Then, he belittled his opponents, calling their views a superstitious devotion to a free press.

Here was Edward Everett not only condoning but also pressing that mobs destroy newspapers. "Shall we hesitate in such a crisis, and split hairs about possible abuses of authority..." the Republican politician screamed.[36] Of course not.

We could dismiss Edward Everett as an administration mouth-piece. Yet as befitting a man who carried some sort of real or imagined weight within the current administration, his words were important. He would have been a perfect choice to make such comments, though it seems that his words were all his own. They just happened to come at a perfect time

A public discourse sprang up on the merits of Everett's column. His words were warmly received by the mainstream press, despite his condemnation of the freedom of the press. "The liberty of the press is to be enjoyed so long as it does not aid in the destruction of the government," seconded Occasional, the pseudonym John Forney used when writing from Washington.[37]

Wrote Henry Raymond's *New-York Times*, "It seems to us that Mr. Everett's position on this subject is clearly just, and that editors of newspapers should be allowed no more impunity than is accorded to any other men in assailing the existence of their government."

And then astonishingly, "Speech should only be free when it is loyal.... Whenever the press becomes dangerous to the existence of the government, it must be checked by the law."[38]

Attacks by Civil War soldiers against editors as called for by
Everett was a masterful cover. Guilty parties did not have to suffer the
consequences of civilian law. If there was no bodily harm inflicted,
then there was usually no need for punishment. Besides, Republican
editors usually applauded the efforts. Republican newspapers were
pushing for more decisive intervention, which would give the mobs
legitimacy and wipe away their crimes as acts of passion and justice. It
seemed, though, that in these early cases newspapers had trumped the
so-far-defensive activity of the government, and single-handedly took
responsibility for persuading mobs to destroy Democratic dissension.
Disturbingly, Republican papers flexed their muscle in the face of
their newspaper counterparts, but even more disturbingly, flaunted
their power over the government.

Others were happy to jump on the bandwagon. Also speaking in
defense of the administration was Daniel Dickinson. The former
senator was no stranger to the passion of politics, having once been
forced to disarm a colleague who had drawn a pistol against another
senator during a heated discussion on the Compromise of 1850. A
brilliant public speaker, he began traveling the country delivering fiery
condemnations of those opposed to the Lincoln Administration.

Thundered Dickinson to a large crowd:

> But to suspend the "Liberty of the Press!" Oh, how bad that
> is—to have the press suspended. (Laughter) The liberty of
> the press! You say anything to them on the subject of the
> government—"liberty of the press" is the first thing you
> hear. The press has liberty enough; and here let us shake the
> wrinkles out of this befogged and pettifogged question a
> little. The liberty of the press is a great and sacred right and
> blessing. But the liberty of the press is no greater a right
> than individual liberty, and than a thousand other rights.

The liberty of the press is to enjoyed so long as it does not aid in the destruction of the government...In my opinion, Mr. Lincoln ought to have laid his hand upon a great many treasonable journals which he has not done. (Cheers) A more abominable abuse never existed. If Satan had been let loose after his confinement of a thousand years, he could not have done more mischief that these miserable treasonable journals.[39]

Carefully, a few Democratic voices could be heard in opposition. Frank Howard, from Baltimore, took on the famous orator directly. It is worth reading as he would soon find himself muzzled, joining his colleagues in a federal prison. The anger and frustration that Howard felt can be read through these lines, which are unusually sarcastic for a column of the time.

The "enforcement of the laws" is getting on famously. Newspaper offices are "gutted"—as the term is—with great success, by "loyal" multitudes. Congressmen are burnt in effigy, in the most creditable and satisfactory way. In Massachusetts, where they always do such things best and where the influence of Mr. Everett's eloquent precepts is likely to be greatest, because of his proximity, they add tarring and feathering, and riding on a rail, to the list of their efforts on the behalf of the Constitution. Nothing can surpass the noble and generous patriotism with which the citizen of Haverhill possessed themselves of the person of the "the editor of a secession sheet" (meaning an unhappy man, who dared to oppose abolitionism and war)—they covered him with a "coat of tar and feather"—rode him on a rail through the town and then compelled him to make recantation of his opinions, on his knees, in the midst of brutal and horrible indignities. "I am sorry," the wretched victim was made to say, "that I have published what I have and promise that I will never again wrote or publish articles against the North."

What a triumph of reason and free institutions!

Upon the heads of such men as Everett, and those who united with him in his crusade against freedom of opinion and speech is the sin and the shame of such outrages.[40]

Three days prior, Howard had taken on the president, asking for a discussion "in plain English. When Mr. Lincoln says—or his advisors say for him—that he has a right to suspend or violate the Constitution in order to preserve the government…[he] means that the powers conferred on him by the Constitution are not sufficient, and he must assume other powers which the Constitution does not confer." In other words, he must govern the country for the time outside the Constitution. But that is not all, added the paper. "Mr. Lincoln claims…[i]t is treason to take up arms against him. It is rebellion to oppose his authority. He may be wrong, he admits. [But] if Congress is on his side, and will not impeach him or find him guilty, there is no remedy at all. This is the sum and substance of the famous opinion of Mr. Attorney General Bates."[41]

The mob madness continued throughout August. Egged on by the rumors of the August cabinet endorsement of the street actions, blessed by the leading orators of the day and the major newspapers, it became the summer of rage against the antiwar newspapers. Surely the violent attacks justified discussions by Lincoln and his cabinet? Was that the topic of the cabinet meetings that occurred the week of August 19 as reported by the *Philadelphia Inquirer*? And would all the mob action and newspaper closings that followed been condoned if it had not been quietly endorsed by the cabinet? Surely someone close to the president should have expressed concern.[42]

Until now, the action had been confined to mob action. In mid-August, postmaster Blair supported Seward's strong-armed tactics with his own: he began a provocative policy of throwing Democratic newspapers off the trains. This had the immediate effect of preventing the antiwar newspapers from New York or Philadelphia from being read outside the home region. The effect may or may not have been a safer Union; but without a doubt it brought a windfall to loyal men like Forney and Weed. Boasted Forney in late August, "*The Press* was the only paper received in Washington. Owing to the stoppage of all the New York papers in Philadelphia yesterday to search for the packages of the *Daily News,* no papers came through last night but the *Philadelphia Press* and the five or six hundred copies of your sheet were all brought up in fifteen or twenty minutes after their arrival."[43] For Forney, the crackdown was turning into an economic windfall.

Throughout the summer, there existed a muted response from the political opposition. One can only imagine their fear and concerns for their personal safety. Few were willing to join with editors like Howard in publicly debating the administration's supporters and its draconian policies. Instead, it fell to the international community to show condemnation for the wanton disregard of basic constitutional rights. One such pointed example could be found to the north, in Canada.

Warned the *Toronto Globe* in response to the summer of rage:

> This is not only an exceedingly foolish way of proceeding—it not only insures its own punishment by encouraging a race of journalists who will never speak the truth except when likely to please, but it does more than almost anything else to lower the American people in the

estimation of all civilized nations. We care not what the destroyed journals published. If treasonable matter, then the writers ought to have been punished in due course of law, and not by a mob....

At the present time, especially, the assumption of power by illegally constituted tribunals ought to be sternly checked, or the great republic will be resolved into chaos from which there is no return, except by "the purchase of order at the expense of liberty."[44]

Equally concerned as their colleagues in Canada were the British newspapers, several of which reported with surprise on the use of jail time and mob tactics to silence editors and politicians. As the news of the summer madness trickled to England through "Mr. Reuter's Express," the *British Daily News* published a long and articulate examination on the merits of the silencing of the opposition press in America. Wrote the editor, "The case of the press has already become one of the chief difficulties of the new situation. And it is not only a grave embarrassment in itself, it indicates a series of perils which will have to be dealt with, however the war may terminate."

The editor asked the question that was on the minds and lips of many in the Union. What should be, he wondered, "the fate of an opposition press, in a time of civil war, in a democratic Republic?"

Now that the policy of compromise and connivance with the South is at an end, must all the newspaper accord with their renewed minds, or will they tolerate journals which speak now as they all spoke and thought two years ago? If they can bear to have everything told, and every man allowed to say in print what he thinks, believes, and senses, the political regeneration will be proved to be real and complete; and the best patriots may well rejoice. This is, however, too much to expect.

Hedging his bets, still unsure if the latest news was true, he reasoned that:

> In a country with democratic institutions, where every man has a voice and a part in the government, mob tyranny would be a deeper disgrace than it could ever be in any of the old countries of Europe; and all true patriots in the free states should dread its uprising more than all the forces of the South. If it is true...that a newspaper editor has been tarred and feathered for his opinions in Massachusetts, the citizen will have to decide immediately what course they will take.

The editor reached a surprising conclusion, preferring "censorship of the press than to a mob carrying tar and feathers to punish opinions." In other words, the silence of the loyal opposition should come from the American institutions and not the violence of the streets.[45]

No matter the international condemnation, by summer's end the administration enjoyed the greater support from just about all walks of the society. Men like Everett encouraged the angry returning soldiers to mob the antiwar newspapers while newspapers carefully laid out the argument as a just need on the part of the Union. The attorney general proclaimed the entire proceedings legal, and the Congress endorsed the behavior by providing a legal umbrella with their passage of the Confiscation Act, even if the suppression of the press was not the primary objective of the measure. Apparently others, like John Hickman, recognized other uses for the bill, especially confiscation of newspapers that had pro-Southern sentiments.

Still, there were concerns. Even pro-administration papers echoed Hodgson's published fears that, once introduced to a new climate of oppression, there would be no turning back. "We bear in mind whatever has at any time been proven in favor of the utmost latitude of opinion," the *Philadelphia Inquirer's* William W. Harding editorialized, "and of the hazard of interfering with its prescriptive freedom in this country, without erecting precedents which may, in the future, wantonly control its just expression."[46]

Seward, Weed, Cameron, and others, like Forney and the radical congressman John Hickman, had developed a well-reasoned plan of attack. The Confiscation Act appeared to provide legal justification for closing the newspapers, and as of yet editors were too scared to contest that justification. Respected leaders whipped up crowds of returning solders into a mob that served as the first battering ram against any dissenting voices. In this environment of fear, patriotism, valor, and a belief that the very future of the Union was at stake, no one would dare question the activities of the administration.

The president, inevitably swept into the controversy, was in a difficult position that would not only test his own resolve, but the delicacy of his interpretation of the Constitution during times of war. This mass assault on the Constitution seemed within what might be referred to as "the Lincoln doctrine:" that there could be no constitutional freedoms without a full Union. Such strong-armed tactics served his purpose of stifling opposition, especially in the critical states of Maryland and Pennsylvania.

Lincoln clearly left much of the operations to the cabinet. As he did with the military in the early months of the war, he was not inclined to become involved in the details. Yet despite his being uncomfortable with the Confiscation Act and some of his extra-constitutional actions, he also allowed his administration to take those steps necessary to shut out unfavored editors. It is a black mark against his presidency that at no time did he speak out against the mobs attacking unpopular papers. Nor did he speak out in favor of freedom of the press or maintaining America's core values during wartime. Lincoln did not object to the suppression of the loyal opposition and this later caused him and his party to suffer in the mid-term elections. Indeed, it made the presidential election far closer than it need have been.

Loyalists to Lincoln could be forgiven if by the end of the summer they felt comfortable that the voices of dissent would be snuffed out and public opinion controlled. From their perspective, the summer madness had been effective, and any sort of loyal opposition had been efficiently branded unpatriotic.

But overlooked were two factors. The first was the independence of the judicial system. The judicial branch had suffered no wholesale transformation from the exit of the Southern states, though time would reveal how independent the judges of the land would be. Would they crumble as did many of the most articulate antiwar editors?

But the second, and far more unpredictable and so far overlooked factor, was the willingness of one man, John Hodgson, to fight back.

Unknowingly, a British editor summed up Hodgson's dilemma as the summer of rage gathered force. "This same mob power, now used on the 'righteous side,' may be directed, on occasion, against any...person that is unpopular."[47]

And no one was more unpopular to so many powerful men as a stubborn small town editor named John Hodgson.

Chapter Seven

THE JEFFERSONIAN IS MOBBED

"The man does not live who is more devoted to peace than I am. None who would do more to preserve it. But it may be necessary to put the foot down firmly."[1]

—Abraham Lincoln, February 21, 1861

H odgson had to know it was coming, as did everyone connected with the belligerent and outspoken editor and his increasingly anti-Lincoln, antiwar, editorials. But knowing something might happen and having it happen are two very different experiences.

Clearly, Hodgson was visible, outspoken, and showing no signs of moderation given the realities of the war, despite efforts of other Democrats in Chester County. Hodgson made his latest strike in mid-August 1861. Cracks were appearing among local Democrats, many of whom understood that if only for self-preservation, it was time to be more supportive of their neighbors and the war. Hodgson helped curb such weak insolence.

On August 13, West Chester Democrats met at Horticultural Hall. Hard-line Democrats defiantly talked secession, while Joseph Hemphill tried turning the crowd toward a moderate platform. One Democratic supporter sought to introduce a more temperate resolution, blaming the war on the Southern states. It was beaten back and instead a resolution introduced by a frequent contributor to the *Jeffersonian,* elder party leader and Southern sympathizer Nimrod Stickland, was passed. The resolution read, in part, "The American government is founded not upon the sword, but upon the intelligence and virtue of the people. Public measures are to be brought to the test of the Constitution and finally settled by the appropriate civil tribunals. To resort to armies is a fundamental error, and must result in establishing a military despotism."[2]

Hodgson commented on an alternate, more moderate set of resolutions, which were met at the convention with hisses and boos, "the resolutions...express no condemnation of, but, by their silence...would be construed to endorse, the unconstitutional and corrupt doings of Lincoln." Hodgson supported Stickland's heavy-handed condemnation of the Lincoln administration.[3]

Such sentiments were more and more intolerable to the patriotic citizens whose sons and husbands were now fighting to defend the Union. Amidst the Fort Sumter crisis in April, Democrats and Republicans gathered at the courthouse for a recruitment meeting. Though few names were enrolled, West Chester's most influential men made a raucous series of speeches. After P. F. Smith declared that any man who opposed the administration or was even suspected and doing so "must be put down at all hazards," Uriah Pennypacker warned "every man who dares to exercise the right of free speech or free thought, and every man who does not submit to his dictation." Pennypacker singled out John Hodgson. "He went so far as to refer to us," Hodgson included in his report in the next issue of the

Jeffersonian, "in a manner evidently to point out where the mob was to begin its work." If it was to come, Hodgson continued, he hoped "they will do it in the daytime, when we are present, and not sneak to the task...."[4]

Hodgson stayed only long enough to hear the comments of Republican congressman John Hickman, who gave a few remarks in praise of President Lincoln and to convince those present that the loss of Fort Sumter was inconsequential to the United States and the war effort.[5] That Hodgson even attended the event showed his personal courage. It was just after his fistfight in the oyster bar and many in the town had sons and fathers now fighting for the Union. It is difficult to imagine how uncomfortable it must have been for any editor insisting on airing critical comments against the popular Lincoln. Hodgson stubbornly continued to insist he was loyal to the Union and breaking no laws.

The mob that snuck into town to destroy the *Jeffersonian* must have known that West Chester was a quiet town, especially at night. It differed little from most country towns in an America still fifteen years removed from its centennial. The unpaved country streets—witness to the daily traffic of bankers, merchants, journalists, politicians, and vagabonds—were a far cry from life in a thriving city like Chicago, New York, or even Philadelphia, now only a short trip by rail. West Chester was growing up, advertising itself as a quaint railroad stop along the way to the bustle of the big city and their "spacious houses, replete with every convenience." The short commute to the village quickly becoming Philadelphia's newest suburb offered pastoral views of "the spacious farm and buildings of the Friends' West Town Boarding School. Soon after come in view the hills and valleys bordering on Chester Creek" and then "opens a district which presents a variety of scenery, and situations for country seats, rarely to be met with."[6]

Less than five thousand men and women—black and white, African, German, and Irish—called West Chester home. Located in southeastern Pennsylvania, it was settled more than one hundred fifty years before by a group of Quakers who, by the hand of God they claimed, ventured into the colonial wilderness and conquered the untamed, uncivilized forests. Like the surrounding towns, West Chester's founding fathers also conquered the Indian communities that formerly lined the Brandywine River. They were, at that time, mostly Englishmen, the wave of Irish, German, and blacks not coming until the nineteenth century.

The country had changed dramatically since then. Thousands of men were now dead as the United States, united in name only, waged an unholy and unavoidable war against itself. West Chester, no matter what its citizens claimed in times of peace, was no longer a sleepy borough unaffected by the turmoil of the world around it. It was as responsible and as involved in the devastation as anyplace.

The small band of strangers, witnesses would later claim a half dozen or so men, hitched their panting horses and a small wagon on the outskirts of town, only a few blocks from the heart of the borough. Coming through town from the northeast, perhaps traveling on a muddy road from nearby Philadelphia or Doylestown, they would have walked through the towering shadow of the courthouse, both hands of the heavy clock reaching slowly toward the twelve. The center of county justice was a giant structure which, due to a thin layer of peeling white paint, had just been recently covered with an impressive limestone edifice. Instead of marble, its grandeur was framed with thick cast-iron Corinthian columns with a central, massive bell tower that split the heavens.[7]

From the west, only a block away from the courthouse and on the opposite side of the street, stood the Mansion House. Besides the courthouse and the county market, the three-and-a-half story luxury hotel was the borough's greatest claim to respectability. And like all respectable establishments, it also offered the borough's greatest temptation to vice. By day, the borough's lawyers and newspapermen drank coffee and other guilty pleasures on the veranda. At night the well-dressed and well-to-do mingled amidst the thick smell of ink carried in by the local journalists that also congregated in the cellar oyster bar.[8]

Owners of the *Jeffersonian,* the local hard-hitting, punch-in-the-mouth kind of newspaper, knew it well. The paper used to operate out of the cramped basement of the building next door. John Hodgson frequently stopped in for a meal and a drink, though just as often to pick up the latest gossip. And it was here in the Oyster Bar that on April 12 Hodgson made clear to everyone his determination to fight with bare knuckles for his right to disagree with Abraham Lincoln.

From either direction, past law offices, private residences, merchants, taverns, and churches, the mob—which we can now call it as their intention became apparent to the few witnesses still stirring—would have seen signs of what the town had grown to become. Gas lamps, extinguished at such a late hour, lined the streets. Recently laid brick sidewalks framed the wide, compacted dirt streets, providing a dry path under the awnings of storefront windows that advertised the talents of furniture makers, seamstresses, and other merchants. The stores were fronted by bulky signs with thick, heavy lettering, each working to out-do the other and draw business from their nearest competition.

Guided by the moonlit sky, the lawless group of conspirators finally closed in on their destination: the small, two-story office building at 12 South High Street, the home of the prospering West Chester *Jeffersonian.* As the mob walked steadily down the street, finally coming before the front door, the *Jeffersonian*'s ever-slower beating heart gasped for one final breath.

Nearly as the courthouse clock struck midnight, according to newspaper accounts in West Chester and Philadelphia after the fact, the unidentified mob crashed through the front door of the building proudly owned by the Hodgson family and swarmed into the brick office building of West Chester's only remaining Democratic newspaper. Quietly and with little attention, the men quickly and systematically destroyed the press equipment and anything else they stumbled upon. They callously overturned office furniture—chairs, tables, and desks—and smashed the small wood and metal type blocks. So intent were the men on putting the newspaper out of circulation that they made the effort to destroy even the huge cylinder printing press, the paper's very lifeblood. It is not easy to destroy a solid cast-iron press in the thick of night; whomever these men were, we can say they were strong and determined to shut down Hodgson for good.

They quickly climbed the narrow steps in the rear of the building, destroying the paper's most vital business records as if dumping the foul-smelling refuse of a chamber pot into the alley below. Subscription lists were ripped into pieces and thrown through the shattered front window, the bundles catching on the jagged shards of glass that jutted from the wooden frame as notebooks and papers were vaulted out into the dense August air.[9]

A short hour or so later, the echoes of breaking glass and smashing wood unaffecting the slumber of both uninterested and terrified neighbors, the second-generation newspaper was merely an eerie reminder of its former self.

With the destruction complete, the mob dispersed quickly and discretely, wasting little time before streaking out of town. "The thing was managed very quietly, without noise or disturbance, and few people knew of it till this morning," reported the *Evening Bulletin* the next day. Newspaper reports would confirm that there were several witnesses to the crime, but no one attempted to disrupt the attack. And why would they, given the unpopularity of the Hodgsons? Said the *Evening Bulletin:* "The paper was one of the most false and mischievous secession sheets published in the North, denouncing the war as a war to benefit 'niggers' only, and pleading for the right of secession."[10]

The *Jeffersonian,* a country newspaper built on the sweat and determination of its editor, fair-skinned and thick-blooded John Hodgson, was now only the latest victim of the military and philosophical conflict that pitted North versus South. The hysteria gripping the nation, it seemed, had finally swept away West Chester's remaining innocence. The once violently pounding heart of the *Jeffersonian,* now the victim of an abrupt and violent attack, was left only to bleed.

All was quiet again in West Chester, "the seat of justice of Chester County," a railroad advertisement declared. The moist air once held at bay by a field of glass and wood now invaded the devastated building. Its defenses now overwhelmed, the *Jeffersonian* awaited reinforcements at first light. In the meantime, the building sat empty and isolated, the sturdy chairs that embraced a tireless editor earlier that day now lay broken. [11]

The next morning brought sunshine and clear skies to West Chester. The job required an early start, and John and William Hodgson, editor and owner, father and son, both started to work on foot, each leaving their wives from opposite sides of town. It was Tuesday and the day's issue of the *Jeffersonian* had already been delivered to the post office the night before for delivery. Now the process would begin again for their Saturday edition.

There exists no record of when the owners of the *Jeffersonian* arrived on the scene. Whether a witness or a concerned citizen awakened them that night, or if the destruction and chaos were waiting for them unexpectedly the following morning, we will likely never know. Work began at daybreak, so the Hodgsons probably arrived without a hint or a warning of what they would find.

When father and son arrived to start their busy day, a routine they repeated twice a week for the last eighteen years, they were greeted by ruin. Those eighteen years of toil and personal sacrifice now took the form of chaos, two lifetimes of work crushed out by one callous and calculated blow. The sight must have been overwhelming, painful, and confusing all at the same time: Surveying the wreckage, treading softly over familiar ground, finding empty shelves and barren cupboards where paper, ink, and type once rested, the dusty floor now providing a trail of footsteps and torn paper to the office upstairs.

After surveying the scene, John and William Hodgson surely labored over difficult questions: Was the attack a local and isolated act of vigilante justice, or a product of the national crisis knocking on their door? If so, who else in town was made victim?

Were they looking to inflict harm, or just send a warning? Would the perpetrators return? When? And could their homes and wives be targeted next? Then after the initial panic, after a glaring look from father to son, more questions.

Did local politicians control the mob, if that's what occurred here, or were the stakes higher? Then an unthinkable question, but one that, in the early confusion of the war, in a time where the most powerful men in the country were readily accessible by the most common man or woman, had to be asked. Hodgson had recently taken to criticizing John Hickman, Postmaster General Blair, Secretary of War Cameron, and at times the unconstitutional behavior of the president.

One can easily imagine that Hodgson must have wondered whether it was possible that the president of the United States, the awkward looking and, as of yet, outwardly passive Abraham Lincoln, was involved? What about the powerful Thurlow Weed, hiding behind the abolitionist Seward, or some sort of John Hickman and Cameron team? The list of possible perpetrators was long—but all paths and all clues pointed back to Washington and the free reign given to the Republican newspaper men now in power. Men, who Hodgson would darkly warn, "love power more than liberty."[12]

The summer of rage had finally come to John Hodgson and his beloved paper. Could one suspect the president of the United States of involvement in a local mobbing? It seems ridiculous that he would be involved in such a petty crime, but these were different and dangerous times. The Hodgsons knew better than anyone. And now, in the early hours of what they expected to be a normal Tuesday morning, there were no answers. Instead, the Hodgson's stood in isolation, possessed only by a growing, consuming fear.

Shockingly, their neighbors seemed none surprised. More disturbing is that no witness came forward to tell what transpired. Did the mob cover their faces to hide their identities, or were they so confident that the town would invite such a destructive act on the *Jeffersonian* that they felt comfortable under cover of darkness, knowing that fear would prevent the locals from coming forward?

Nobody was talking, and there were no answers.

Despite an apparent lack of witness, local papers in West Chester detailed the destruction of the *Jeffersonian* as if having the full account in hand. Within two days, the first public reports detailing the break-in of the *Jeffersonian* appeared in Simon Cameron's Pennsylvania organ, the *Philadelphia Evening Bulletin,* then was reprinted in John Forney's Philadelphia paper, *The Press.*

> All that is known in the town about the destruction of the
> *Jeffersonian* is that a man living opposite the office saw half
> a dozen men enter the building and throw the type out of
> the upper windows. They afterwards descended to the
> pressroom, but their operations there were invisible to him.
> Soon after wagons drove away from that neighborhood,
> supposed to have contained the party.

Forney's paper, a former Democratic organ, offered a disclaimer
that would become all too familiar, offering little hope to the
Hodgsons that information might still be forthcoming. "No one in
the town knew anything of these men or their project. They evidently
belonged to the country."[13]

Commenting later in the war, Henry Evans of the nearby *Village
Record* summarized the feelings toward the *Jeffersonian,* "Perhaps there
is not a newspaper in the Union that has been a more venomous
enemy of the government...than the *Jeffersonian.* No wonder it has
been regarded by loyal men with detestation."[14] In fact, another
convenient Republican theory soon surfaced; that indeed the attack
was done by Hodgson himself in order to gain fame and funds from
Democratic party leaders![15]

These were glancing blows, but not entirely inaccurate. John
Hodgson, though outspoken and unwavering on many fronts, was in
no way a champion of a more inclusive American society and was
rapidly becoming the "poster-boy" of everything many in the North
had come to dislike about Southern supporters. He was an often foul-
mouthed and always-stubborn defender of an American way of life
that was rapidly disappearing. That he was a racist is too simple to
state; he was hardly extreme in his views on the American slave. He
regarded America through the prism of economic opportunities and
religious and personal freedoms, and everything else was secondary. It

was a land of opportunity for hardworking men like himself and he seemed, at every occasion, to despise and reject the notion of a benevolent government lifting up the weak and needy.

Consider his comments, as the war progressed, on the question of emancipation of the slaves. His concern is for the economic viability of his beloved home state. "She would get off well if she escaped with fewer than five hundred thousand of them. They would come among us poor and dependent upon us for their food and clothing. All the white men we have are not now profitably employed. Add half a million Negroes to the number of our inhabitants, and they cannot possibly maintain themselves, excepted by shoving so many white people out of employment." Concludes Hodgson, "As citizens of Pennsylvania and white working men of the North, we object to having our places usurped by liberated slaves."[16]

It was an American dream for his sort of people alone. His dream of a land unchanged, just as when he arrived as a child. Stubborn is a word that keeps coming to mind. Repugnant is another. So too are courageous and articulate. It was his way or no way at all. In May he even teased the base manhood of Republicans, taunting that "if they dared would mob us, but for want of sufficient courage, sneakingly and stealthily belie and slander us."[17]

The time of the mob had finally arrived.

It took four days for one of West Chester's three Republican papers to report the mob attack on the *Jeffersonian*. Finally, on Saturday, August 24, the *Village Record,* its North Church Street office operating just around the corner from the *Jeffersonian,* reported the incident as quietly and unemotionally as news could be reported in the mid-nineteenth century.

> The office of the *Jeffersonian* in West Chester was entered
> on Monday night last and the newspaper press broken, the
> hand press pitched out of the window, and the type
> knocked into piles and thrown into an adjoining sink. On
> Tuesday morning the office presented a desolate-looking
> spectacle. Nothing but a few bundles of paper was to be
> seen in either the first or second stories of the office.

Reminiscent of the unemotional, outwardly objective view of *The Press,* the *Village Record* wasted little investigative energy. "Who the perpetrators of this act were we have no knowledge," it reported. "The noise in the office, it is said, attracted the notice of some of the neighbors, several men were seen moving about the streets and office; but before any persons in the neighborhood got into the street, the work was done and the men had departed. It is believed they came from the country."[18]

Somehow the fact that this newspaper, hated by *The Press* and despised by the many Republican newspapers in the area, had met with a violent death at the hands of men who "came from the country" made the attack more palatable. Those who know often say little, and this, we suspect, was the case here. For Democrats, it was yet another horrific blow.

The *Village Record* further vented hostility against its in-town rival, offering an editorial disguised as a report of the "sacking of the *Jeffersonian.*" The column was really a warning to other Democratic editors, putting forth one of the first philosophical arguments in favor of the mobbing. "In a state of war, the laws are slow," wrote its highly outspoken editor, Henry Evans. "All depends on the virtue of the people—if they are false, the nation is gone. The wily traitor setting under the forms of law strike a dagger in the vitals of the government before his treason is discovered," he colorfully and fearfully warned his readers. "He is smooth and specious, and while he is carrying out his diabolical plots, his hypocritically clamors for the forms and rights of the Constitution.... Let the leper not go unheeded by the statesman of the country."

The threat was not subtle. "The plot is forming in Pennsylvania for severing the Union [and] for uniting our state with the Southern Confederacy," Evans further warned, seeing the drama as Lincoln must have. "It has its advocates in Chester County—it has its emissaries among us and throughout the state. It has its presses, and its orators, and if they are to persist in their disloyal and malignant designs, the government may as well fold its arms and submit to the yoke with which the rebel leaders have prepared for it."

Evans then turned his attention to John Hodgson. "We make no false charges against men who are our fellow citizens, whether they call themselves 'Democrats' or by any other name. We give our convictions. The republic is in danger. We must rise to the dignity of patriots in this hour of peril. We must defend it with our lives and our property. Liberty itself is at stake. Those who are not for us are against us; every tie of friendship and association must yield to our love of country."[19]

It was clear warning to Hodgson's paper, and, coming from his former colleague and long-time friend, a cowardly way to publicly sever their relationship.

Another Philadelphia paper, the *Inquirer,* also chimed in, offering an answer to the constitutional debate that allowed the *Jeffersonian* and other democratic papers to continue their diatribes. "The method is easy and instant. Wherever they exist, declare martial law, close their printing establishments, seize their persons, and keep them where neither their tongues nor pens can longer sow the disaffection whose harvest is our ruin."

The suppression of the *Jeffersonian* was long overdue, the Philadelphia *Inquirer* contended. "Now," it demanded, "what the cause of present order as well as ultimate natural security demands, is that in Baltimore, New York, and wherever else treason has an organ, it should be crushed out by summary martial process, superseding alike mob outrages, and the tom-foolery—in times like these—of grand jury circumlocution."[20]

Clearly, the fate of the *Jeffersonian* was not left to "summary martial process." Apparently someone felt that the government was too slow, or perhaps they feared that the government would not act at all and the *Jeffersonian* would continue uncensored. Why take the risk when you can take matters into your own hands?

The *Philadelphia Bulletin* put into print the administration's fears regarding Hodgson's paper. "The principal circulation was in the lower part of Chester County and along the Maryland line. Many of the people are touched with secession sentiment. They take but one newspaper, frequently, and they are of course, greatly influenced by its statements."[21] Note the use of the past tense in describing the paper's circulation. The *Jeffersonian* was now dead.

The Civil War was three months old. It was a revolutionary period in a time and a place where the country's first great revolution was still not yet a distant memory. Many of the old-timers in West Chester still remembered when French general Lafayette visited their town in 1825, a farewell tour of sorts to visit the sites and sounds of the great American liberation. He fought at Brandywine, a short distance from West Chester. The battlefield still served as a constant reminder to the townspeople of the blood sacrifices made there.

War offers unique opportunities for aggressive and decisive actions, often at the expense of the innocent. Lafayette witnessed it in the American Revolution, then during his own country's ill-fated revolution. The debate over treasonous behavior, partisan examples of which already littered the infant conscience of American history, would sharpen the double-edged sword now being wielded by influential politicians. And though both sides claimed divine inspiration, the guidance of God and country in their path, the people continued to be swept into a fervor. Only time could tell which side was truly favored, though, and even then may not know which was right. In the interim, the *Jeffersonian,* its editor, owner, and employees, appeared to be overlooked civilian casualties easily condemned.

It should come as no surprise that John Hodgson knew what to do immediately after confronting the destroyed office. By the end of the week, with the identity of their attackers sill a mystery, the Hodgsons had had considerable, albeit uneasy, time to think and regroup. John Hodgson, on normal occasions an energetic and restless powder keg, spent much of the week on the train he helped bring to West Chester, linking the town to its older sister, "the great and growing city of Philadelphia."[22] To make up for lost time, Hodgson was utilizing the presses of the *Christian Observer* at 48 South Fourth Street, "formerly a New School Presbyterian paper, but recently repudiated by that denomination on account of its pro-slavery proclivities."[23] The two papers had much in common.

William Hodgson, John's tall, narrow-shouldered oldest son, and on paper the *Jeffersonian's* proprietor and business manager, remained at home to fan the flames and guard what remained of the family's business, leading the salvage operation. They remained on the lookout for a return strike. With the elder Hodgson running back and forth from Philadelphia, it was clear to all that it was the determined goal of the family to resume publication and to do so quickly. Unlike so many other Democratic papers that had been mobbed, there was no apology from the Hodgson family, no promise to recant their antiwar editorials, and no begging to be allowed to resume the family newspaper with muted tones.

Instead came the screech of metal on plank floors and the pounding of hammer to nail as the *Jeffersonian*'s office was refitted. All in West Chester could hear for themselves that its bleeding heart would be resuscitated. The Hodgsons made plans for a special circular denouncing the cowardly midnight raid, its main objective to openly and defiantly announce that they were still in operation. The circular would go out that Friday, and the *Jeffersonian* would follow the next day with complete details of the event in their normal Saturday edition.

That day, Frank Key Howard's Baltimore *Daily Exchange* reprinted an article from one of its New York exchange papers. Speaking against the recent war on Northern "peace papers," it carried collective sentiments of an angry and disheartened nationwide corps of editors.

> That day indeed will be a most calamitous one, when our people will not permit the utterance of an opinion in opposition to the will of the tyrant majority. If there is to be a suppression of free discussion at all, let it be done by some spiritual or secular autocrat—some emperor, king, or pontiff—not by the people themselves.
>
> The people of Concord, Bangor, Haverhill, and lastly, of West Chester county, Pennsylvania, would seem alike destitute of faith in the power of truth and of the first principles of toleration. May these be the last outrages committed at the North which it will be our duty to chronicle.[24]

It was a desperate plea against a seemingly unstoppable undertow. John Hodgson spent Friday in Philadelphia finalizing the Saturday edition when the most unexpected event of the week, or even of the summer of 1861, transpired. That afternoon at the *Jeffersonian* office on High Street, where William was finalizing the circular denouncing the mob attack, he answered a knock on the door. There before him stood two United States marshal's deputies. They handed William a document.

In part, it called for the deputies to "take, hold, and keep possession of the building, as well as all property of every kind whatsoever, used in and about the publication of said newspaper."

In the months to come, Hodgson realized that Lincoln and his administration were testing the Confiscation Act, which gave the administration the right to strip away any property used to support the Confederate cause, whether by intention or not. Hodgson thought the Republican party the greatest of hypocrites. "If a Northern Democrat wrote to the Confederate president, Jefferson Davis, that Chester County was comprised of Southern sympathizers," Hodgson later argued, "that person would be held guilty of treason, because the information conveyed would tend to encourage the rebellion. But the Republican press, for mere party purpose, untruthfully, and in the face of the protestations of the Democrats, and in spite of all the men and money they are contributing to the war, persist in asserting that the Northern Democrats are secessionists and Southern sympathizers."[25]

The angry mobs had not eliminated John Hodgson. The fistfights with old friends had no seeming effect, and the general feelings of patriotism sweeping the Union had changed his antiwar stance not one bit. No, the man was too foolish and now it seemed that someone in the administration had decided to act. But who?

When first closed by an apparent mob, most antiwar proprietors simply closed their doors for good and prayed that that was the end of their troubles. Some found other employment, some converted to the Republican Party, and some fled to the South. It must have been unbelievably unsettling for so many of the Democratic editors to go from political dissenters to social outcasts, stripped of their jobs and businesses.

Hodgson could have walked away, but he refused. Instead he mobilized friends, allies, and family and without hesitation plotted to resume publication. Indeed, the subscription rolls jumped as a result of the publicity. Hodgson even laid plans to advertise via a broadside.

Then the improbable took place. On Friday, August 23, 1861, the *Jeffersonian* was closed not by an angry mob, but rather the administration of Abraham Lincoln. Now the question becomes far more realistic. Were these federal marshals acting with the permission of the cabinet? From how far inside the Executive Mansion came the authority to "take, hold, and keep possession of the building" that published the antiwar, anti-Lincoln newspaper? That was now a very appropriate question.

In the normal course of exploring a singular moment in the history of the Civil War one might expect that the involvement of the president in a particular event would forever remain a mystery. Especially in the nineteenth century, when so many political decisions were made informally, without the paper trails of more recent administrations. Was the president involved in the federal marshals taking control of the *Jeffersonian?* What do we know?

Well, we know exactly what the Hodgsons knew. The document handed to them revealed that the takeover of the building and the suppression of the newspaper were being taken "upon the authority of the president of the United States."

The rage had only just begun.

Chapter Eight

SUFFERING FOR LIBERTIES

"Where be those who, twelve months ago, thought 'honest Abe' the right man in the right place, and who denied [sic] to the people the right to question his wisdom or his motives? Where now are those who, even six months ago, with bare-faced, shameless mendacity, persecuted and imprisoned the people, who did not believe either in this honesty or his capacity?"[1]

—John Hodgson, January 17, 1863

There was a structure in the harbor of Baltimore that brought to life the fears of the antiwar editors. Though conceived as a fort, it was transformed in the opening days of the Civil War into a prison—a place to house the men who opposed Lincoln and his war.

Rarely in American history have there been prisons like Fort McHenry in Baltimore and Fort Monroe in New York and a dozen more scattered through the Union. Through their gates passed the entire spectrum of American society of the 1860s, apparently united only in their ability to sway voters to turn against the conduct of the war.

"Among the prisoners may be found representatives of every grade of society," wrote the author of the 1863 pamphlet *Bastilles of the North*. "Governors of state, foreign ministers, members of Congress and of different state legislatures, mayors and police commissioners...doctors, civil, naval, and military...mechanics (especially machinists and inventors, whom the government regards as a dangerous class); editors of newspapers, religious and political (Governments don't like them)..."[2]

Those taken to these prisons were all the living embodiment of the power of the Confiscation Act. As explained by one prisoner, these men were referred to as "prisoners of state, a term happily hitherto unknown on this side of the Atlantic, the very sound of which instinctively carries us to Italy and Austria, or the blackest period in the history of France."[3]

The *Official Records of the War of the Rebellion* document the correspondence, much of it confidential at the time, which triggered the wave of arrests that continued throughout the war. They exemplify the dire consequences of wartime opposition, and showed citizens that no one, from a country editor to a national politician, was exempt from the wrath of the government in wartime. Overall, it is estimated that more than twelve thousand arrests of noncombatant citizens were made during the Civil War.[4]

The evolution of the government's attempts to curb dissension at home had made every Republican a defacto secretary of war, especially district attorneys, marshals, and their deputies. The prison system, already bulging with prisoners of war, was also bulging with prisoners of state. Different regions called for different methods, and differing styles had led to strings of midnight raids and violence upon persons who continued to hide under the thin veneer of the Constitution.

The opposition press that dared to speak was angry toward the decentralized and seemingly random actions on the part of the administration. It was a very valid point. Hodgson reprinted one such comment: "What were we coming to if arrests might be made at the whim or caprice of a cabinet minister? Might not a senator be sent to prison? Might not the commanding general of the army send the president of the United States to Fortress Monroe, simply because he has the power?…This thing should be regulated by law, despotism creeps upon the people unawares, under the plea of necessity, and it became proper to make the inquiry which was proposed."[5]

Although Lincoln had temporarily calmed the secession storm that brewed in Baltimore in April 1861, leading to his justification of events before a joint session of Congress on the fourth of July, another dragnet had been required later that year. Attention had actually never left Maryland, but the president's fragile grip on the war machine continued to prompt secession activities in the state that Lincoln told Congress was one of "those who favor a policy which they call 'armed neutrality;' that is, an arming of those states to prevent the Union forces passing one way, or the disunion the other, over their soil."[6]

Baltimore was still a watched pot ready to boil. In early September 1861, a few weeks after the seizure of the *Jeffersonian*, the city remained under military occupation, and predictably remained openly hostile and uneasily volatile. Lincoln, hesitant at first to interfere with the daily operations of city and state government, now took to the other extreme and began eliminating even potential dissension.

A few days after the Union route at Manassas, just outside of Washington, DC, in late August 1861, sixty-three-year-old Major General John Dix replaced Nathaniel Banks as commander of the Department of Maryland. Dix was thrust into the difficult position of quelling the already seething Southern sympathies in and around Baltimore. At the outbreak of the Civil War, he was the highest-ranking volunteer in service, being one of three men originally recognized by Congress with the rank of major general at the outbreak of hostilities.[7] He was a veteran of the War of 1812, and was admitted to the bar upon his return, practicing law for a time in New York. Later he served in Mexico, but returned to civilian life until the outbreak of the mid-century conflict. His long, illustrious resume boasted terms as a United States senator, adjutant general and secretary of state of New York, United States postmaster general, and secretary of the treasury under President Buchanan. As a civilian he served as president of the Chicago and Rock Island and the Mississippi and Missouri Railroads. Among it all, he had also found time to publish several books on his foreign travels.[8]

Dix, a Democrat, did not want the job in Baltimore, but answered his president's call.

Like the general soon to be in charge of all Union armies, Democrat George B. McClellan, John Dix also believed in the necessity of war. He was a nationalist, and during times of crisis thought that party politics should take a back seat to the interests of the country, an ideology largely foreign in this domestic war. Dix proved his loyalty, and his iron will, time and again. In January 1861, while serving as the United States secretary of treasury, Dix ordered the arrest of a Southern ship captain who refused to surrender to federal forces. Dix added to his order, "If anyone attempts to haul down the American flag, shoot him on the spot."[9]

Dix and Lincoln agreed on the use of force during war, though the president had proven reluctant until events in Baltimore forced him, he told Congress, to the other extreme. Arriving in Baltimore, General Dix recognized the required immediacy of peace in the city if the war effort were to be successful.

At the top of the list was devising a strategy to equalize belligerent newspapers.

"There is no city in the Union in which domestic disturbances have been more frequent or carried to more fatal extremes, from 1812 to the present day," Dix would write in 1862.

> Although the great body of the people are eminently distinguished for their moral virtues, Baltimore has always contained a mass of inflammable material, which ignites on the slightest provocation. A city so prone to burst out into flame, and thus become dangerous to its neighbors, should be controlled by the strong arm of the government whenever these paroxysms of excitement occur.[10]

When the general arrived in Baltimore, he found the command, with headquarters at Fort McHenry on Baltimore harbor, to be in complete disarray. On the day of his arrival he wrote to the assistant adjutant general, Colonel E. D. Townsend, outlining the danger of the situation. One regiment from Massachusetts whose enlistments had expired was convinced to stay another week, as was the Thirteenth New York who had "resolved unanimously this morning to go home tomorrow." Of eight regiments in the fort, only three would remain at the end of the week where "there ought to be ten thousand men." To push his point across, Dix warned that "the late reverse at Manassas has brought out manifestations of a most hostile and vindictive feeling in Annapolis as well as in Baltimore."[11]

Dix reinforced Fort McHenry from within with both men and weapons, and created two other garrisons at strategic points overlooking the city. The Confederate flag was banned from the city, and further fortifications were made along the city's main avenues and railroad lines.[12]

Dix then took on the press. Although convinced of the necessity of censoring democratic papers, their suppression posed a difficult case for the general, one that he warned be prosecuted with extreme caution. In August 1861, an order was issued via the War Department for the suppression of several newspapers, though it was abandoned "in consequence of strong remonstrances from Union men in Baltimore."[13]

Unsure of the potential consequences, Dix recommended to his superiors, specifically Secretary of State Seward, that "a measure of so much gravity as the suppression of a newspaper by military force should carry with it the whole weight of the influence and authority of the government, especially when the publication is made almost under its eye."

Seward, as well as Secretary of War Cameron, persisted. Perhaps having learned a lesson from the recent chaos in West Chester, Bangor, and New York, the general proceeded with caution. "There is a good deal of impatience among some of the Union men," he wrote. "They wish to have something done. The feeling is very much like that which prevailed in Washington before the movement against Manassas. It would not be difficult to get up a political Bull Run disaster in this state."[14]

Bull Run was still fresh on everyone's minds. Overconfidence and inexperience created a dangerous confusion on the Virginia battlefield. The result was several thousand casualties, political panic, and above all, a heavy realization of what they had created. The lessons of that battle lingered, and General Dix moved forward cautiously.

Chief among the aged general's concerns were the eight newspapers operating in the heart of the city. The *Daily Exchange,* having reported diligently on the mob activity in the North, was at the top of the list, refusing to tone down its demonstrations. "If the individuals who now countenance the government in its efforts to silence the press, [sic] were all like the ignorant fanatics with whom they are at present acting," Frank Key Howard reported late in

Abraham Lincoln, c. 1858. Lincoln supporter and *Chicago Tribune* editor Joseph Medill had a photographer create this ambrotype from the original daguerreotype, with the masthead of the *Press and Tribune* skillfully placed onto the paper. (Courtesy of Abraham Lincoln Book Shop, Inc., Chicago, IL)

This broadside circulated in West Chester after an altercation in the Mansion House Oyster Bar between John Hodgson and Charley Springer, coinciding with the attack on Fort Sumter in June 1861. (Chester County Historical Society, West Chester, PA)

West Chester, Friday Evening, April 12th, 1861.
An important dispatch from *MOSE*, the former correspondent of the Jeffersonian.

WAR BEGUN!
HOSTILITIES COMMENCED!!
IN AN OYSTER CELLAR.
HODGSON vs. SPRINGER,
OTHERWISE
Secessionist against Republican!

Secessionist fires first shot—Republican answers beautifully. Field of action an oyster cellar.

The Major was Upholstered.—MOSE.

John Hodgson. This photo captures the fiery, uncompromising editor of the *Jeffersonian,* posed in his local militia uniform, probably prior to the Civil War. (Courtesy of Douglas Harper)

William Hodgson. Although he unsuccessfully attempted to steer the *Jeffersonian* toward a more conservative course during the early months of the war, William was unable to control his father's cutting editorials. (Chester County Historical Society, West Chester, PA)

John Hickman, 1855. The West Chester, Pennsylvania, congressman left the Democratic Party prior to the election of Lincoln, and became one of the most outspoken radical Republicans in Congress. A brilliant orator and attorney who at one point was being considered for Lincoln's vice president, Hickman was John Hodgson's fiercest antagonist. (Picture History, Meserve-Kunhardt Collection)

John Forney, c. 1860. The founding editor of Philadephia's *The Press*, Forney founded the *Washington Chronicle* at Lincoln's request—after the president got him elected as secretary of the Senate. (Library of Congress, Prints & Photographs Division, LC-DIG-cwpbh-00084)

Newspaper Row was the home of about sixty out-of-town newspapers during the Civil War. Correspondents, politicians, office seekers, and any one else of importance gathered across the street at Willard's Hotel. (Washingtoniana Division, DC Public Library)

Abraham Lincoln, 1860. This famous Matthew Brady photograph of Lincoln was taken on the morning of his Cooper Union speech in New York on February 27, 1860. (Picture History, Meserve-Kunhardt Collection)

Fort McHenry, Baltimore, c.1861. The federal fort where Frank Key Howard and other Baltimore editors and Maryland legislators were detained in September 1861. (Library of Congress, Prints & Photographs Division, LC-USZ62-3677)

William Bradford Reed, 1865. A popular Philadelphia statesman and attorney—and well-known Southern sympathizer—Reed published anonymously and refused to speak in public until representing the Hodgsons in their case against the United States. (Picture History, Meserve-Kunhardt Collection)

George Washington Biddle. The more conservative partner of William B. Reed, Biddle was from one of Philadelphia's most important families. Whereas Reed was disgraced after the war, Biddle would have a long and distinguished legal career. (The Historical Society of Pennsylvania (HSP), Society Print Collection)

Walter Hoge Lowrie. The Pennsylvania supreme court justice lost his position on the court largely due to the unpopular verdict in the Hodgsons' case. (The Historical Society of Pennsylvania (HSP), Society Print Collection)

William Seward, c. 1861–1865. Seward joined Lincoln's cabinet with the expectation that the president would soon fail in his quest to preserve the Union, though they would soon develop a mutual admiration. Seward was responsible for many of the political arrests during the first year of the war. (Library of Congress, Prints & Photographs Division, Civil War Photographs, LC-DIG-cwpb-04948)

Horace Greeley, editor of the *New York Tribune*. Lincoln considered Greeley to be as helpful to him as "an army of one hundred thousand men." (Library of Congress, Prints & Photographs Division, LC-USZ62-8776)

In Lincoln's handwriting is the tally of endorsements for Philadelphia patronage positions, including Philadelphia District Attorney George Coffey and U.S. Marshal for the Eastern District William Millward, the two local officials most directly responsible for the seizure of the *Jeffersonian*. Lincoln appointed more men to patronage positions than any president in history. (Abraham Lincoln Papers, Library of Congress, Manuscript Division)

"Abraham the Last." Among the themes in this graphic cartoon are Lincoln's trampling of the freedom of the press and the privilege of the writ of habeas corpus, while Secretary of State William Seward wields the power to arrest opponents at will. *(Picture History, Meserve-Kunhardt Collection)*

August, "there might be room to hope that the North would yet struggle out of the abyss into which it is so blindly and madly plunging. But unfortunately those who should have been foremost to defend our constitutional liberties are most clamorous in insisting upon the suppression of the journals which oppose this war."[15]

The *Daily Exchange,* one of the most vocal Northern papers sympathetic to the South, had published its inaugural issue on February 22, 1858. Founded by Charles Kerr and Thomas Hall, they were joined a few years later by a third party, Henry Fitzhugh. Located on the southwest corner of Baltimore and Calvert Streets, with an office in the Carroll Hall building, its columns were outspoken from the beginning. In short time, its verbal exchanges with the "violent, prescriptive, and corrupt Know-Nothing faction and its satellites, minions, and bullies" became inevitably destructive. On August 12, 1858, in a scene prophetic of recent events in the North, the editors of the *Exchange* were "invaded by a gang of notorious roughs and outlaws, all armed, who forced their way into the counting-room, where the leader put a pistol to the head of the chief clerk and threatened to shoot him, while his comrades commenced their work of destruction." The windows were smashed, and the furniture and papers thrown throughout the room.

But this time, citizens rallied around the paper.

"Apprehending that the attack would be renewed at night, a body-guard of citizens volunteered to defend the office, and assembled for that purpose for several nights in succession, but no further demonstration was made."[16]

Later in 1859, William Carpenter and Frank Key Howard bought interests in the paper. Howard, a member of the Baltimore bar, was "soon recognized as the leading editorial writer of the staff, and the paper now attained a front rank among the leading journals of the country." The *Exchange* was recognized as the organ of the Baltimore

Reform movement which, by enactment of the legislature in February 1860, established a new court system, a new police force, and elected a Reform mayor.

In the meanwhile, the paper's following grew substantially. In early 1860, Kerr and Hall were bought out, and Fitzhugh sold his interest to William Wilkens Glenn, son of a Baltimore judge. The new proprietorship, Glenn & Co., now included Glenn, Frank Key Howard, and William Carpenter.

Howard had gained a reputation with his sharp editorial style. His flare and color were a lethal combination. Like the *Jeffersonian,* the *Daily Exchange* promoted the presidential candidacy of Democrat John Breckinridge.

Howard enticed his readers with an affinity for sarcasm that spared Lincoln little:

> Surely Mr. Lincoln presumes over much upon the patience or the stupidity of the nation when he gravely addresses it…how could he have ventured thus to speak in view of the acts which he has done or sanctioned within the past three months. It can only be explained upon the theory that he imagined himself to dealing with an "artificial crisis" and therefore privileged to treat it as flippantly as he pleases.[17]

Ultimately, Howard shared a fear of the dilution of the press and its ultimate ability to report accurate news. In addition, censorship of the press would inevitably be only the first step in a military occupation of all Northern institutions at the hands of the Republican Party.

Conscious of the ever-present ability of newspapers to incite a mass rebellion, General Dix had other considerations as well. The

Maryland state legislature was scheduled to meet again in a few weeks, and the issues first raised by Lincoln before their last meeting in May were revisited. Lincoln had allowed that meeting, with reservation, and the legislators voted down secession. Disaster had been averted for the time being. But could Lincoln take such a risk four months later?

By September, with the prospects of a long, drawn-out war becoming a reality, the climate continued to change dramatically. Much had occurred since May, including the arrest of the Baltimore police commissioners and others considered to be spies or sympathizers. The summer of rage had swept through the North, and many Democratic editors had been silenced by citizen mobs. But the large military presence in Baltimore may have prevented such activity there, and consequently Baltimore's eight Southern newspapers continued to provoke the president and his commander in Baltimore with an inflated sense of protection.

On September 4, Secretary of State William Seward received a worried letter from Frederick Schley, editor of a Republican paper, the *Baltimore Examiner.* Schley warned of an upcoming "adjourned session" of the Maryland legislature on the seventeenth.

"Many loyal citizens believe that at the coming session some effort will be made on the part of the 'Tory' majority to convulse the state and force it into an attitude of hostility to the government. Already," he wrote convincingly, "it is believed in intelligent quarters that at the last extra session it was decided in a caucus of the majority to pass an ordinance of secession at their next meeting at all hazards." Schley considered a prevention of a meeting of the legislature a "prevention of evil," which was "what the loyal citizens of Maryland desire and this is almost secured by the interposition of the federal government."

Twelve senators represented a majority, he reported, and of the "present senators eight are loyal and reliable, leaving fourteen in whom I have no faith and I speak the sentiment of many." The editor offered advice. It is the "duty of the federal government under its constitutional obligation…to guarantee to Maryland a Republican form of government and protect her from domestic violence; to interpose and cause the arrest of those senators whose notorious disaffection to the government causes popular alarm here and is calculated to produce civil strife under pretext of law." [18]

Schley did not know that decisive action had already begun. A flurry of letters had already changed hands between Dix, Simon Cameron, General Nathaniel Banks, and the soon to be named general in chief of all Union armies, General George B. McClellan.

"The passage of any act of secession by the legislature of Maryland must be prevented," Cameron wrote to Banks. "If necessary, all or any part of the members must be arrested. Exercise your own judgment as to the time and manner, but do the work efficiently."[19]

McClellan sent word to Cameron that because the arrests would be made in General Dix's jurisdiction, all should be made on his recommendation. "I have indicated Fort Monroe as their first destination in order to get them away from Baltimore as quietly as possible, and would suggest that they ultimately be sent North," McClellan further suggested.[20]

True to form, Dix was also receiving orders from William Seward, with whom Secretary Cameron had been entangled over the responsibility of citizen arrests since the opening of the war. Authority over the arrests of citizens was normally a domestic matter and therefore a responsibility of the State Department, but now, in a domestic war, Cameron considered the responsibility to be his alone. Neither Seward nor Cameron were willing to relinquish control, and so both assumed the power.

Seward and Cameron were still entangled as fall began to blanket Maryland and Pennsylvania. On the evening of September 11, secret service agent Alan Pinkerton delivered Simon Cameron's final order concerning the upcoming meeting of the Maryland legislature. In it, Cameron authorized the arrest of six men: T. Parkin Scott, Severn Teackle Wallis, Henry Warfield, Frank Key Howard, Thomas Hall Jr., and Henry May. They were to be kept in "close custody" and denied any communication upon their imprisonment at Fort Monroe. "The exigencies of the government demand a prompt and successful execution of this order," Dix was told of the arrests, which were to take place under the direction of Mr. E. J. Allen, Pinkerton's code name, with the "necessary military force" to be supplied by Dix.[21]

At 11 p.m., Dix wired Cameron. "No effort or precaution will be spared to carry out your order into execution promptly and effectually."[22]

That evening, the leading citizens of Baltimore turned in, ignorant of what lay ahead. Earlier that day, oblivious to what the next day few days would hold, Frank Key Howard's *Daily Exchange* hurled further criticisms at Washington. "The course which a despotic and foresworn administration has pursued towards us will not in the slightest degree influence our conduct.... As we have violated no law we can afford to despise Mr. Lincoln's warnings or menaces."[23]

The day before, the *Daily Exchange* was denied use of the mail by the local post office on direct orders from Washington. "I believe the *Exchange, Republican,* and *South* should be suppressed," directed the postmaster general, Montgomery Blair. "They are open disunionists."[24]

The caution and deliberateness of the planning of arrests in Baltimore could very easily have occurred in Philadelphia or West Chester, but there is no record of any such correspondence or alignment of forces. General Dix warned of the consequences of moving without complete autonomy.

In the early hours of September 13, a short time after midnight, Lincoln's campaign in Baltimore began. *Daily Exchange* editor Frank Key Howard was awakened by a knock at his front door. Not deaf to the whirling rumors of a potential crackdown, he came groggily to his second floor bedroom window. Looking down, he was unable to recognize the features of a lone man standing below. Pushing a whisper up the side of the house, the stranger reported that he had a message from Severn Teackle Wallis, a prominent Baltimore attorney, member of the state legislature and a frequent contributor to the *Daily Exchange*. Expecting a message of warning or other news of importance, the editor moved hurriedly to the front door. When it opened, two men pushed their way inside. Several others followed brandishing revolvers, and when Howard, an attorney by training, demanded a warrant, he was refused and dragged into the library.

The rest of the household—Howard's wife, two young children, and a servant—were pulled from their beds and likewise ushered into the library as the soldiers ransacked their home. Finally, Howard was escorted back upstairs and into his bedroom to dress and pack a bag. His destination, according to the leader, was nearby Fort McHenry.

Men moved in and out of rooms at a frantic pace, dumping the contents of drawers into large canvas bags; "private memoranda, bills, note-books, and letters."

They drove through Baltimore to the outskirts of the city. The entrance to Fort McHenry, where he had visited his father, Charles Howard, president of the Baltimore police commissioners, many times after his arrest a few months earlier, was littered with bridled horses and their carriages. Others had arrived before him.

Fort McHenry was situated three miles from the heart of Baltimore, separated by two long drawbridges on either side, its five main buildings otherwise secluded by the prison's twenty-foot-high brick walls. The buildings formed a perfect five-point star, a brick labyrinth that offered a stark contrast to the unassuming cityscape just miles from its gates, though extending the manicured setting and earthworks surrounding the outer walls. Escorted by two men "wearing the badges of the police force which the government had organized," he was pushed through the enormous front gates.

Once inside, Howard was escorted into a small room. It had whitewashed brick walls, a dark timber frame ceiling, and a plain plank floor, scuffed and warped by the dangling chains of traitors from the past. Lining the wall on one side were long benches, the other, ten-foot-deep cells that measured only four feet in width. Light struggled through six three-inch holes in the rear wall near the expansive ceiling, fourteen feet high.

To his bitter surprise, Howard saw many old friends before him, the victims of similar intrusions. The cast was a veritable who's who of the Maryland Reform party: Coleman Yellott, Stephen Dennis, Ross Winans, Severn Teackle Wallis, Henry Warfield, Dr. J. Hanson Thomas, T. Parkin Scott, Henry Morfit, Charles Pitts, William Harrison. Each was a member of the House of Delegates from Baltimore. Besides the legislators were the mayor of Baltimore, George Brown, and United States congressmen Henry May.

The record books of the State Department, under "arrests for disloyalty," provide the activities of the victims. The biography of attorney Severn Teackle Wallis is an example:

> S. Teackle Wallis, of Baltimore, was a member of the Maryland legislature and was publicly esteemed as the leader of the band of conspirators who were known to be plotting to pass an act of secession.... Wallis openly advocated the recognition of the rebel government and his correspondence and manuscripts were full of arguments in their justification. His arrest was a measure of precaution to

preserve the public peace and to prevent the consummation
of the treasonable purposes entertained by the conspirators
in the Legislature.[25]

Another victim of the midnight raid, Henry May, was one of
Maryland's six representatives in the United States Congress. He had
also been arrested in July for "holding criminal intercourse and
correspondence with a person in armed rebellion against the
government." The case came before the House Judiciary Committee
and its chairman, West Chester native John Hickman. Fortunately
for May, the man levying the charge proved "ignorant of and unable
to produce any evidence tending to prove any of the matters referred
to in the resolution." In addition, the charges that had brought them
before Congress "were grounded upon newspaper articles only." May
was admonished, and the Judiciary Committee had appeared to set a
precedent that, due to the nature of newspapers, accusations and
purported evidence did not warrant persecution without further
evidential support. Already that had seemed to have been thrown
out. Democrats began to use the word "arbitrary" to describe the
arrests.[26]

Alan Pinkerton reported the success of the Baltimore arrests to
William Seward ten days later as General Nathaniel Banks, encamped
near Darnestown, mobilized the Third Wisconsin. "It becomes
necessary that any meeting of this legislature at any place or time shall
be prevented," he wrote to the regiment's commander three days after
the arrests. If the session leaned toward secession, they would arrest
the "presiding officers of the two houses, secretaries, clerks, and all
subordinate officials.... The process of arrest should be to enter both
houses at the same time announcing that they were arrested by orders
of the government. Command them to remain," he wrote sternly, "as
they are subject to your orders."[27]

"Let the arrest[s] be certain and allow no chance of failure," Banks told a subordinate. If representatives did show the tenacity to appear, orders were to find and arrest them.[28]

With Maryland's Democratic representatives now in prison, the legislature would be allowed to meet without fears of secession. And with the leading sympathetic newspaper editors now confined at Fort McHenry, the city seemed suddenly very quiet. Meanwhile, the victims waited. None had been charged with a crime nor served with a warrant.

Another man swept up in the arrests was Lawrence Sangston, a member of the Maryland legislature. Once released, he published a diary of his time in prison. He insisted that there had been no plans for secession and that the real reason for the arrests had been disclosed by a letter from Lord Lyons of Great Britain, in which he stated that Mr. Seward had informed him the arrests were "made in view of the Maryland elections." The Republican newspapers, on the other hand, continued to insist the arrests had been made to strike "terror into the hearts of the people of Maryland."[29]

Editor Frank Key Howard was confined with three "companions" who shared "three or four chairs and an old ricketty [sic] bedstead, upon which was the filthiest apology for a bed I ever saw" and "a tolerably clean-looking mattress lying in one corner." He "could not help being struck by an unpleasant coincidence." Forty-seven years prior to the very day, his grandfather, Francis Scott Key, then a prisoner aboard a British warship, witnessed the bombardment that led to his writing of the "Star Spangled Banner" the following day. The irony did not escape him. "The flag which he had then so proudly hailed, I saw waving, at the same place, over the victims of as vulgar and brutal a despotism as modern times have witnessed."[30]

A few days later, the group took the steamer *Adelaide* to Fort Monroe, near Old Point Comfort, Virginia, then ten days later were transferred to Fort Lafayette.

While family, friends, and colleagues wrote furiously to state and federal officials petitioning for the release of the prisoners, Lincoln at last responded. His medium, as was his tendency on matters of such importance, was a loyal newspaper: this time the *Baltimore American.* The president took responsibility for the wave of arrests occurring in Maryland, but told citizens that they were on a need-to-know basis. "The public safety renders it necessary that the grounds of these arrests should at present be withheld," he wrote, "but at the proper time they will be made public."

> Of one thing the people of Maryland may rest assured: that no arrest has been made, or will be made, not based on substantial and unmistakable complicity with those in armed rebellion against the government of the United States. In no case has an arrest been made on mere suspicion, or through personal or partisan animosities, but in all cases the government is in possession of tangible and unmistakable evidence, which will, when made public, be satisfactory to every loyal citizen.[31]

On September 26, Frank Key Howard and the members of the Maryland legislature arrived at Fort Lafayette in New York Harbor. Howard's partner at the *Baltimore Exchange,* William Wilkins Glenn, now joined them. After Howard's arrest, two articles were courageously printed in condemnation of the arrests, and Major General Dix acted on behalf of the government in Glenn's arrest.

Fort Lafayette was on a narrow stretch of rock in New York Harbor nestled between Staten Island and Long Island (eight miles south of New York City). Formerly called Fort Diamond, Fort Lafayette was the smallest of three forts lined up in the harbor. The thirty-foot-high octagonal walls loomed down at its new arrivals, a double line of batteries on the side facing Long Island greeting the weary group of prisoners. Above those, on the second story, sat a row of smaller twenty-four pounders, protected by a frail looking wooden roof, on top of which sat firepower the prisoners could only imagine.

On September 30, William Seward ordered the release of W. W. Glenn "on taking the oath of allegiance to the government of the United States."[32] Glenn refused, having "already more than once taken an oath to bear allegiance to my state and to support the Constitution...and never having violated this oath in the slightest particular...know of no ground upon which any other could be demanded of me."

It was a stand to be taken by most of those confined.

Glenn was a special case, Seward was convinced, as he held only a financial interest in the *Daily Exchange*. Glenn was then released without taking the oath. "The *Daily Exchange* has been stopped by force," he wrote to Dix. "Though disputing the right to commit the act I still submit to the superior power of the government." Upon conditions of his parole, Glenn agreed not to "edit the *Exchange* nor republish it nor contribute to any paper so long as the censorship of the press is exercised in Baltimore." He concluded his letter of acceptance sarcastically.

> Denying the right of the government to hold me under arrest without trial I still acknowledge the fact which is patent that I am a prisoner. As such I should be glad to accept my release under conditional parole, pledging myself also not to connect myself with any anti-administration

newspaper until I am in a position to express my views freely and unrestrictedly.[33]

Frank Howard disagreed with Glenn's actions. Instead, he sat in protest by refusing not only the oath of allegiance, but also any conditional release that forced an admission of guilt by the United States government.

"I fear I am destined to undergo confinement some time longer," Howard wrote to his wife from prison, "for I will make no substantial compromise with the despotic power which has trampled my rights and the laws and constitution of my state under foot; neither will I accept the intervention in my behalf of any man in Maryland who can regard the tyranny to which I am subjected as other than a brutal, unjustifiable, and infamous exercise of arbitrary power."

> Let it be your consolation as it is mine to know that I am suffering in behalf of constitutional liberty, and this country will yet regret the day when it undertook to intimidate or punish without the form of law the Southern men who have dared to vindicate Southern rights. There are those whom a banded world cannot coerce into submission, and some such spirits are in Fort Lafayette.[34]

Howard's wife, Lydia, never received the communication. The post commander returned it, along with other letters of similar topic, to Howard "with notice that if he was not more respectful in his letters it would be my duty to stop his correspondence."[35]

Lieutenant Colonel Martin Burke, commanding general at Fort Hamilton and Fort Lafayette, concurred. "I am surprised that a member of the Howard family," he wrote, "which from the time of the Revolution to the commencement of our present troubles, were gentlemanly and patriotic, should now by infringing these rules endeavor to embarrass his custodians from whom he has received every kindness consistent with public duty." In addition, Burke wanted to "call Mr. Howard's attention to the indelicacy (to use the mildest term) of his course in applying unbecoming epithets to our commander in chief."[36]

Wood showed a copy of Burke's letter to Howard, who responded candidly as always, writing that "if you have duties to discharge I have rights to vindicate." And with an ironic and desperate sarcasm, Howard confessed that the only one of his rights "which has not been absolutely destroyed is the right of free speech within the narrow bounds of my prison and this it is my duty and purpose to defend to the last."[37]

The arrests of Frank Howard, Thomas Hall, and the Maryland legislators were a clear and unprecedented deterrent against secessionists living in the North. In hindsight, the strategy also illustrates a major difference between calculated government attacks and the seemingly random way in which the *Jeffersonian* was mobbed and then seized. But at the time, such occurrences struck fear into men like John and William Hodgson. There seemed neither justification nor pattern to the arrests, and there was no thought that they would avoid such persecution. All they could do was move ahead.

Nor was the randomness of the *Jeffersonian's* seizure an isolated incident reserved for editors only. Attacks against prominent politicians were well known, though those arrested did share one commonality with John Hodgson: they were often newspaper contributors.

Arriving at Fort Lafayette on September 26, the delegation of Baltimore lawmakers and editors missed by one day the release of one such man from New Jersey, James Wall. His story was also becoming a familiar one. Wall was not an editor nor a controlling interest in a newspaper. He was merely a contributor to a number of papers, though his political lineage with the Democratic Party was deep.

Wall was born in Trenton, New Jersey, on May 26, 1820. The son of a United States senator and former district attorney of the United States, Garret Dorset Wall, he spent his youth educated by private tutors in New York, graduating from the College of New Jersey in 1838.[38] After college, James Wall studied law. He was admitted to the bar in 1841, and began immediately to practice in his hometown. In 1847, he moved to Burlington where four years later he was elected its first mayor under a new city charter, which he had written in his own hand. In his duties as mayor the congressional son spearheaded the construction of a new farmer's market house, and was one of three men who incorporated the Burlington Gas Company, bringing artificial lighting to the city for the first time.

In 1854, Wall looked to follow in his father's footsteps and ran for a congressional seat. He was defeated, but tried again two years later and lost a second time. Between elections he found other diversions, publishing a small book of "Foreign Etchings," the observations of a recent European tour. In literary circles he had a growing reputation, having become a regular contributor to the *Knickerbocker* magazine, *Bentley's* magazine, and the *Edinburgh Review*.[39]

Wall lived in the home owned by his father at 210 High Street, a three-and-a-half-story home on Burlington's busiest street. He was respected, dignified, outspoken, and always on the inside of the latest news and political movements. Like the other Democrats pushed to the verge of submission, publicity would prove his greatest burden. Wall's power at home and in the national media made him a dangerous figure to the Lincoln administration. The rest of the story followed the new "Lincoln Doctrine."

On September 11, two days before an unannounced caller forced Baltimore editor Frank Key Howard from his bed, James Wall, on an unseasonably hot and sticky late-summer day, was notified that he had visitors waiting in his office. Wall left the company of his wife and two children at the supper table and walked through the house to his first floor office on the opposite end. There he found two men waiting: Benejah Deacon, the United States marshal for the District of New Jersey, and Burlington's mayor, William Allen.

Wall asked his predecessor why they had come. The marshal handed him a telegram. "You will please forthwith arrest James W. Wall, of Burlington, NJ, and convey him to Fort Lafayette, New York Harbor," it read, "and deliver him to the commanding officer at that place." The order came from the secretary of war, Simon Cameron.

Like Frank Key Howard, Wall was a trained lawyer. He refused to accept the legality of a warrant sent by telegram and without a signature. He told his unwelcome guests that they had no legal right to be there, and refused to accompany them from the house. The marshal stood and moved to the window, pulled back the venetian blind, and pointed to five more men standing in front of the house. Wall panicked and lunged for the marshal. He grabbed Deacon by the throat and pushed him back, and then broke for the door. The illustrious former mayor was now a lost rat in his own house, escaping to the hallway where several men, converging from the front and rear doors, wrestled him to the ground. He managed to knock one down before being knocked to the ground himself and beaten, his shirt mangled and halfway torn from his convulsing chest.

With his family in witness to the scene, one of the town's foremost citizens was dragged to Steven's Station, a short ride through town, and pushed onto a train destined for New York. Aboard the train, Wall, consumed by anger and rage, had time to consider the full impact of the arrest. Despite the wave of mob justice, he had continued to print his opinions. For several months he was the primary editorial contributor to the *New York Daily News,* one of the newspapers singled out by the New York grand jury that inaugurated the summer of rage. Wall's articles condemned the administration's usurpation of constitutionally guaranteed freedoms.

Like Hodgson, Wall addressed his protest directly to the postmaster general, Montgomery Blair. "Your recent high handed, unconstitutional act in stopping certain newspapers from being circulated through the mails will meet, as it deserves, the indignant protest of every free man," he wrote in a published letter to Blair. "If the proscribed papers have reflected severely upon the conduct of the administration, they had a right to do so in a republic where it has been our most cherished boast that the acts of our rulers are open to the freest scrutiny. If the people relinquish that, they richly deserve to be slaves."

> Now Sir, I defy you to lay your finger upon a line of the editorials of the *Daily News* (one of the organs under the government ban), that by the most forced construction could be declared treasonable to the country. That journal has labored for peace, for a cessation of this unnatural war, for an appeal to the people for the acts of the government, or 'an appeal from Philip drunk to Philip sober.' It had a perfectly constitutional right to do this; and in that direction I trust it will continue to labor, undismayed by either the menaces of government or the threats of the mob. In fact, had the government listened to the repeated warnings of the *New York Daily News,* instead of giving credence to those journals that were pretending to sustain it, the disgrace at Manassas Plains would not now stain the national (e)scutcheon.

Wall pressed his luck and had made an outward threat in defense of his friends and colleagues who sat in Northern prisons. He pressed Blair further.

> Our fathers were intimate friends; and although your father today belongs to the Republican party, I cannot believe that he endorses the recent arbitrary act of your department, or else he must prove recreant to the doctrines he proclaimed, years ago, in the *Globe*... "Under no possible emergency, not even in insurrection or amid the throes of civil war, can this government justify official interference with the freedom of speech or the press any more than it can with the freedom of the ballot."
>
> Little could he have then supposed that one of his own sons should lend himself to carry out an arbitrary edict that prostrated this boasted freedom at a blow.
>
> You, by such an edict, have assumed to dictate to me what political papers I may receive. Where do you derive your power?

Blair called his bluff. The postmaster general's response was just as pointed. "I did not give the order to which you refer because I thought the papers very dangerous," Blair responded from Washington on the last day in August. "From what I have heard of the ability and temper of the most offensive, I doubt if any great harm could be done by them. As, however, the objects [written] were traitorous, the demand of the people that they should be aided by the machinery of the government in those objects, could not be disregarded."[40]

Yet another part of the censorship puzzle, Montgomery Blair had been preventing newspapers from using the United States mail system for the past month as an alternative means to stopping opposition newspapers. The appointment of lucrative postmastership positions to loyal Republicans by the administration was paying dividends. August and September newspapers were littered with notices of other papers whose circulation was stopped by the postmaster general. In Philadelphia, United States marshals met steamers and railcars, confiscating newspapers labeled as traitorous by Blair and local postmasters. Like the *Jeffersonian,* the *Daily Exchange* lost their mail privileges, though its editors, Frank Key Howard and Thomas Hall were arrested a few days after. The *New York Daily News,* together with each of the papers identified by the New York grand jury, was barred from the mail on August 22, for being "dangerous for their disloyalty."[41]

The *Chicago Tribune* reported that "a force of deputy marshals were sent to the office of the American Express Co., where was understood to be a large edition of disloyal newspapers that had been lodged for transmission by express. The officers seized six packages of the *Daily News.* The publishers of the *News* finding themselves excluded from the post office, Adams Express, and Rose & Toucey's agencies, had endeavored to employ the American Express Co., which they supposed were not watched."[42] The *New York Daily News,* like so many other papers, found government agents one step ahead.

The War Department's General Order No. 67, the same order cited in the seizure of newspapers after being named by a New York grand jury in June, provided legitimacy for the acts.

> By the fifty-seventh article of the Act of Congress, entitled "An Act for establishing rules and regulations for the government of the armies of the United States," approved April 10, 1806, holding correspondence with or giving intelligence to the enemy, either directly or indirectly, is made punishable by death, or such punishment as shall be ordered by the sentence of a court-martial.

Like the general language of the Confiscation Act, General Order No. 67 gave local authorities great liberty to cause the arrest of Democratic editors who printed anything against the government, though the War Department's directive was created to avoid the publication of troop movements and other military measures. Most papers knew better, and on only a few occasions were military matters discussed with consequences. Many of them occurred in Republican papers.

> The public safety requires a strict enforcement of this article. It is therefore ordered that all correspondence and communications verbally, or by writing, printing, or telegraphing, respecting the operations of the army, or military movements on land or water, or respecting the troops, camps, arsenals, intrenchments [sic], or military affairs within the several military districts, by which intelligence shall be directly or indirectly given to the enemy, without the authority or sanction of the general in command, be and the same are absolutely prohibited, and from and after the date of this order, persons violating the same will be proceeded against under the 57 article of war.[43]

Wall knew that his letter to Blair had caused his arrest, but under what justification, if any, he was unsure. Having moved from the jostling discomfort of the train to the jostling discomfort of a steamboat for the final leg of his journey to Fort Lafayette, he wrote a scathing letter to the secretary of war, whose name was attached to the warrant carried by the marshal.

"Suddenly this afternoon I was torn from my home," he wrote to Simon Cameron, "from a sick wife and frantic children by an order signed by yourself. What is my offense? I have been in favor of peace and have written in its favor, but I defy the world to lay their finger upon a single act that can by the most violent construction be tortured into treason." He was innocent of traitorous charges, he contended. "I come of Revolutionary blood on both sides and would scorn to do an act that would compromise or cast dishonor on such a birthright." His only crime was to "long for peace and a cessation of this terrible conflict."[44]

"The arrest of Colonel Wall has produced a most intense feeling of excitement among the people," printed the *New York Herald,* "as he has been a leading man among them.... There is great excitement here in consequence" of Wall's arrest, he being "charged with secession proclivities."[45]

Few other newspapers noticed.

In response to the case, the situation in Washington became further entangled. As was becoming more the case, Seward was actually in the dark on the matter. Concerned citizens asked "by what authority under the laws and Constitution of the United States the numerous arrests have been made throughout the North, especially the arrest of Col. James W. Wall...a man whose only offense appears to the public to be a letter addressed to Secretary Blair on the freedom of the press."[46]

Others thought the arrest long overdue. "You have done the loyal Union people of this [city] a great service by sending away that brawling, noisy secessionist James W. Wall," wrote a Burlington resident who signed his letter to Cameron, "Union Now and Forever." Wall was a "perfect pest to the Union...He exalted in our defeat at Bull Run...He said the d—d Black Republicans dare not arrest him. Do look after these folks," the anonymous author asked sternly. "They talk of Mr. Lincoln and his cabinet as if they were robbers."[47]

Meanwhile, Wall continued to write relentlessly to Cameron from prison. "I have just received a letter from my wife informing me that

Captain Burling had charged me with attempting to prevent his men from enlisting and that this was the cause of my arrest," he wrote a week after his capture. "I pronounce the whole charge an infamous fabrication."

And just in case Cameron was unconvinced, he enclosed a copy of a letter sent to Captain Burling on the matter. As to the charge of corruption, "I shall hold you personally responsible," he scathingly warned the captain. "I will follow you like a sleuthhound, and your blood or mine shall expiate this offense." A frustrated week in prison, without charges and without answers or any contact with the outside world, besides limited correspondence, was evident. "I pronounce the whole charge a base, contemptible lie," he persisted, "invented for malicious purposes and utterly unworthy your character as an officer or a gentleman."[48]

Cameron passed responsibility for Wall's arrest to Seward in a letter from his chief clerk on September 19. Four days later, Seward responded to an inquiry from New Jersey governor Charles Olden. The governor was concerned that "persons of entire credibility" were vouching for a number of those arrested. "In other cases the friends of the prisoners assert positively that they have been guilty of no act against the government and that if they were permitted to know only why they have been arrested they could satisfy the government of their innocence." He pressed the necessity to "justify these arrests."

In the case of Wall, Seward responded. "It is to be regretted that you have not given me more precise information in regard to the…arrest…represented to have been made upon insufficient grounds."[49]

Apparently, Seward thought the situation too politically charged to continue Wall's detainment, or perhaps even he thought the situation had gotten out of hand. Seward had had little involvement, knew few of the facts, and had no evidence of wrongdoing. "Let him be released on taking the oath of allegiance," Seward ordered, no doubt to the displeasure of Blair and Cameron.[50]

It was a surprising move by Seward. More representative was an exchange of conversation said to have taken place between men seeking the release of a Fort Lafayette prisoner. Seward abruptly replied that the prisoner would not be released. The brother of the prisoner asked what the charges were, adding that there were no charges on him on file.

"Seward answered hastily: 'I don't care a d—n whether they are guilty or innocent. I saved Maryland by similar arrests, and so I mean to hold Kentucky.' Then (Seward) turned on his guests; 'Why the hell are you not at home fighting traitors, instead of seeking their release here?'"[51]

On September 24, Wall took an oath of allegiance, the normal process of release.

> I, James W. Wall, do solemnly swear that I will support, protect, and defend the Constitution and government of the United States against all enemies whether domestic or foreign, and that I will bear true faith, allegiance, and loyalty to the same any ordinance, resolution, or law of any state convention or legislature to the contrary notwithstanding; and further that I do this with a full determination, pledge, and purpose without any mental reservation or evasion whatsoever. So help me God.[52]

He arrived home on a stormy Friday evening, September 24, 1861, and despite being ill, spoke to a crowd of hundreds gathered around a banner that read, "James W. Wall, the Defender of the Constitution, Welcome Home." The American flag was flowing behind it, pressed against the weight of the rain.

The Burlington Cornet Band played as they rode slowly down the street. The procession ended at the house where thirty-four young girls dressed in their Sunday whites greeted them, one representing each of the thirty-four states (North and South). The girls formed two lines from the carriage to the door.

Wall stood on a small podium that had been built in front of the house, the stone porch its base, and addressed the crowd. "What a study in contrast to the melancholy scene," he began after thanking the crowd, "hardly a fortnight ago, when I was dragged ruthlessly from these steps, torn mercilessly from the clinging embraces of the dear ones at home, and consigned to the tender mercies of the brutal military despotism that rules with iron sway within the gloomy walls of the American Bastille. I have been imprisoned for two weeks, against my will, and I have not been able to learn what these charges are."

> If by a simple mandate of any cabinet officer, in a state loyal to the Union as this has been, and when the courts of law are open, you or I may be torn from our homes, without cause shown, and consigned to the gloomy walls of a government fortress, the same mandate, only altered in its phraseology, may deprive us of our properties, (or send us to the executioner), confiscating the rights of the states.
>
> The right to have our lives secure against interference and unreasonable searches is guaranteed. Do you know, my friends, how old these privileges are? They can trace this lineage back to the days of the mailed-clad baron, and these feet have stood reverentially upon the grassy lawns of Runnemede, where these great privileges were born six hundred years ago.
>
> The freeman who secured their Petition of Rights from Charles in 1628, never ceased their importunities until

they made the king confess, "My maxim is, that the peoples' liberties strengthen the king's prerogatives, and the king's prerogative is to defend the peoples liberties, and so it is with the states, it can only be used to defend and strengthen our liberties, not to destroy them."

"I, for my part," he continued, now almost thirty minutes later, "will demand at the hands of the legal tribunals of my country full redress for all the wrongs and outrages that I have been made to suffer. There are dastardly wretches in your midst, who, I understand, have been instrumental in this arrest, and for whom I have no regard and utterly despise. They will be sheltered by their own insignificance."[53]

It was obvious that Wall, a representative of the radical Democratic press, would not be deterred from the wave of overt acts perpetrated on himself and his colleagues. Just how they could continue to fight and avoid imprisonment seemed a delicate, if even possible, proposition; and, as previous operations indicated, there was no rhyme or reason to the attacks. Why did the Hodgsons remain free while Howard rotted in prison?

When Wall finally reacclimated himself to life at home, he wasted little time getting back into the fold. He sent a letter to William Bradford Reed. "I have understood from a reliable source that it is the intention of a number of prominent Democrats to start a Democratic journal shortly in Philadelphia. If so I should like very much to be attached to the editorial corps...I think the dawn and the cry of 'Watchman, what of the night,' will soon cease," he continued. "Permit me to congratulate you on the result in Pennsylvania. We shall show you the virtue of a good example in New Jersey in November."

Wall was probably referring to the recent mid-term elections in Pennsylvania, which were held earlier than in New Jersey. Democrats had taken many of the local seats up for election.

Unfortunately for him, Wall's activities were still under surveillance. State Department agents intercepted his letter, and Reed never saw it.[54] The watchman was still looking over their shoulders.

In November 1862, Frank Key Howard was released from prison. Lincoln had promised the citizens of Baltimore that "in all cases [of arrest] the government is in possession of tangible and unmistakable evidence, which will, when made public, be satisfactory to every loyal citizen." Upon his release after fourteen months in prison, Howard was yet to be charged with a crime.[55]

Though reassuring words would often come from Lincoln, his actions were a bit more docile and troubling. Wrote one prisoner, "The wives of several of the prisoners at Fort Monroe visited the president regarding the fate of their husbands. The president received them very politely, listened to all they had to say, and informed them that he had nothing to do with the Baltimore prisoners, they were Seward's prisoners, and declined interference."

From this exchange we may infer that each member of the government has his own set of captives, over whom he exercised exclusive jurisdiction and control.[56]

The summer of rage, the wave of mob justice, the government seizures and arrests, and the confiscation of property under the endorsement of the United States Congress and the signature of the president, led to a courtroom in Philadelphia. John and William Hodgson, as will be seen, had taken it upon themselves to fight back. There was no chance or point to use force. The weapon—or tool— was the court and, as usual, the Constitution.

So much had happened that it seemed little chance that justice would be enjoyed by the likes of those on the wrong side of the administration. Like the war itself, the case was playing out to be a battle of wills. It was a battle John Hodgson could not lose.

Part Two

A TRUE ACCOUNT OF THE UNITED STATES OF AMERICA VS. THE **JEFFERSONIAN** NEWSPAPER

In the Supreme Court in and for the Eastern District of Pennsylvania

William Millward, William Schuyler, and John Jenkins, Defendants, were attached to answer William H. Hodgson late of said country Plaintiff, of a plea of trespass.

Whereupon the said Plaintiff, by his attorney William B. Reed and George W. Biddle, Esquires, complains, for that the said defendants on the twenty-second day of August AD 1861 and on other days and times between that day and the commence of this suit with force and arms seized and took goods of the plaintiff then being his peaceable possession to with one power press of the value of $600, one hand press of the value of $200, forty printing cases of the value of $80, printing utensils comprising jobbing type, galley sacks, etc. to the value of $250, thirteen reams of paper of the value of $50, office furniture…The subscription list of a paper called The *Jeffersonian* of the value of $4,000, books of accounting for jobbing of the value of $200 being in all of great value, to wit, of the value of $7,334.

And the said plaintiff further complains for that the said defendants on the said 22nd of August 1861 with force and arms, broke and entered a certain house and office of the plaintiff, situated in the country aforesaid and the county of Philadelphia and then and there ejected and expelled the said plaintiff and his agents and servants from the possession and enjoyment of the said house and office and kept him so ejected and expelled for a long time, from the said 22nd day of August until the 14th day of October, whereby the plaintiff during all that time lost and was deprived of the use and benefit of his said home and office. Whereby and by reason of the premise and by the wrongful acts and doings the said defendants saith he hath suffered damage to the amount of twenty thousand dollars and therefore he brings suit.

W. B. Reed
G. W. Biddle for plaintiff
Filed November 19, 1861

Defendants plead "not guilty" with leave to give the special matter in evidence.

John G. Knox
David Webster
Filed December 5, 1861
—*Taken from the opening pages of the court transcript*

Chapter Nine

THE COST OF THEIR CONVICTIONS

The freedom of the press is a wholesome check upon public officers, and should be sustained.[1]

—John Hodgson, December 28, 1861

I f there was any doubt to John Hodgson that the seizure of the *Jeffersonian* was the work of congressman John Hickman, the appearance of federal marshals armed with a summons and invoking the name of Abraham Lincoln would have settled the issue.

Hodgson and Hickman knew each other well—in fact, in 1848 the rising attorney and the young journalist had met in court, with Hickman defending Hodgson's right to publish. Hodgson, even then not one to shy from scandal, was being sued by John T. Haines, a local justice of the peace, for "an alleged libel" in response to an article Hodgson printed in the *Jeffersonian*. In it, Hodgson questioned Haines's personal and professional integrity.

According to Hodgson, the incident began in a local bar when a former West Chester resident, the highly intoxicated John M. Evans, "boasted of having been in Mexico, and of giving Uncle Sam and his nephews the slip." Within earshot sat a local recruiting officer who promptly arrested the loose-tongued Evans as a deserter and led him to the local jail in chains. The next day Evans tried to escape the confines of his West Chester holding cell and was again shackled. The *Jeffersonian* reported that in the process Evans made "some rhetorical jestures [sic], and ugly words not found in Webster's parlor dictionary."[2]

Later that day, another shouting match ensued during which Evans's attorney chased the recruiting officer out of his office with a fire poker. The commotion caused a crowd to gather outside, and most reveled in the disgraceful situation that developed. The rambunctious crowd screamed for Lewis, the attorney, to beat the recruiting officer with the poker, a request for which Lewis showed great restraint.

In a hearing the following day, "the panorama underwent a rapid change." The case hinged on whether or not the recruiting officer had a legal right to hold Evans on suspicion of desertion. Surprisingly, Haines, the justice of the peace, released the deserter on the grounds that the officer did not first consult Haines on the arrest. As a federal official, explained Haines, the officer was obligated to ask his permission to make the arrest.

Hodgson defended the recruiting officer in his paper, charging that Haines made his decision because he was offended that his authority was not properly recognized. Hodgson, always frankly critical and outspoken, saw no room for splitting fine hairs when it came to interpretation of the law. As such, he openly criticized Haines for abusing his position on the bench by hiding behind a technicality. In response, Haines filed suit against Hodgson and the *Jeffersonian* for the public condemnation. Hodgson turned to his friend John Hickman for legal support.

In his closing argument of the trial, Hickman conceded that indeed the article printed by Hodgson was libelous. However, he pointed out, "In point of law and fact a justice of the peace is a servant of the people and amenable to them. His acts are public property, and the fit and proper subject of investigation the right to examine and report which, is granted to every editor by the constitution of the Commonwealth." Even though the report may have been "ludicrous or otherwise," Hickman admitted, it would be "necessary to show a malicious motive to prove a libel."[3] Hickman won the jury and upheld Hodgson's right to publish freely.

Hickman also read, verbatim, Article IX, Section VII of the Pennsylvania State Constitution, dedicated to the freedom of the press to "examine the proceedings of the legislature, or any branch of government." Hodgson would have known well the spirit of this right, if not the words themselves. He was building a journalistic career by searching without fear into "any branch of government," something not many journalists cared to do in the mid-nineteenth century.

Hodgson bragged of their defense of a free and open press. The *Jeffersonian*—in typical Hodgson modesty—reprinted the entire article for which he had been sued for originally printing. He also added two additional columns of "notes and comments." If any reader still missed his point, Hodgson also included an itemized list of the costs of the suit "which the taxable citizens of the county have to pay."[4]

Ironically, more than twenty years later, it was Hickman's legislative weapon, the Confiscation Act, that provided the justification for the seizure of the *Jeffersonian*. Hodgson certainly had Hickman on his mind when the federal marshals came to close the *Jeffersonian*. On that August day in 1861, the United States government had used the Confiscation Act, which Hickman had helped push through Congress, to muffle Hodgson's voice.

Confronted with the full force of the federal government, both John and William Hodgson, father and son, together reacted with an unpredictable move—or perhaps not so unpredictable. Instead of closing the newspaper or changing the editorial tone, as did many of their colleagues, they sought out two of the best Democratic lawyers in Philadelphia and sued the federal marshals who had closed the paper. The case—known initially as the *United States of America vs the* Jeffersonian *newspaper* wound its way through the Philadelphia circuit court, where Hodgson battled for the return of his office and equipment. Later, turning the tables, the government was sued for trespassing on private property, and the overall question of freedom of the press would hang over the deliberations. This case came to the docket of the Pennsylvania Supreme Court where the case would be heard in February 1863 before Walter H. Lowrie, Chief Justice of the Supreme Court at Philadelphia.

The start of 1863, more than a year after the mobbing and seizure of the *Jeffersonian,* found the country in depression. With the war entering its third year, it was a far different atmosphere from the optimistic summer days of two years earlier. In tiny country towns and villages North and South, thousands of soldiers had been killed in some of the most memorable battles on American soil. In August 1862, Confederate General Robert E. Lee defeated Lincoln's army at the second battle of Manassas just outside of Washington, DC. Afterward, he turned toward Maryland. In September 1862, battling near the town of Sharpsurg, near Antietam Creek, Lee's forty-thousand-man army clashed against a Union army twice that size. The result was the bloodiest day in American history. Almost thirty thousand men were left dead. Lee's invasion of Maryland had failed, but he retreated to fight again. The war seemed to be on the doorsteps of Union families not only in Maryland but even Pennsylvania, as J. E. B. Stuart and his band of raiders looted Chambersburg, Pennsylvania, a town north of the Mason-Dixon line.

Regardless of who fired and who fell, an American lost his life. No man, not a newspaper editor, a battlefield general, or Lincoln himself saw an end to the bloody war.

Politically, a series of setbacks in mid-term elections throughout the North threatened Lincoln's prosecution of the war. In fact, elections were one of the greatest threats all along to the Union's battle for survival. A major election was held somewhere in the North in at least half of the forty-eight months the war would last through 1865. In 1862, Republicans lost thirty-five seats in Congress and both New York and New Jersey elected Democratic governors.[5] Closer to home, the lower house of the Pennsylvania state legislature was now in Democratic hands as well as several key state positions formerly held by Republicans. Without a doubt there was a resurgence in the political fortunes of the Democratic Party from the dark days of two years prior, and it heartened the likes of the antiwar Democrats throughout Pennsylvania.

It can well be argued that, of course, many voters were weary of the war and desiring to put into office men who were more open to negotiations than the stubborn Lincoln. Whether they agreed with the political events or not, it can also be stated that voters in the state elections were even then using the American tradition of sending a message to those in power. Hodgson's subscribers voted. So too his colleagues in Philadelphia and New York, in Boston and in Baltimore. Though more and more were fearful of any public dissent, thanks to the draconian actions of the Lincoln administration, most Democrats, and apparently some Republicans, felt that the administration had moved too far in their heavy-handed assaults on civil liberties. After all, no matter the emotions of war, it is difficult to watch friends and neighbors locked in jail solely for their sympathies to the enemy.

Secretary of State Seward's tumultuous year of responsibility for citizen arrests put fear into the hearts of many an editor and legislator. Until, the War Department took responsibility for "prisoners of state," it is estimated that Seward oversaw the arrest of just under one thousand Northern citizens. Equally disturbing, many of the arrests took place without his knowledge and certainly without his consent. The processes in place gave local authorities enough excuse to make the arrests on their own, often on a whim and often for their own personal gain. The arrest of newspaper editors was a very real occurrence, and the randomness of the arrests struck fear into men like John Hodgson who lived every day of the war thinking he would be next to suffer.[6]

In Ohio, the 1863 elections went strongly for the Democrats and many felt part of the reason was the effort to suppress the political opposition. Boasted the *Democratic Crisis:*

> Mrs. McGregor, whose husband is in a military prison for no cause whatever but that he is a Democrat, is filling her husband's post admirably. She is pouring hot shot into the sides of the lack traitors, that must make them wince, if they have the least manhood left. From her paper of last week we clip the following:
>
> A Noble Wife—A True Woman—
>
> Let Tyrants Blush!
>
> THE LATE MILITARY ARRESTS IN CANTON
>
> I cannot help thanking the people of Stark County, for giving so decided and so emphatic an expression at the polls on the 14th inst.
>
> Among the matters, passed upon by the people, was unquestionably the reign of terror, the mob rule, and the

late arbitrary arrests, inaugurated and enforced by the abolition leaders in Canton and Massillon. These men…procured a military force of two hundred guns…to force away two peaceable law abiding citizens from their wives and children. Drunk with power, reveling in the ruin of their country, they seemed to imagine they could go on in their career of depravity, and the people would tamely submit.

But the people have spurned them, and condemned their acts. How little these men know the people! Only two days after these proceedings, the people of Stark County administered the rebuke.

Attack the Confederate troops, the voters from Missouri to Maryland seemed to say, not me or my neighbors. James Gordon Bennett's *New York Herald* agreed:

Now, what are the causes of this wonderful revolution? There had been little or no canvass; the press and free speech had been under rigid restriction and censorship. The influence of money and contracts was all on the Republican side.

Yet the people voted on the opposite side. Why have they done so? Because the Republican Party, which ousted the democracy from power on the ground of its corruption, has proved itself ten times more corrupt, while at the same time its tyranny and utter incapacity for rule have brought the nation to the verge of ruin.[7]

Bennett believed Lincoln to be honest despite a long list of corrupt practices cited in his paper. His analysis was unique: he felt the Democratic victories in the mid-term elections were good news for Lincoln as it showed the radical Republicans to be weak at the ballot box. "But now that it is proven by the elections that the radicals are powerless, and that he has the people to stand by him in defense of the Constitution, he can get rid of his imbecile cabinet."[8] Bennett, who had supported the institution of slavery, welcomed any sign that the radical Republicans did not reflect the views of Northern voters, and instead that Lincoln's moderation was the choice of the average citizen.

It seemed that a critical moment in the fate of the Union and the Lincoln administration was fast approaching, and Pennsylvania was now the center of all the calculations. Lee was, by early 1863, making the decision to focus his efforts in southern Pennsylvania, to pressure Pennsylvania and Maryland. A Confederate invasion could alter a critical gubernatorial election in Pennsylvania in October, inviting a Democratic victory not only in Pennsylvania, but later in the presidential election the next year. Pro-Southern Democrats knew this. So too the Republicans. The political stakes had never been higher.

Political changes were not limited to the states—there had been changes in Lincoln's cabinet as well. The corrupt Simon Cameron of Pennsylvania had been kicked out in 1862 and replaced by Edwin Stanton, a hawkish Democrat who made William Seward's uncoordinated system of citizen arrests, as well as the number of arrests made, look pathetic. Stanton also had publishing connections; he was a friend of George Harding, the brother of the publisher of the *Philadelphia Inquirer,* the leading Philadelphia paper at the time. The paper was regarded at the time as the political organ of another business-political team: the infamous financier Jay Cooke and Secretary of Treasury Salmon Chase.

In late October 1861, Hodgson's legal actions against the government gave him at least a temporary reprieve, and his paper was reinstated without explanation. He again had his voice, and had plenty to say after a two-month hiatus. Hodgson wasted no time saying goodbye to Cameron and taking a good swipe at John Forney's growing publishing fiefdom:

> Simon Cameron is no longer secretary of war. He has virtually been removed from office, although the president tries to let him down easy by sending him out of this country and into one, Russia, where plunderers of the government treasury are punished, as they are not, but should be here. Hon. E. M. Stanton…has been called to Simon's place, and his first duty should be to look after Cummings, Lebos, Brookes, Laumans, and others of Simon's favorite operators who are occupying quartermasterships, paymasterships, inspectorships, contractorships, &c. The sooner the whole gang is routed out the better for the public treasury, although Forney & Co. might lose a percentage of spoils thereby.[9]

Another Democratic editor was kinder to the departing secretary, sarcastically commenting that "in one thing the people have been very much disappointed. They had a right to expect that, during the existence of a devastating civil war, the politicians and demagogues would confine their stealing to the army." But, went on the editor, "the corruption of the Republican Party was such that those in power were stealing from every place they could." He went on to highlight an attempt by Secretary Chase to pass a provision providing that one half the monetary value of all forfeited vessels seized would be given to three officials in the New York ports.

Concluded the *Crisis* of Columbus, Ohio, "it comes the nearest to Cameron's shoddy contracts of anything we have seen. Such facts as these develop the real causes of the prolongation of the war. The people's servants are unfaithful to their trust. The misery of the people, the very misfortunes of the country, is their gain."[10]

But little did Lincoln know how much of a role Stanton had played in Cameron's War Department. Stanton had helped Cameron draft his yearly report, which he submitted to Lincoln in January 1862. The report included Stanton's strategy to arm freed slaves, which Lincoln flatly refused; then Lincoln appointed Stanton as Cameron's replacement where he would unknowingly see more of the same. Stanton also soon took control of telegraph lines and inaugurated a dragnet assault on the opposition press.[11]

The Union landscape had changed dramatically in the direction desired by Lincoln. Dozens of newspapers had been destroyed forever, the victims of mob justice. Others had been targeted by United States marshals and their property seized, while yet others languished in federal prisons without charge or hope of trial. John Hodgson had survived the mob, and was now fighting for the life of his beloved *Jeffersonian.* The brutal tactics of the administration had won—many dissenting voices were silenced.

But many were also weary of these unprecedented actions. As the war dragged into its third year, intense public scrutiny was forcing an overhaul within the Lincoln administration.

Hodgson's views were suddenly more popular than at any time since the start of the war, this because of the one dramatic act of Abraham Lincoln that terrified many in the North.

The most anticipated change of war strategy occurred on the first day of 1863, when all of the emotional fears of Southern sympathizers—and more than a few Republicans—came to fruition. On Thursday, January 1, 1863, Abraham Lincoln's Emancipation Proclamation came into effect. Born out of the apparent Union victory at Antietam, the Proclamation legally did not free any slaves, but it did create a moral and nobler justification of the war. It was now a war for liberation. From this day forward, when the federal army marched through Southern towns, they would bring with them the hope of freedom, a more tangible cause than the political struggle of the federal government to suppress the right of a state to break away.

To an observer, the evolution of Abraham Lincoln on this issue is like watching the struggling maturation of a great poet. His first actions taken on emancipation are shallow. He had hastily squashed Frémont's efforts to liberate slaves in Missouri, and refused to approve Simon Cameron's attempts to arm freed slaves and muster them into the Union army. He had also hesitated on signing the Confiscation Act of 1861, which called for the seizure of all property connected to any person engaging in any activity that could be defined as treasonable. The initial version called for slaves to be included in the list of property, but that was removed in order to pass the bill. The issue of emancipation, from Lincoln's wary perspective, had not yet been a politically viable option, or a strategic benefit to the war effort.[12]

During this time, the president had been prodded by the actions of the radicals in Congress, by the actions of some potential political competitors like General John Fremont (the Republican party's presidential candidate in 1856), by the desires of his cabinet, and by the loud voice of *New York Tribune* editor Horace Greeley, among others. And still his progression was deliberate.

Lincoln's famous response to "The Prayer of Twenty Millions," in which Greeley attacked Lincoln for acting too slowly to destroy slavery, best relate his views on the slavery question, and to his approach on the entire war.

My paramount object in this struggle *is* to save the Union, and is *not* either to save or destroy slavery. If I could save the Union without freeing *any* slave, I would do it, and if I could save it by freeing *all* the slaves, I would do it; and if I could save it by freeing some and leaving others alone I would also do that. What I do about slavery, and the colored race, I do because I believe it helps to save the Union; and what I forbear, I forbear because I do *not* believe it would help to save the Union. I shall do *less* whenever I shall believe what I am doing hurts the cause, and I shall do *more* whenever I shall believe doing more will help the cause.[13]

When Lincoln did respond to Greeley, it was vintage Abraham Lincoln. Perfect in timing; and perfect in accomplishing desperately needed military goals without costing the beleaguered Union much of anything. Despite the fact that Lincoln had the ultimate response to Greeley's charges, the Emancipation Proclamation, ready in a desk drawer, he refused to release it because of Greeley's pressure.

When Lincoln did respond, he did not respond directly to the New York editor. Seeking maximum publicity, he wrote instead to the *National Intelligencer* and forced Greeley to reprint his comments. By involving two newspapers, the media-savvy Lincoln invited more response, and dialogue, than he would have by responding to Greeley only through the *Tribune*.[14]

The complexity of the reaction of the public—as well as fellow politicians—to the Emancipation Proclamation goes far in explaining where exactly men like John Hodgson stood in the political spectrum of the day. And the sad answer is that Hodgson's views on keeping the institution of slavery alive and blocking any evolution of civil rights for blacks were not that far removed from the mainstream.

Hodgson considered the Emancipation Proclamation, like Lincoln himself, a political and military tool for winning the war, not an act of humanity.

Consider that Hodgson's bitter Republican foe John Forney, writing in *The Press,* supported the Emancipation Proclamation in political terms, but expressed no sympathy for the freedom of the slaves. In 1862, Forney called for the colonization of the blacks back to Africa "on the grounds of their permanent inferiority."[15]

Nor did politicians on the other side hesitate to voice their displeasure. Ohio's Democratic congressman, Samuel S. Cox, warned that soldiers from his state would not fight "if the result shall be flight and movement of the black race by millions northward." Attempts by several entrepreneurs to bring freed blacks north sparked rioting and violence in southern Indiana and in Cincinnati, Ohio.

The *Crisis* articulated the fears of many a Democrat in warning that "the enormous rise in the price of everything a laboring man has to buy, while his wages are nominally the same, with the prospect of a great reduction through Negro competitions, would cause the free Negroites to reflect. Had they the least wisdom or common sense, they might wonder what they are doing, without waiting to try the experiment…the excitement is getting very high."

Such was "the excitement" flooding through the country that even the Cabinet reacted with concern. A message sent from Washington to General Ulysses Grant tried to temper the rising emotions:

> WASHINGTON, January 19, 1863. Major General GRANT, Memphis, Tenn.: I am directed by the secretary of war to say that if you have ordered the shipment of Negroes from the slave states to Cincinnati, you will countermand the order. H. W. HALLECK, General in Chief.[16]

The public mood toward Lincoln's proclamation covered the spectrum of emotions. Radical Republicans thought the act accomplished too little, as it did not address the rights of slaves in the Union. Democrats thought Lincoln had sold out his country and many feared the economic and social backlash of tens of thousands of slaves sweeping North for freedom. There was also tremendous confusion as to what the Emancipation Proclamation actually meant to accomplish. This confusion included many of the Union troops. Typical of the comments was a letter from A. J. Juckett, a loyal soldier on the frontlines:

"I don't think Mr. Lincoln's proclamation is going to do any particular good as we cannot free the slaves until we capture the territory they are in. We don't seem to be having much success now," he wrote. "As for a colored army, I don't care if they do make them fight. It will not hurt them any more than it will me."[17]

And it was not just the men in the trenches who were less than enthused. General Henry Halleck dryly commented in a backhanded complement to Horace Greeley, "the conflict is now a damned *Tribune* abolition war."[18]

Despite concerns even in the Union army, many Republicans gladly saw the proclamation as a military tool that undermined Southern strength, and as an adept political move that froze Great Britain from inching closer to recognizing its economic trading partner to the South. But social equality for the freed slaves remained a concern only to a minority of the population, a handful of radical Republicans and genuine abolitionists like Harriett Beecher Stowe and Horace Greeley.

The implementation of the Emancipation Proclamation and the failure of Northern military efforts alienated many moderate Democrats, throwing them into closer alliance with their party's extreme wing.[19] The result was a tangible victory for Philadelphia peace radicals like William B. Reed, and allowed Hodgson to assume a greater voice to a growing subscriber base. For Lincoln and his supporters, though they had held border states like Maryland and Missouri in the Union for the time being, there was a fear that continued strength among Democrats could spell doom in Pennsylvania and hence the Union.

The result by the start of 1863 was a society depressed, unable to see the end of the war, and lacking in confidence towards Union leaders.

A diary-keeping Philadelphian summed up the gloomy mood felt by all patriotic Northerners. Offering a rare contemporary view of the Union in the days before the Hodgson trial, banker George W. Fahnstock feared that "the worst is yet before us and democracy will complete the ruin and disintegration of our republic."[20]

And two days later, on the thirty-first of January, he expanded his pessimistic thoughts toward the power of the opposition party and their public dissent of the war.

> The government are perplexed. I begin to think Lincoln unfit for the emergency. We are bordering upon anarchy. The rebels are full of spirit and taking every advantage of our weakness, whilst our people are wrangling over shadows. The Democrats are assisting the rebels to break up our government. They avow their perfidy with unblushing effrontery, and give utterance to their treason on the street.
>
> The *Evening Journal,* a disloyal sheet, was suppressed here a day or two since, and the editor carried by order of Gen. Schenek to Ft. McHenry. Judge Ludlow, a pettifogged Democrat, takes notice of the arrest, calls in the grand jury, and lashes himself into a wrath about it, when in fact it is none of his business.

Sadly, concludes Fahnstock, "Congress is demoralized—so is the army—the navy—the government."[21]

Observers in Great Britain agreed, one editor writing that "the Democrats are gradually developing their plan of attack, and the more we see of it the more desperate and unscrupulous it appeared. After they had been emboldened by their success in the elections in the west last autumn, the leaders…determined upon a system of resistance to the general government.[22]

In other words, the Union suffered from too much democracy; allowing political opponents to aid the enemy. Hodgson would beg to differ. So too the editors tarred and feathered, and the many editors locked in the "American Bastilles," as the jails in Baltimore, New York, and other Northern locations became known. But for supporters of Lincoln and of the Union as it was—there was just too much opportunity for the supporters of the South to sway public opinion against the war. The opposition had to be stopped.

It was in this context that a trial took place to determine if the American government had the legal right to suppress a paper that opposed the government's war. It was John Hodgson's fight, and he stood alone.

Chapter Ten

"HAVE WE
A GOVERNMENT?"

*"This question has been repeatedly asked. Many people in this country
seem to have been laboring under a false idea that this was a
government of the people, that we the people, were the sovereigns, and
that presidents, governors, (and) congressmen were our servants.
Mr. Lincoln will show you that you have a government, independent of
'we, the people.'"*[1]

—John Hodgson, April 20, 1861

L ike any legal conflict, the path to the February 1863 trial
involved several preliminary clashes. During their initial circuit
court case in October 1861, the United States district attorney,
George Coffey, had failed to appear on behalf of the state. Therefore,
failing to prove any illegal activity by the *Jeffersonian,* the government
was ordered to return the Hodgsons' property.

Interestingly enough, the first question posed by a judge was
whether the district attorney meant to construe that the government
had a legal right for censoring the press. After a discussion, the judge

concluded that he understood the government believed it *was* authorized to censor the press.[2]

Another judge believed the only question was whether the Confiscation Act was meant to include newspaper presses.

And a third judge thought it "important" to know whether the destroyed type of the *Jeffersonian* had been cast into bullets![3]

But having their property returned proved of little value for the paper's ability to reach its subscribers. Immediately following the case's dismissal, the Hodgsons' mail privileges were suspended by the United States post office, and it would not be until January 1862, five months after its seizure by the government, that the *Jeffersonian* was again delivered unmolested. In the meantime, they would publish and circulate their papers through alternative methods, adding time, labor, and expense to the already tedious task of distribution.

As usual, the *Jeffersonian* did not take the government action lightly. Postmaster General Montgomery Blair was accused by the *Jeffersonian* of being a pawn of congressman John Hickman, and for taking action without any legal precedent. The postmaster had issued a report stating that he took the actions against more than a dozen Democratic newspapers because of the slowness of the judicial system. "To await the results of slow judicial prosecution was to allow crime to be consummated, with the expectation of subsequent punishment."

Blair lectured to the Democratic editors, "the freedom of the press is secured by a high constructional sanction. But it is a freedom and not license that is guaranteed. It is to be used only for lawful purposes. It cannot aim blows at the existence of the government, the Constitution, and the Union, and at the same time claim its protection."[4]

Hodgson begged to differ, pointing out that "Mr. Blair knows...that [my] journal had not been...presented by any grand jury."

And further, Blair knew that the legal case against the *Jeffersonian* had been thrown out of court.

Reasoned Hodgson, "having been publicly vindicated in court, we had a right to believe that, after a suppression of our journal of nearly two months…we would be permitted to resume and continue its publication."[5]

Hodgson was ready to go public with his suspicions. The blame, confided the publisher, "rests with the strings pulled on the postmaster general. How long Mr. Blair, controlled by the consuls of Hickman & Co, will continue his edict, or how long President Lincoln will permit it, we cannot presume to say."[6]

Hodgson was surprisingly conciliatory toward Lincoln, believing that the prohibition against use of the mails "is so clearly unjust that we cannot think it was authorized by, or can for a moment, receive the sanction of President Lincoln and his cabinet."

Hodgson warned, "We shall at once take steps to ascertain the truth…John Hickman & Co may, on our streets charge the Lincoln administration with being 'weak and vacillating,' and it appears that they can induce the postmaster general to prohibit the mail circulation of a democratic newspaper."[7]

The threat to "take steps to ascertain the truth" began immediately.

The *Jeffersonian* was well armed for what lay ahead. Hodgson's legal team consisted of a young man named George W. Biddle and the well-known and in some circles, infamous, William B. Reed.

Petite and balding, with sculpted, almost feminine cheekbones, William Bradford Reed was better known for his sulfuric tongue and an unwavering support for Southern causes than his outward appearance. But in this time of crisis, Reed, like his clients, was caught on the wrong side of loyal. Reed was representing several unpopular defendants, most of them Confederate sympathizers arrested and incarcerated without charge. One, Pierce Butler, was arrested in August 1861, a few days before the mobbing of the *Jeffersonian,* and would remain in Fort Lafayette for a full month until pledging not to conduct hostile acts against the Union. With the help of Reed and other attorneys, Butler began legal proceedings against Secretary of War Simon Cameron, even causing his arrest and indictment by the Pennsylvania Supreme Court in Philadelphia on the charges of trespass, false imprisonment, and assault and battery. Ultimately, Lincoln interceded on Cameron's behalf by endorsing Butler's arrest and asking both the Senate and House judiciary committees to make the suit disappear, which they did.[8]

In taking on the case of the *Jeffersonian,* Reed saw another opportunity to correct a number of wrongs forced against him since the war broke out, and an opportunity to prove once and for all the fraud of the Lincoln administration. But above all else, this complex man saw in the Hodgsons a chance to further his beliefs that all men had the right to oppose the government and receive a fair trial. Though a time-honored American tradition, it was, to put it mildly, a tradition out of favor in the fall of 1861.

Reed's resume was long and distinguished. A proficient statesman, attorney, and writer, he was again spending most of his time practicing law. When war loomed in 1860, Reed gave what he then considered his final public address. His ties to the South before the war were well known, and his sympathies at the outset of war equally understood by Northern Republicans. He was fifty-four years old, an old-line Whig who joined the Democratic Party in the tumultuous 1850s. An experienced statesman, even he thought he could have no influence on the war should the ambitions of men make a reality of a bloody conflict.

Reed's family had come to America on the *Mayflower*. His family line, his own contributions included, was unrivaled in social circles; and his colleagues knew it.

A graduate from the University of Pennsylvania at the age of sixteen, Reed was admitted to the bar four years later. Before the age of twenty-one, he was appointed the Secretary of the American Mission to the Congress of the Spanish-American Republics at Panama, then spent several months in Mexico in the same capacity. A year later he returned home, fluent in Spanish, and began to write a series of essays for the *American Quarterly Review*, a journal to which he would contribute for the next ten years.

In 1834, at an age when most men were settling into their first meaningful job, he was elected to the Lower House of the legislature in Philadelphia. In 1841 he was appointed the city's attorney general, and then a state senator.

Soon after, he was again offered the post of attorney general, but turned it down and instead won election as the district attorney of Philadelphia. He served in that capacity until the time came, as a loyal Democrat now with heavy political ties, to campaign for James Buchanan in 1856.

A former history professor at the University of Pennsylvania, Reed's leisure hours were passed studying the American Revolution. He published numerous articles and books on the roles of his own ancestors, specifically his grandfather, General Joseph Reed, who was, as everyone knew, George Washington's first secretary and a member of Congress. An in-depth student of history, the grandson had studied the complex relationship between General Reed and Benedict Arnold. The story so inspired Reed that he was working on a manuscript about the country's most infamous traitor.

Like any good politician, Reed also had his favorite newspaper organ. His columns, where he shared both his satisfactions and fears of country and state to the public, appeared in the copperhead *New York World.* He had published a number of pamphlets as well, and in the years preceding the war was a featured speaker at most Democratic rallies in Pennsylvania.[9]

Over the years he had had the privilege of traveling to the world's great centers of learning, and he returned to the United States with all of the respect, insight, and humbleness of a man who had seen much through so many foreign eyes. On his return trip from China, serving in the Buchanan administration as the United States' first ambassador to that country, Reed traveled overland through India and most of Europe, gazing upon sites unbelievable. But amidst this journey it remained home, and the familiar institutions, that were missed most.[10]

"Returning from abroad in the spring of 1859," he wrote in a self-published pamphlet in 1862, "I took relatively little part in the presidential canvass of the next year, though feeling a deep interest, for I saw in the future, as clearly as I see in the ghastly present, that the triumph of the 'Republican' Party, with its aggressive doctrines and the radical and fanatical spirit which animated it, threatened the disruption and downfall of the Republic itself." Upon his return, he was shocked to discover that the country whose reputation for liberty and democracy he had proudly carried across the world was now, believed the ambassador, destroying the very foundations of its most time-honored traditions.[11]

After his return to the states, Reed lectured regularly. At the National Democratic Association meeting, held in Philadelphia in September of 1860, he warned of the dangers of republicanism. He was preaching to the converted, speaking with the agenda of maintaining unity within the Democratic Party. But even that hope was starting to lapse, the Breckinridge and Douglas Democrats gnawing at each other over whether peace or war was the means to mend broken ties. All told, "Mr. Lincoln's election would endanger Southern rights and interests" he told the crowd.[12]

He spoke from the heart, "of Mr. Lincoln, whose election I consider full of threatened evil to the Union and the Pennsylvania." He told those who listened.

> The sad conviction presses on me that the animating spirit of the Republican Party, however individuals may honestly disclaim it, is antislavery fanaticism, enthusiastic sentimentalism, founded on the false ethical principle that slavery, as it exists in this country is wrong, per se, and that under Lincoln, there can be no covenant or constitution, which binds us to protect it…
>
> I still revere the authority of those who have gone before me; I still swear by the Constitution, as it is judicially construed, and I dread that social and political revolution, now so imminent, which is to inaugurate the new school of political obedience to a higher law than the Constitution, to which Mr. Seward has pledged Mr. Lincoln and his administration.[13]

This reflected the view at the time that Secretary of State Seward was shaping Lincoln's stance on the Constitution. But as we have seen and will see further, Lincoln was his own man and knew well the consequences of his muzzling the opposition.

After Lincoln's election, on January 17, 1861, Reed joined a town meeting at National Hall in Philadelphia. The group of "distinguished fellow citizens" passed a number of resolutions which, by his own admission, Reed had relatively little input. One of them, though, he wrote exclusively, denouncing the "fanaticism" that had brought them to the brink of war and calling for an assembly if the South were to secede so that the commonwealth of Pennsylvania could "determine with whom their lot shall be cast; whether with the North and East, whose fanaticism has precipitated this misery upon us, or with our brethren of the South, whose wrongs we feel as our own, or whether Pennsylvania shall stand by herself, ready, when occasion offers, to bind together the broken Union, and resume her place of loyalty and devotion."[14]

Since that day, Reed himself later wrote, he "never attended a political meeting or opened my lips in public." He had said and done enough, and it was clear that words would no longer persuade. Instead, he isolated himself within his mansion on Chestnut Hill in Philadelphia and in the courtrooms just down the street.

Reed continued to write, but fearful of the new Republican administration, insisted on writing columns anonymously in newspapers. A number of pamphlets appeared as well. Each attacked with insight the constitutionality of the administration's actions against antiwar newspapers and pro-Southern supporters, but cautiously. Reed published the pamphlets also anonymously until he could no longer refrain from avoiding the increasingly anemic public debate.

The former diplomat and statesman knew that he was being watched closely by the administration. As John Hodgson knew all too well, the chaos of the war offered unparalleled opportunities for those in power to bury old enemies. Reed too had experienced the rage sweeping through the Union. A mob had targeted his house after the fall of Fort Sumter in April 1861, while he was in court. His terrified wife and children were at home, and not until a servant found an American flag in the attic and unfurled it from the window did the mob disperse. Reed tried to overlook the encounter as the act of hot-tempered men, but upon hearing of its endorsement by some members of the Republican party "regarded this outrage on my home with deep and yet contemptuous resentment."[15]

Despite his reclusiveness during the outbreak of the war, through the early battles and through the summer of rage, Reed remained favored newspaper fodder. He continued to be disliked by many for his conciliatory words toward the South. A full eight months after his last public appearance, on August 20, 1861, the day after the *Jeffersonian* was first attacked, the *New York Herald* ran a report that Reed had been arrested. Like reports of John Hodgson's arrest a week later, the story was not true, another example of the eagerness of the press to print breaking news, whether accurate or not. Or to harass and keep unsettled those not in favor.

Reed was a rigid man whose family honor was a driving force in his life. Still after the war, in 1866, noted historian George Bancroft, riding the continued public anger toward Reed's support of the Confederacy, pictured his grandfather Joseph Reed as nothing short of a traitor. This may well have prompted Reed to write a two-volume defense of his father—and it was not until 1876, ten years later, that it was discovered that the allegations were based on the mistaken identity with a Colonel Charles Read. For the lawyer, honor and family were the bedrock of one's identity and this man would rise in defense of both.[16] Yet, he sought no refuge from casting himself at odds with his neighbors and his government.

Reed was furious at the reports of his alleged arrest, and probably realized that he could no longer afford to remain on the sidelines. The noose was closing around his neck—newspapers were reporting of his arrest, his friends were in jail, and to do nothing was to suffer a similar fate. Though hard to prove, it seems that for this man who wrote an unpublished book filled with admiration for a lost soul such as Benedict Arnold, the situation provided motivation to act. Reed was ready to fight the only way he knew how to fight: in the courts.[17]

William B. Reed was not alone in his desire to join the fight with Hodgson; he would make up only half of the defense team that represented the Hodgsons for the next two years. Unlike the fragile-looking Reed, George Washington Biddle was an imposing man. He had a rectangular-shaped head and a tall and narrow face proportionate to a solid, round frame. Graying eyebrows matched his thin hair and full white beard, a stark contrast to a smooth chin and upper lip that accentuated sunken, piercing eyes. Low ears and a high, sculpted forehead contradicted his otherwise bulbous proportions.

Biddle and Reed worked together on many an occasion, a strange arrangement to the outsider. Biddle believed in a firm persecution of the war and a Union victory. Reed, on the other hand, argued vehemently for an immediate end to the war, even if that meant capitulation to the confederacy. Where they came together was in their agreement on the rights of all citizens.[18]

Like Reed, Biddle too came from an elite Philadelphia family with strong ties to the father of the country. His grandfather, Clement Biddle, was born in Philadelphia. At the onset of the Revolutionary War, he and his brother began working toward the raising of troops, helping to organize the "Quaker Blues," a Philadelphia volunteer regiment. A year later, Congress appointed him deputy quartermaster general. By war's end, his battlefield service included the battles of Trenton, Brandywine, Germantown, and Monmouth. Years later, in honor of distinguished service, he was appointed justice of the court of common pleas, and then, in 1789, United States marshall of Pennsylvania, a position to which he was appointed directly by George Washington.

George's uncle, Nicholas Biddle, played a role in the Lewis and Clark expedition—not in the expedition itself, but in the all-important publication of their findings. When Captain Meriwether Lewis died in 1809, William Clark, then Nicholas Biddle, and journalist Paul Allen edited and finally published the Lewis and Clark journals in 1812.

At the outbreak of the Civil War, the Biddles of Philadelphia defended the Union. George's first cousin, Henry, was serving with the Union army, and when war came in 1861, George, the forty-one-year-old attorney, answered the call as well. When a reserve unit, which had been initially created almost two decades earlier in 1844, was reactivated in 1861 to defend Philadelphia in case of Confederate attack, Biddle volunteered. Battery A of the First Pennsylvania Artillery was comprised of volunteers from the Philadelphia bar, including a future chief justice of the Pennsylvania Supreme Court.[19]

Biddle's law office was located at 204 South Fifth Street, a plain, four-story brick row house with dark green shutters that framed the windows of the second, third, and fourth stories. The inside was more representative of its occupant. A prominent marble banister led to the upper three floors where more marble dominated in the form of six mantles, one framing the fireplace in each of the six rooms on the third floor. The luster of the yellow pine floor was a far cry from the worn, scuffled floors of the *Jeffersonian* office, its luster having been worn away years before, the floor itself now covered over, no doubt, by the accumulation of dirt from the weeks of inactivity. Biddle's work was respected nationwide. Even a lawyer named Abraham Lincoln in Springfield, Illinois, purchased a two-volume book of English common law that Biddle had coauthored.[20]

Of the two men, Reed, thirteen years his elder, was certainly the veteran of the Democratic Party while Biddle was only just beginning to come into his own.

Having aligned themselves with the much-hated John Hodgson, both Reed and Biddle were immediately attacked by Lincoln's favorite editor and longtime Hodgson antagonist, John Forney, who was, not surprisingly, keeping the public apprised of the impending court proceedings in *The Press* with his usual combativeness. Forney's well-known relationship with John Hickman continued to bother John Hodgson, and so it was no surprise that it was Forney who seemed to make the greatest effort to diminish the importance of the case. Forney introduced the duo to his readers before their initial circuit court appearance in October 1861. It began:

> We notice that Messrs. William B. Reed and George W. Biddle, well known Breckinridge leaders in this city, have taken charge of the West Chester *Jeffersonian,* which was suppressed by order of the federal government (because of its persistent attacks upon the war), and that they are to appear this morning in the U.S. district court, for the purpose of securing such action as will authorize the republication of that pestilential journal.
>
> Mr. Reed is probably the ablest, most crafty, and most industrious enemy of the government in this quarter; and he will attempt today—as he has attempted before—to invoke, in defense of his client, the very laws against which all his movements are directed. Relying upon the assumption that a lawyer may espouse the cause of his client—no matter how treasonable that client may be—he shields himself under this usage, in order to defend one of the worst enemies of the government. There are exceptions to every general rule; and, in a crisis like this, we unhesitatingly assert that no attorney should be permitted to appear before any court as the advocate of a known, published traitor to his country—particularly when that attorney is himself believed to be in sympathy with the enemies of his country. We have no right to challenge the impartiality of our judiciary; but at a moment when the American Union is

attacked by its worst foes—when the despots of the Old World are waiting to see it overthrown, and ready to exult in its destruction, we trust that, if the civil tribunals refuse to crush the enemies of the country, the military arm will be invoked to do the work in which they have failed.

"We hope," Forney concluded, "that in the absence of the gifted United States district attorney, Mr. Coffey, his representative will not fail to take the highest ground against the men who, under the cover of professional usage, are attempting to make a precedent which may encourage treason in its vilest forms."[21]

After the war, when tensions had dissipated, Forney offered his disappointment in Reed's activities, writing that "nobody in Philadelphia who knows W. B. Reed, whatever his present feelings, will deny that if he had followed this record he would have been among the dictators of the Republican party."[22]

Forney's words in 1861 are in an extraordinary column written by the administration's Philadelphia mouthpiece. On a personal level, Forney knew Reed well, and was airing his disappointment in Reed for staying loyal to the Democratic Party, especially considering his antislavery leanings. But he was doing more in this editorial. He also seems to be calling on the angry young men, the sort who returned from their time on the battlefield and mobbed antiwar editors, to take violent action against Hodgson's legal team, should the outcome not go as Forney might desire.

One can only imagine the added pressure this put on everyone connected with the case. At the height of the summer of rage, a public call by a man like Forney might well have inspired a new round of violence.

It was not uncommon for Forney to publicly lash a person for whom he held personal admiration. Forney, like any politician, knew how to pacify the crowd's appetite.

∽

As a student of American history, Reed must have considered it entirely appropriate that the courtroom battle was taking place in Philadelphia.

From 1790 to 1800, Philadelphia was the center of United States government. George Washington lived in an executive mansion on Market Street, between Fifth and Sixth streets. The United States Supreme Court met in Old City Hall, and Congress met in Congress Hall. In 1800, John Adams moved into the not-yet-completed Executive Mansion in Washington, DC, the city that was being built on a swamp near the Potomac River, near George Washington's beloved Mount Vernon.

With the nation's capital moved to Washington, Philadelphia continued to thrive, replacing the workings of government with the business of industrialization as it was transformed into the manufacturing center of the nation.

Philadelphia, the city that had become the second home of Hodgson and his editor son William as they met with their attorneys and government officials after the seizure of their paper in late 1861, had assumed more than its share of the burden of war. Through March 1862, Philadelphia had provided more than thirty thousand of the state's one hundred thousand soldiers.

The court system in Philadelphia, home of Independence Hall, home of Benjamin Franklin and some of the greatest intellectual minds of the eighteenth and nineteenth centuries, was established in 1773 with the creation of four separate courts of general jurisdiction, each with one president judge and two subordinate judges. This system was still in place during the Civil War, but the number of courts had more than doubled. Another important event had occurred in 1850 that changed the fabric of the Philadelphia courts. Against the lobbying of the Philadelphia Law Association, judgeships became an elected office. Judges were now politicians with agendas and political parties to support, threatening the objectivity of which was until recently the last nonpartisan branch of the United States government. This was a crucial development in the chess game between the anti-war Democrats and the pro-Lincoln Republicans.[23]

Courtrooms did not yet possess the noble grandeur of the later court. Judges did not dress in the formal black robe: it was not adopted until the 1880s. Courtrooms were not formal palaces reminiscent of Greek and Roman architecture, but were dark, small offices created in available space. The location of the courts, at Fifth and Chestnut streets near Independence Hall, the Second National Bank of the United States, and other important legal and financial institutions, was more important than the physical buildings themselves. Most attorneys resided within walking distance, their homes doubling as their offices.

A typical week in the court included trials from Monday through Friday, and the filing of motions on Saturday morning. The court year was divided into two terms, a May term, which actually ended in May and gave both judges and attorneys a break until the opening of sessions again in September.[24]

Hodgson's trial opened with formal motions on February 3, 1863. The first witness appeared the following day in the courtroom of the chief justice of Pennsylvania, Walter H. Lowrie. Reflecting the many political troubles faced by the Lincoln administration, the chief justice was a Democrat.

Pennsylvania Supreme Court Justice Walter Hoge Lowrie was the nephew of United States Senator and twelve-year Senate Secretary Walter Lowrie. Judge Lowrie, who was fifty-four years old when the Civil War began, was one of the few members of his family not to enter the service of the church.[25] Lowrie was an elected judge and would face reelection the following fall. The verdict here would very much determine Lowrie's political future as well.

The witness list was short and to the point. Witnesses called by the plaintiff were Charles Hodgson, John Hodgson, the newspaper compositor Benjamin Mills, and deputy district attorney William Lynch. It also appears that William Hodgson took the stand, though he is not listed as an official witness in the transcript. The only witness for the defendants was George A. Coffey.

As the witnesses took the stand, the tone of the lawyers on both sides was polite and respectful. The case unfolded in an eerily calm manner.

One of the first surprising facts to come out of the trial was that the idea to take on the administration via the courts was not John Hodgson's. "It is proper to state that the employment of counsel in the case of the *Jeffersonian* was forced upon the proprietor by George A. Coffey, United States district attorney," wrote William Hodgson angrily in his first issue back after being seized.[26]

During the first day of the three-day trial, when called to testify on his own behalf, John Hodgson recounted how he and his son William visited District Attorney George Coffey to ask that the paper be reopened. Coffey demanded a written pledge of obedience. Hodgson refused.

The district attorney, in his testimony, confirmed their exchange.

Coffey: "He came to see me a half a dozen times with the view to have the property restored."

Regarding his requiring a written pledge, Coffey states that Hodgson was willing to sign a pledge to defend the Constitution. But that was not enough for the district attorney. He insisted on a written pledge to fight for the Union.

And how did John Hodgson answer?

Coffey: "He said he would rather die than support the war. Did not say this in reference to this property."

Hodgson's testimony is more specific:

John Hodgson: "I called on Mr. Coffey. On the tenth of September my son and I came to the city. I saw Mr. Coffey. He said if I came in again on Thursday, in the meantime, he would have communication with gentlemen in West Chester and then we could settle it. On Thursday I went, and Mr. Coffey required a written pledge, and I told him I was not prepared to make any pledge, as the paper had been illegally seized and ought to be given up."

All Hodgson had to do was beg forgiveness from the business establishment in West Chester, those with ties to radicals like his old colleague and attorney, Congressman John Hickman. All he had to do was refrain from publishing the sort of emotional yet prophetic editorials that had captivated Democrats and sign a pledge.

Hodgson: "He then wrote off a copy of a pledge, the closing part of which was this: that I believe the only way to put down the rebellion and restore the Union is by war. I said to him that whatever my private opinion might be I would rather die than give my pledge to a paper of that kind in order to get the property back.

"I took the copy of the pledge but have lost it."

The district attorney was requiring that Hodgson sign a pledge not to disavow an anti-Union stance, but to become pro-war. The administration from top to bottom was preoccupied with only one objective: putting down the rebellion in the battlefield, not through negotiations.

Hodgson: "On Friday my son and I were there again, and Mr. Coffey told us we could do no more, and said we must employ lawyers. My reply was that it was a plain case and ought to be settled without going to law. Mr. Coffey recommended us to employ a Mr. Harrison."

Mr. Knox: "Did not Mr. Coffey say that he did not want a pledge that you would support the war, but simply a pledge that you would not oppose it?"

Hodgson: "No sir. He said he did not want me to support the administration, but he wished me to support the war, and I told him I would not give any pledge."

It seems, therefore, that Hodgson took the advice of the district attorney, but as usual for the editor, on his own terms.

He not only decided to fight to have the paper reopened, but soon made the extraordinary decision to sue the government officials that had shut down his paper, charging them with illegal trespass. Perhaps it was done to learn the exact involvement of John Hickman or to cause embarrassment to the local Republican Party. Partly it may have been to prove the illegality of the actions taken by the zealous federal marshals. It was not done to embarrass the president. Strangely, Hodgson had developed a patriotic attitude toward the president— lashing out at times, but also a defender on many an occasion.

Regardless of his benign treatment of the president, the year-and-a-half interval between the attacks on his paper and the trial did nothing to dull the anger and fine writing of John Hodgson. As the 1863 trial date approached, he wrote as usual without fear, lashing out in some of his strongest language yet. While the nation was filled with self-doubt, Hodgson never hesitated. Speaking about the Republicans around Lincoln, Hodgson reduced them to cartoonish characters. "They are flatters of office holders, the despised pimps and scored sycophants of place and patronage.... The day of retribution is not far off, the hand on the dial is nearing the hour which is to strike the doom of these already terror-stricken and infamous wretches."[27]

Reed too seemed to be growing in confidence as the trial date approached. A few months before he had published a pamphlet called *A Statement and Vindication of Certain Political Opinions* in which he predicted that the war was bankrupting the Union. Furthermore, he called on the North to recognize the Confederacy since even a military victory, argued Reed, would not end the battle between North and South. For a time, *Vindication* was hugely popular and made Reed the target for administration papers throughout the North. The *Pittsburgh Dispatch* was just one newspaper branding Reed as "an enemy of the country."[28]

On January 28, just a week before the trial began, the publisher of Philadelphia's only Democratic daily newspaper, the *Evening Journal,* was arrested and sent to Fort McHenry. The newly opened Democratic Club met to protest his arrest and five-day confinement when suddenly the editor, Albert Boileau, appeared. He had gained his freedom by pleading ignorance: he wrote an apology for the offending editorial and stated that it was the work of W. B. Reed and had been inserted into his paper without his knowledge. This was enough to give Boileau his freedom.[29]

Reed had become the catalyst and the scapegoat for much of Philadelphia's antiwar agenda.

Hodgson's infamous legal team had spent sixteen months in preparation for the showdown in the Philadelphia courtroom. At stake was not necessarily the right of a small town publisher to circulate his paper. Nor was it a battle solely to insure that the federal government had no right to strip a man's property based on personal beliefs.

No, this was about accountability. Who was in charge of the administration's assault on the opposition press? Did the chain of command go to the president in all cases or only a selected few? If so, then Hodgson's paranoia may indeed have been correct: local federal officials hungry for power and patronage may indeed have taken liberties to shut down whomever they chose. But in the intervening year and a half, this action had alienated many moderate voters, threatening the reelection of the president.

Hodgson had to learn who was responsible for unleashing a mob on his office, and then who sent the government to seize what was left. He had to know if it was his bitter enemy, Congressman John Hickman and his editorial partner, John Forney. But in the process, Hodgson's efforts took on an importance that he had championed his entire career. At stake was a fundamental question, one posed by Abraham Lincoln on the fourth of July, 1861, "Must a government, of necessity, be too strong for the liberties of its own people, or too weak to maintain its own existence?"[30] Hodgson must have been fearful of even asking the question regarding the president's involvement. But he was also not afraid of any answer that would result.

Bull-headed Hodgson had stormed his way into the very nexus of the problem facing Lincoln as he battled not only to destroy the Confederacy, but to sway the wavering voters closer to home. Hodgson needed an answer. For himself, and for the country.

Chapter Eleven

THE GOVERNMENT CONSPIRACY

*"Citizens are committed and imprisoned because in the public
newspapers they dare criticize the acts of the government. Newspapers
have been suspended, and the whole power of the government
despotically exercised without a public murmur."*[1]

—John Hodgson, December 28, 1861

John Hodgson knew in his gut that he was the victim of old
enemies who had taken advantage of the confusion of the war and
the hands-off approach of Lincoln for their own benefit. The war
increased this power by creating thousands of new clerkships,
paymasters, and other jobs on the government payroll. It also diluted
the talent pool in many cases, with appointments going to incapable
men hired as a favor. For the hungriest politicians of the day, such
chaos provided just the cover they needed to carry out personal plans
to their own benefit. Increasingly, in the Lincoln administration, men
lower and lower on the scale of power were given the license to act as
they wished in the name of military security.

What was left to reconcile was how the vendetta against Hodgson played into a larger conspiracy against newspaper editors, and all opponents of the war, in the North. Hodgson would have been the first to admit that he could not substantiate many of his attacks on Republicans, and understood the difference between suspecting a conspiracy and proving a conspiracy. And he understood his enemies enough to know that proving anything, especially in wartime, would be a formidable task. Hodgson started with what he knew: newspapers and politics.

It is difficult to understand today how far-reaching the patronage system was. Lincoln's extensive use of patronage had put not only United States marshal William Millward and Philadelphia district attorney George Coffey in their positions, but also men like deputies John Jenkins and William Schuyler, and thousands of other loyal Republicans into positions across the Northern states. Lincoln would call himself "rich with honorable and fat offices."[2]

Congressmen, colleagues, acquaintances, and complete strangers would offer themselves or provide the president with recommendations for anything from minister to a foreign country to a local clerkship. When sent directly to Lincoln, he would pass them along to the administering office with his own notes on a particular endorsement. Often his own recommendations were in the form of hash marks on an envelope stuffed with forwarded recommendation letters. This method, more a tally sheet than a recommendation, continued throughout the war.

Oftentimes, political leaders from a particular territory would meet and agree on who they would endorse for particular jobs, thereby completing their compromise so that the president had only to sign off. In some cases, positions were used as a training ground for up-and-coming politicians.

John Hodgson pointed to the corruption of two men as the architects of his struggle against the government: Congressman John Hickman and editor John Forney.

It was John Hickman and his radical Republican colleagues who played such a critical role in the passage of the Confiscation Act that Lincoln hesitated before signing, and it was Hickman who had led the effort to define the punishments for crimes against the Union. It was Hickman who sought to legally silence any dissenting opinion from being voiced publicly in the Union—coupled with the fear of losing all of one's earthly possessions. And it seems the ability of Hickman and Forney to prod Lincoln in their direction may have been the web that trapped Hodgson.

By 1861, Hickman hated Hodgson. Of course, he was not alone in that hatred, but Hickman had the political motivation for making sure Hodgson was finally silenced and made a model for other publishers who might consider defying the administration's policies.

And Hickman disliked Lincoln, believing him weak and conciliatory toward the South and toward traitors like John Hodgson. For Hickman and other Congressional radicals, the summer of 1861 was a time for the suppression of dissent and destruction of any opposition, both within and outside the Executive Mansion.

Certainly, Hickman came to be one symbol for a new generation of Northern politicians who were determined to stamp out slavery. Yet it seems clear in looking at the steps taken by Hickman that the most charitable statement should be that perhaps the noble ends justified the day-to-day means. Hickman loved power and attacked everyone, from Hodgson to Mrs. Lincoln, in pursuit of obtaining greater influence. He and Forney seemed smitten by the power to appoint friends to lucrative positions and to later have the favor returned. They were of the breed that in the strange times of the Civil War used the most noble of goals to obtain political power.

It was not uncommon in this time of war for long-time friends and colleagues to become sworn and bitter enemies. Relatives lobbed cannon balls and exchanged musket fire from opposing lines, while on the home front, politics fractured once secure relationships. But the feud between Hodgson and Hickman had taken on a life of its own, having played itself out on the pages of the *Jeffersonian* and *The Press*. Every statement made by a Republican represented John Hickman, and every effort to destroy the Union stunk of John Hodgson.

Hickman's defection from the Democratic Party in the years leading to Lincoln's election was gradual, but by the outbreak of the war he was amongst the most radical of Lincoln's party. Hickman and Hodgson now represented the prevailing views of the old and the new guard. But even then, how could two longtime colleagues come to represent such opposing worlds? Hodgson's hatred for Hickman had grown so uncontrollable by late 1861 that the editor began to rationalize the behaviors of Abraham Lincoln, who too seemed to be unable to protect himself from the power of the radicals in his own party.

Nothing illustrates more the tensions between the radical Republicans—driven by a desire for immediate emancipation of the slaves and a more effective war campaign—and the more moderate path chosen by Lincoln than an incident with the *New York Herald*.

At the end of 1861, James Gordon Bennett's paper had leaked an advance text of a presidential address. Hickman suspected the source of the leak was none other than Mrs. Lincoln. The reporter was quite close to Mrs. Lincoln and was often her guest at the Executive

Mansion. Here was a chance not only to embarrass the president, but also to punish Mrs. Lincoln, whose Kentucky roots and Confederate connections, as well as her "airing her French,"[3] made her suspect to many radical Republicans.

A congressional hearing was held, and the offending reporter was locked in the capital jail for refusing to reveal his source. The next morning he finally agreed to tell the truth. He was called back before the eager congressmen who waited for the scandalous information.

But all he would say is that his source was the White House gardener.

The gardener was called in and he swore his memory was so good he remembered the president's text. No one believed this story. Though unknown at the time, the president was forced to testify before Hickman's judiciary committee. It was an historic moment for the separation of powers, representing the first time a sitting president testified before a congressional committee. More than likely, Lincoln was forced to beg the radical Republicans to let the matter lie. Hickman's brash use of power infuriated even the traditionalist John Hodgson, who heaped scorn on the congressional chairman for probing into the "private, social, and family affairs of the White House."[4]

> [Hickman] has screwed his eye to the White House keyholes and pinched his ears in the cracks of the office doors in vain. His questions about the dinners, the breakfasts, the table talk, the visitors, the social chit chat of the White House, are unanswered. His dishonorable and too evident suspicions of the president and Mrs. Lincoln strike only himself and his fellow committeemen. They have grossly insulted the president and his wife, even while they were mournfully watching the last agonies of their dying son. They have disgraced the Congress to which they belong, and slandered the people

they profess to represent. Having voluntarily relinquished all claim to the titles of Americans and gentlemen, the country will esteem them at their own base valuation.[5]

Hickman went after Hodgson like a lover scorned, and based on their past history, in many ways they both were. Hickman was taking advantage of his position in Congress, which according to Hodgson he had gained under false pretenses. Voters had put him in office as a Democrat, not as the Republican he had become.

When Hickman turned on the Democratic Party, he did not look back. In 1859, he blasted them with hard-nailed accusations of corruption and greed. "They have done more," he told them, "they have gone farther; they have come amongst us, and bribed cupidity with gold, ambition with promotion, and vanity with temporary consequence, to do violence to justice. Longer forbearance not only ceases to be virtuous, but it becomes cowardly and base. The North has rights, long in abeyance truly, yet not lost; we will save them; by walls of fire and blood, if needs be, we will save them."[6]

Framed by an American flag draped directly behind him and flanked by portraits of Lafayette and George Washington to either side, Hickman stood with his back to the rostrum and vocalized his position to the House of Representatives in January 1858.

In opposition to the proposed policy of forcing upon the people what they do not want, I place the Democratic doctrine of popular sovereignty, which will give to the people what they do not want. The president requires us to take a new but ragged garment, and attempts to comfort us by saying it can be patched and made sound. I will never traffic in goods which are defective, and will not wear, if I know it, notwithstanding I may buy, others if I do not like

them. I will never barter truths for errors, knowing that I
may support the latter by sophistries.

In his flair for the dramatic, he quoted the great poet Milton, his
knowledge of history and literature a potent weapon he exploited at
every possible occasion. "Truth is strong!" he implored his fellow
congressmen, "Next to the Almighty, she needs no policies, no
stratagems, no licensings to make her victorious."

More and more, Hickman was convinced that Lincoln would
succeed. Hodgson thought Hickman no longer a man of integrity, but
one of opportunity. And if Hickman's hunch played out, a long-
awaited opportunity might present itself. In fact, he had already been
playing his hand toward that end. By all indications, his play was
working. In 1860, Hickman was on the short list of vice presidential
candidates. He was eventually passed over, but he was without a doubt
becoming a force of change in the emerging Republican Party.[7]

Hodgson publicly chided Hickman's hypocrisy for trying to
muster support from all voters, even the Irish whom the congressman
had scorned in years past. According to the *Jeffersonian,* Hickman had,
years before, fought the election of a judge "because he was the son of
an Irishman and a Catholic." In addition, in 1852, Hickman
"denounced the Irish as Paddy O'Raffs." Two years later Hickman
"bargained with the Know-Nothings…for their votes; and held
frequent communions with that proscriptive order upon the subject of
his election to Congress," during which he maintained how much "he
loves them—how dearly he loves them—how truly he loves them—
how devotedly he loves them—how great a friend he is of theirs."[8]

The more tolerant, though some might say power-hungry,
Hickman can be seen in this extraordinary letter in June of 1859
when he asks leading West Chester Irishmen for their support and
apologizing profusely for any past bigotry.

In all sincerity, the congressman pledged his loyalty, being in "favor of you doing all our work, of building all our railroads, of digging all our canals, of clearing all our forests, of being pioneers of our rapidly extending territories, preparing the ground for rich farms, of digging all our potatoes, of planting all our cabbage, and cleaning all our streets." Hickman even charitably went as far as to "agree that you shall hold some of the smaller offices—not such as president, &c. &c."

The United States was the land of freedom, he contended, where there "is but one kind of citizenship. It is absolute, and confers a perfect equality of social, religious (except Catholic), legal, and political (if you, my dear Irish and German fellow-citizens, have been born in this country) rights."[9]

Hodgson had grown sick of how Hickman was pandering to each power block of the time. "The game of...the special friends of Hickman, is to keep him before the people in a double posture," Hodgson jabbed. "To the Democrats, he is a Buchanan man; to the Black Republican leaders, a congressman who has served their cause."[10] In fact, this is primarily what made Hickman so attractive to voters. He squeezed out reelection in 1856, losing West Chester but winning the county. Outside of Hodgson's home territory, voters saw an independent politician out to serve his constituents, and not prone to bend to party pressures.

Two old allies were divided by the great issues of the day. And for the small town publisher, he was overcome by the conviction that his former friend was motivated by far more than a sense of ethics and morality. Hickman, he was convinced, wanted revenge. The mob had brought it, and Hodgson was trying to prove that Hickman was the source.

◡

John Hickman had openly become an enemy of everything Hodgson believed in. But while Hodgson was straying further into isolation in West Chester, Hickman was building his base. Most importantly, he had found an editor who not only ran Philadelphia, but had taken over the press in Washington and secured the ear of the president. John Forney complemented Hickman as Weed complemented Seward.

"We notice that the Republican papers are rejoicing largely over the fact that John Hickman, a 'Democrat,' advocates the same doctrines as the abolitionist, W. H. Seward," Hodgson pondered publicly. Although Hickman was not closely involved with Seward personally, the platform had brought the congressman into a more disturbing partnership with Pennsylvania editor and Washington insider John Forney. Like Hickman, Forney had been teetering between the outgoing Democratic administration and the yet entirely unknown party that it would soon follow. Perhaps learning from the maneuverings of Hickman, John Forney, in the interim, was also carefully playing both sides.

Forney bridged the differences between Seward and Hickman, though Democratic newspapers were eager to "expose Forney's hypocrisy" at every opportunity. When it became clear that Lincoln would be the Republican nominee, Hickman and Forney embarked on an infamous partnership, the connections and political weight of each leveraged for the other. Hodgson, rather egotistically but not wrongly, predicted that it would be at his expense.[11]

The *Jeffersonian* reprinted an article from the *National Vedette* that highlighted the hypocrisy of the relationship: "Mr. Forney has held up his hands in hypocritical horror at what he affected to believe to be the treasonable doctrines of Mr. Seward; and now, forsooth, when the same doctrine is put forth by Mr. Hickman, this immaculate politician can endorse it as the soundest principle of political philosophy! Others may deem such men worthy of confidence," the article confided, "but we cannot."[12]

Hickman, like Lincoln, recognized the power of the press, likely having learned its value first from Hodgson. In Washington, he was without an ally that could provide unfettered access to the masses. He found such an ally in Forney. They were now hard at work, and began to court Lincoln months before his nomination in Chicago.

By September of 1860, as Hickman's transformation into a Republican advocate became clearer, Lincoln seemed still unable to determine what to make of him. To a crowd in Columbus, Ohio, Lincoln asked for three cheers for Hickman, who Lincoln admitted to having never seen and knew little about. But "of all the Anti-Lecompton Democracy that have been brought to my notice, he alone has the true, genuine ring of the metal."[13] However, Lincoln made it a point to make clear that he advocated none of Hickman's causes, and in personal notes in two speeches a few days later, Lincoln copied his previous statement of Hickman being a "small" man.[14]

The fiery politician held views too radical for Lincoln, and the feelings were returned. Hickman seemed to use Lincoln for providing jobs and political favors but had no respect for his careful approach to the political issues.

Hickman was always blunt. Now that he aligned himself with the radicals in Congress, in many ways both Lincoln and Hodgson would be viewed as standing in the way.

While John Hickman was to many a loose cannon, Lincoln had been sold on the importance of Philadelphia editor John Forney since early 1860 when he began to understand the editor's strategy for leaving the Democratic Party. A letter to Lincoln from Alexander McClure, chairman of Pennsylvania's State Republican Committee, in

June of that year clearly explained Forney's efforts. Unsure as to how Stephen Douglas became so unfavorably looked upon by fellow Democrats, McClure finally clued Lincoln into the source. McClure revealed Forney's plans to destroy Douglas's presidential hopes, despite the fact that Forney still appeared to support Lincoln's old foe. "He is a deadly foe of Douglas!" wrote McClure of Forney's true intentions.

> He not only regards him as faithless to principle: but has a personal grudge to gratify because of Douglas's perfidy to himself…. You may have observed that after sustaining Douglas in his issue with Buchanan until he was nominated, the same number of *The Press* that announced the nomination of Douglas at Baltimore, also announced that thenceforth *The Press* "would be in no respects a party paper": and to this day it has never named you but in kindness.

It was a glowing recommendation that Lincoln, with his uncanny ability to work with editors, apparently took to heart. The criticisms of Forney were ignored in several Philadelphia papers. A month after Forney put forward his support for Hickman, the Democratic *Pennsylvanian* came out against Forney's paper, *The Press*. "From the moment it took its position in the late canvass, it has been gravitating with constant approaches to Black Republicanism. It hoped, by adroit management, to draw its partisans on with it, imperceptibly to themselves, and at the lucky moment to betray them all into the hands of the enemy. How many it has succeeded in debauching and selling we have no means of knowing," the paper admitted, but "enough perhaps to fill its contract and to entitle it to its reward from the abolitionists."[15] The president seemed to equally impress Forney. Or perhaps Forney would have been drawn toward any man he thought soon to assume the role of chief patronage officer for the United States.

This patronage came to fruition when it came time to choose Lincoln's cabinet. James Gordon Bennett, the affable, adversarial, and pro-slavery proprietor of the *New York Herald,* had come out in favor of John Hickman as well. *Chicago Tribune* editor Joseph Medill sat down with Bennett in New York in July to discuss potential cabinet appointments. Both agreed on the necessity of including a Pennsylvania man, with Bennett pushing for Hickman. "I asked him why he named Hickman for a place in the cabinet," Medill told Lincoln in a long letter recounting two conversations he had with the New York editor. "He said because Pennsylvania would expect a seat in that body, and that Hickman would have a powerful congressional influence to back him." Besides, "Hickman stood higher with the Republican party of Pennsylvania" than almost anyone, and would go well with "the Forney element" that "would demand recognition."

Medill, unaware of Forney's true intentions, plainly stated that "J Forney goes for Douglas."

"Yes, nominally," responded Bennett who knew the inside truth, "but he will take good care to prevent the naming of a joint electoral ticket, for the purpose of giving the state to Lincoln."

Medill, in his letter to the future president, also provided blunt warnings as to the power of the New York press. "He said he had but little doubt of your election," Medill wrote of Bennett. The New Yorker predicted that "a combination in New York would beat you, but such a fusion would not be made, and you would get the state— although Weed would rather see you loose it." He said that, "Weed would have made a million dollars out of Seward's election in the sale [of] offices, as cattle were sold at the shambles—that he would have blackmailed any job and contract, and retired after amassing a vast fortune, and sending his party to the d---l."

In a few short months, Hickman would be part of those radical Republicans Bennett warned about. In December, Medill wrote to Lincoln for the first time since his election. Still the *Chicago Tribune* editor was propping up the urgency for a nonsectional cabinet, recommending someone from Pennsylvania for the post of secretary of the treasury or the interior, though it should most definitely not be Simon Cameron, noting "that Simon Cameron and Honest Abe don't sound well together," and "[a]s Senator Bingham observed to me, Lincoln don't want a thief in his cabinet, to have charge of the treasury," especially when there are "other sound men to pick from," namely Hickman.[16]

The election went as Bennett predicted, with Lincoln taking the torch of the upstart Republican Party, and though Hickman failed to receive either the vice presidential nod or a cabinet position, the West Chester congressman was not entirely left out of the spoils, masterfully gaining a few far-reaching favors from the White House. Forney was not left out either, and though his road was more difficult, it allowed him to exploit his newfound relationship with the president. Hickman was in the most advantageous position of his career, and though Forney seemed to be in limbo, a little help from his new party affiliation would soon rescue him. And in true form, Forney, like Hickman, preferred to work from the inside.

Forney wrote to Lincoln on March 25, 1861, from Philadelphia, shortly after Lincoln took office. As far as he could tell, and "so far as the public can understand it," Lincoln's policy "meets with almost universal approbation. Our people recognise in your administration the only emblem of the Union, and I am happy to add that the Democrats, as well as the Republicans, stand ready to sustain you, by their means and their physical energies, in the path you have marked out. As an evidence of this the paper which I own and conduct has risen to an unprecedented circulation, and commands an influence which it has never hertofore [sic] wielded, even in the days when I was opposing the proscriptive policy of your immediate predecessor."

Then the doting editor, after the accolades for the recently inaugurated president, used the letter to slide his generosity to his most trusted ally. "I have just left John Hickman, your gallant and devoted friend who was reelected to Congress by an unequalled majority, after a contest historical in political annals. He deserves peculiar and immediate recognition at your hands," Forney insisted. "He will be a host in the next House of Representatives. He intended to resign but has now determined to remain for the purpose of sustaining you in your glorious efforts to preserve the Union."[17]

Yet Hickman and Forney stumbled out of the gate in their effort to at least have the illusion of power in Washington. Hickman nominated Francis Blair Jr. of Missouri, son of Washington publishing icon Francis Blair Sr. and brother of Lincoln's postmaster general, Montgomery Blair, for Speaker of the House. But Hickman could not rally the support, and Blair withdrew after a sound defeat on the first vote. Blair then nominated Forney for reelection to his position as clerk of the House. Forney was also beaten. But he had one more card to play.

Besides his newspaper empire and his decade of work for Congress, Forney played an important social role in Washington, which catered to the political egos of the leading men of the day. His late-night parties at his residence, in the Mill's House behind the capitol, became legendary. "We met like a band of brothers," he would later write, "the lawyer, the clergyman, the editor, the reporter, the poet, the painter, the inventor, the politician, the stranger, the old citizen, the Southerner and the Northerner, the soldier and the statesman, the clerk and the cabinet minister, and last, not least, President Lincoln himself." At times they would hear recitations, sing songs like

"John Brown's Body," and discuss the issues. On one occasion, most all of Lincoln's cabinet held an "exceedingly animated" debate over whether to arm Negroes.[18]

Lincoln liked Forney and appreciated his behind-the-scenes efforts. Although Lincoln had not yet met Forney, immediately after his election in 1860 he sent Forney a letter "thanking me for what he was pleased to call my services in resisting the proscriptions of the Buchanan administration, and proffering a friendship which never abated." Not everyone was as easily sold, though, as Lincoln tried desperately to secure a job for Forney in the Senate.[19]

Forney had never found election as clerk easy, though he had served in that position in the House since 1852. When put forward for clerk of the House in 1859, it took the organizational prowess of Henry Wilson, Charles Francis Adams, John Haskin, John Schwartz, and John Hickman to push it through. In February 1860, Forney retained his position by one vote. It would be his last term in the House. In July 1861, Forney was looking for a new position—but he had friends in high places.[20]

"[James] Grimes is dead set against Forney," wrote Orville Browning, "but I think we can elect him—Have not yet acted upon the matter in caucus."[21]

Lincoln received word from Indiana congressman Schuyler Colfax that Forney's election was also troubling to some Republicans. But when it came to taking care of his favorite editors and publishers, Lincoln was far from passive, being actively engaged in the rough-and-tumble of politics. From documents showing him fighting for patronage for favorite editors, from Forney to Greeley, it is clear that he was involved in the minutiae of the Civil War battle for influencing public opinion on the war.[22]

This was, therefore, just one more example. Largely due to Lincoln's efforts on his behalf, Forney was named the new secretary of the Senate on July 15. From there he could keep track of every act conducted by Congress. For Forney, not only was he now back on the inside, but at the public expense of $2,500 a year.[23] Forney was double-dipping his pen, but it was common practice. Lincoln needed Forney and his close friend Hickman, and the first session of Congress was an opportunity for all agendas to be filled.

Forney had nearly bankrupted himself establishing his Philadelphia newspaper, *The Press,* and Lincoln understood how he could use that to his advantage. In the midst of Lincoln's struggle to retain Forney's services to Congress, the editor had also founded the *Washington Sunday Chronicle,* a weekly paper that would become Abraham Lincoln's press voice. Soon, Forney turned the weekly into a daily paper. The president, the former secret publisher of a German language newspaper in Illinois, suggested he do so and Forney readily responded. Lincoln needed a way to directly reach Union soldiers, and Forney was the medium. In 1862, the *Washington Chronicle* was reaching thirty thousand Union soldiers a day, and it was said that he could have sold one hundred thousand a day if he had the facilities to print that many.

A year later, Forney hosted a "blow-out" party at the dedication for his new printing office, the Chronicle Building. The president was in attendance.[24]

In fact, Lincoln had by now become a frequent unnamed contributor to many columns. A somewhat secret new publishing/political partnership had now been created. Forney was an active voice for the president in the press.[25]

Like many under Lincoln, John Hickman and John Forney, the "twin renegades" as Hodgson called them, were constantly jostling for even more power and more influence. The stakes were high: to reap the rewards of the greatest patronage system of all time, to fend off feints from competitors like Weed and Cameron, and to try to codify the "advances" made toward consolidating their commercial gains. Lincoln may have viewed the suspension of habeas corpus and other wartime measures as temporary, but not so many of those who had profited handsomely.[26]

Hickman had been responsible for setting the stage. Hodgson screamed this out in rough language, but as usual, there was truth in his writings. Hickman introduced and pushed through a bill that gave district and circuit court judges the power to try local cases of treason. Afterward, it was his massaging of the language of the Confiscation Act that carried it from a split vote in Congress to passage in both the House and the Senate. John Forney, working the vote in the Senate, brought the bill to the president where, after great hesitation, the Confiscation Act was signed into law.

These actions by Hickman provided lower Republican officials with extraordinary powers to act as either they wished or were nudged. Did Hickman work on the Confiscation Act to punish Hodgson? Of course not. But he did understand that should the bill be enacted, they would control the levers of true political power. And why not, at the same time, settle old scores like that of the loud-mouthed old man Hodgson who just knew too much? Let Lincoln use noble rhetoric to justify the suppression of dissident voices, and let the Republican machine reap the rewards. Thurlow Weed knew how much the presidency would have been worth to him had Seward won—millions of dollars. If Lincoln did not want his share, all the better.

Less than two years had passed since the passage of the first Confiscation Act in 1861, but beneath the dry rhetoric of the Philadelphia courtroom was a lifetime of anger. Hodgson must have seethed that he was the first victim of the Confiscation Act, an act that put the administration one step closer to a total victory over their worst political enemies. For Hickman, it was a chance to put John Hodgson away for good.

"I would rather die than sign a pledge to support the war," John Hodgson had fumed at George Coffey. He might also have been saying he would rather die than give in to the likes of Forney and Hickman.[27]

Rarely, if ever, had such Civil War emotions spilled over into the dry arena of our judicial system.

Chapter Twelve

HODGSON VS. THE UNITED STATES OF AMERICA

"Was it possible to lose the nation, and yet preserve the Constitution? By general law life and limb must be protected; yet often a limb must be amputated to save a life; but a life is never wisely given to save a limb. I felt that measures, otherwise unconstitutional, might become lawful, by becoming indispensable to the preservation of the Constitution, through the preservation of the nation. Right or wrong I assumed this ground, and now avow it."[1]

—Abraham Lincoln, April 4, 1864

It was the hottest ticket in town. Everyone who could crammed into the small courtroom on Fifth and Chestnut streets for the opening of the trial. They were not assured a place, however, as by the time the trial was underway, latecomers found themselves without anywhere to sit.

No doubt the very fact that administration figures were being held accountable for the closing of a pro-Southern newspaper accounted for the packed courtroom. The men gathered inside the courtroom must have known each other as the audience was composed mostly of lawyers, according to John Forney's account in *The Press*.[2]

There was also an "elephant" in the courtroom. It is an expression of uncertain origin, meaning something big that fills the room, yet no one is speaking about it.

The conversation was more than likely the usual trading of careful rumors and gossip of any group of competitors. Speculation must have been high in the courtroom and the nearby bars regarding just how the trial might hurt or help the political career of the judge, who would soon run for reelection. And whether John Hodgson and his lawyers were still marked by the administration— or if the notoriety afforded them some degree of protection from revenge.

Packed courtrooms carry a certain level of anticipation, and there is little reason not to believe that just seeing the Hodgsons and the administration figures in one packed room did not seem unreal to many of the lawyers and friends present.

For the first time, the issues that had ignited the summer of rage, in many ways an investigation into the powers of Congress to censor criticism, were now being played out in an American courtroom, not on the streets of towns and cities under the cover of darkness. Instead of frenzied mobs bearing torches, the instigators wore well-tailored suits. Instead of cowering in the shadows, they thrived in the spotlight. Instead of anonymity, their names would be repeated for all time as saviors—or enemies—of the republic.

For eighteen months these men had played an intricate game of chess, each side seeking to aid their side of the struggle. For the defendants, the federal officials, the government was wagering an unpopular war and popular opinion had to be swayed toward supporting Lincoln. This meant using the Confiscation Act to silence men like Hodgson.

For Democrats, they were fighting for the Constitution and the right to openly criticize the war, the president, and the centralization of power in the hands of what they saw as corrupt politicians taking personal advantage of the war.

Specifically, the Confiscation Act, drafted with the prodding of John Hickman, was front and center in the government's strategy to defend itself against the charge of trespass filed by Reed and Biddle on behalf of their clients. The Confiscation Act was the pivotal point of Hodgson's case against the United States government.

In legal terms, the case revolved around whether the administration had correctly followed the laws of the land in seeking to shut down dissenting newspapers. Had Congress, and specifically the radical Republicans, provided the administration and its army of local supporters with the cover to silence the opposition as it saw fit? If so, had the law been adhered to when the *Jeffersonian* was closed under orders from the president? Most importantly, did the president, in fact, order the seizure?

Those were the questions before the jury and Pennsylvania supreme court justice Walter H. Lowrie.

The reality was a bit different. In three days, a jury of "mixed politics" would decide not the issue before them, but whether freedom of speech could be tolerated during a time of national crisis.

That was the elephant in the room.

The trial finally began early on Wednesday morning. First were the statements from the government's lawyers, former judge John Knox and David Webster, who immediately went to the very heart of their defense.

Seated next to them and intently listening were the twelve men who would decide this unusual case. Included were a butcher named

Nicholas Bornman, a farmer Philip Hagner, and the other bricklayers, shoemakers, clerks, and tailors that comprised the jury. Not exactly a jury of John Hodgson's peers, and even more ominously, one that may well have mirrored the sort of men who were passionate in their defense of the Union and the war. The Hodgsons needed defenders of the freedom of the press, not necessarily butchers and clerks. It may have given the administration some degree of comfort, despite the political leanings of Judge Lowrie.

Knox, the former judge, began the trial by turning to Judge Lowrie and remarking that "it is obvious to the court that this case will turn chiefly upon your Honor's construction of the law."[3]

Knox forcefully argued that the jury was about to hear a case that rested on a trail of evidence that supported his clients. The act of Congress of August 6, 1861, the Confiscation Act, made it the "duty of the president of the United States to cause and to be seized, confiscated, and condemned, all property of whatsoever kind and description which the owner thereof knowingly uses and employs or permits to be used and employed in aiding, abetting, or promoting the existing rebellion against the government of the United States."[4]

The lawyer took the legal cover provided by John Hickman and made clear that it was an obligation of the president to carry out this act of Congress.

Knox firmly concluded his opening remarks by announcing that the rest of the case was merely a matter of proving that the president had made the order. Knox spoke carefully to the jury in laying down the logic of his argument, in a voice that was even and polite.

> That if the jury believed that the district attorney requested
> by telegraphic dispatch, addressed to the president of the
> United States, authority to seize the *Jeffersonian* newspaper

establishment preparatory to its condemnation and confiscation under the said act of Congress, and that the president, through the secretary of war, gave such authority, the order issued by the district attorney is in lawful justification for the act of the marshall and his deputies in seizing and detaining the property aforesaid.[5]

It is a clever and simple defense. Knox was arguing that the United States marshal was only doing his duty when he seized property that aided the Southern cause, that property being the *Jeffersonian* newspaper. The Confiscation Act of 1861 gave him not only the right, but the responsibility. It was not his decision, but came through the chain of command from the commander in chief himself. Marshal William Millward, one of three named defendants in the case, therefore, could not be guilty of actions taken on behalf of the president of the United States.

Knox attacked the primary question of the trial; could the government prove that Abraham Lincoln sanctioned the seizure of the *Jeffersonian,* or was it a local act of vigilante justice carried out with less noble aims? Sworn testimony by Coffey affirmed that their marching orders had come from President Lincoln, and the smoke-screen offered by the defense in the form of the Confiscation Act would seek to provide cause. What really mattered was whether solid evidence, not just hearsay, could be produced to prove such an order had been made. Absence of such an order would prove that Lincoln had no involvement. This would demonstrate that others had enacted a conspiracy under the false pretense that the seizure had been ordered by the president.

Lincoln already knew the weakness of the first Confiscation Act. In the time after the warrants were first served on the government defendants, the Confiscation Act signed by Lincoln in August 1861 had taken on more meaning. Congress had since passed a second Confiscation Act, this one with the language that John Hickman removed from the first act in order to get it passed for the president. The Second Confiscation Act, passed on July 17, 1862, was clearer in its intentions, that "every person who shall hereafter commit the crime of treason against the United States, and shall be adjudged guilty thereof, shall suffer death, and all his slaves, if any, shall be declared and made free."[6]

Unlike the first Confiscation Act, the second had helped lead the way for Lincoln's Emancipation Proclamation, and had, as Hodgson and the radical Republicans predicted, made the war one of slavery, not of government. The second act was more specific in its goal to "seize and confiscate the property of rebels," a clear distinction between the first that generalized the confiscation of property from anyone interfering with the war effort, North or South. It was a legislative bomb aimed right at the heart of any Northerner who legally supported the Southern cause. The effect would be to completely silence dissenters.

The government's attorneys laid down an argument that was straightforward:
- Congress passed the Confiscation Act
- The Confiscation Act was meant to include antiwar newspapers
- The defendant told the administration they were acting under the Confiscation Act
- They received approval from the president

Therefore, they cannot be found guilty finding of trespassing.

Now it fell to the prosecution. The strategy of Reed and Biddle was first to make real the plight of the confiscated newspaper. The first order in their presentation was to have the Hodgsons take the witness stand. The first Hodgson to testify in the packed courtroom was

Charles Hodgson, the second son of John Hodgson. Living in Washington, he had come to the family's defense when the office was attacked by the mob and was helping his brother and father to get the paper publishing again. There must have been a great deal of anticipation as the talented William B. Reed found himself once again in the public's eye. Charles spoke first of the moment when the marshals arrived at the office.

> I am not connected with the paper at present; I am not interested either directly or indirectly. While working, the defendant, Marshall Jenkins, came into the office and demanded that my proceedings should stop. I asked his authority and he showed me a paper, signed, I think, by Mr. Coffey. It remained closed until I asked Deputy Marshal Schuyler whether the subscription lists came under that authority. I told him it was unjust that we could not collect our debts.
>
> But Coffey insisted that nothing could come out of the office. He allowed us neither books nor anything to be taken out of the office.[7]

Under cross-examination by John Knox, Hodgson estimated the paper's expenses to be "running about four thousand dollars a year, and our income is about seven thousand dollars. Our profit is therefore about three thousand dollars."[8] One can only imagine why this was considered vital information for the government defendants. Perhaps it was to show that the paper was doing quite well, and hence, dangerous for the administration.

John Hodgson testified next. The courtroom finally had the moment it had long waited for. The stubborn patriot and constitutional defender was on the witness stand.

He first explained the legality of the ownership of the paper. According to Hodgson, he leased it to his sons in 1858, then sold it to them outright in early 1861, just before the outbreak of the war. Soon after the sale, his stepson died, and Charles chose to leave for Washington, DC, leaving the whole concern to William.[9]

Hodgson continued, tracing the events on the night of the seizure of the paper. He did not, however, state whether he divested himself of the property for fear of what was to come and prevent an inevitable attack, or if there were less compelling motivations.

> On the evening of the twenty-third I was met at my office by a large crowd of citizens, including John Jenkins and Schuyler. They took me into a room and examined through my luggage. They instructed me they were under orders from Marshal Millward to seize the office and papers. They demanded all of the papers I had.
>
> We then went up to the office. My son said all the books had been taken. I appealed to the marshal, but he said they would keep my books. I returned the next morning to the office and was refused admittance.
>
> The office was in the hands of Constable Lynch. My son had no access to our office.
>
> We had at the time about six thousand subscribers. Some demanded their money back once we couldn't publish. I would estimate that during the seven weeks we were shut we lost about six hundred to eight hundred dollars.[10]

Son Charles had also confronted the issue of money, but in a far simpler way. The paper, he said, was "very evidently a making business because [my father] supported a large family." John Hodgson also revealed that the onset of the Civil War had been good for the bottom line. From January of 1861 to August, the profits, he testified, had nearly doubled.[11]

Subscriptions were up and so too revenue. In all respects, it would seem that the censorship actions, like that of the *Brooklyn Eagle,* had backfired. But in terms of money, it is not the sort of case that on the surface warrants two of the nation's top lawyers and scholars.

So why did the top Democratic lawyers in the state of Pennsylvania take Hodgson's case? One answer goes to the heart of Hodgson's belief in American institutions. One is hard pressed to find other examples—whether in Pennsylvania or the entire Union— where an antiwar editor chose to fight back.

Part of the answer may also lie in the complex character that was William B. Reed. Reed's bitterness toward his country and his government were painfully visible to all who knew him. He suffered deeply from a career being lost to the tide of history, publishing anonymously until 1862 for fear of further conflict, and from a paralyzing feeling of betrayal for his old friend James Buchanan, who proved too weak to prevent the future bloodshed. Reed wanted a Confederate victory. He wanted a society where white people continued to dominate. He wanted to live in a Pennsylvania where state rules were superior to those of the federal government.

He had a tragic career that suffered greatly due to his own personal convictions.[12]

Here, at last, was a chance to strike back at the radicals in Congress and the patronage grabbers in Washington and throughout Pennsylvania. Here was a chance to stop editor John Forney from his march to greater and greater power. And here was a chance to wound the Confiscation Act, which had been used repeatedly to provide legitimacy for the arrests and other abuses Lincoln's men had perpetrated upon dissenters.

It was not for fame that the two lawyers, Reed and Biddle, signed on to defend the *Jeffersonian*. Reed especially was avoiding the limelight since his return from China and dissatisfaction with the new administration. It was not for any money; there is no record that they asked for nor did Hodgson pay his legal team. No, there was perhaps another reason, perhaps the most compelling: fear and self-protection. Even then, both Reed and Biddle seemed driven by a more patriotic impulse, an indescribable sense of duty for country and a responsibility to defend those who were not receiving due process.[13]

Their point of contention was the Confiscation Act, a singular piece of legislation that was inspired in part by the likes of Congressman John Hickman. It could also be called the most potent weapon devised yet against outspoken comments against the war. The Confiscation Act of 1861 was so broad that it effectively would silence any critic.

The Confiscation Act itself underwent changes and modifications. The first version did not include the provisions taking away any slaves owned by those deemed "treasonists" against the Union. It was the second version that added these clauses. As such, the second act was the first official legislation of the Civil War that sought to stamp out slavery throughout the nation. It predated the Emancipation Proclamation and can be viewed in a very moral light in our nation's march toward equality for all citizens. But that is only half the story, for the notorious act, from the Democrats' perspective, also provided, as usual during the Civil War, far more basic rewards for those in power under the cover of a noble morality.

For William B. Reed and other Democrats, it was not for the issue of slavery that he leapt to test the constitutionally of the Confiscation Act in the courts. Yes, Reed supported slavery. Yes, he seemed eager for a Confederate victory. But still again, it was the concern that the act violated the basic tenets of the right of every American to speak their mind without fear of political and economic repression.

A year later, in 1862, the stakes were raised still higher. The newly passed version of the Confiscation Act included amidst the wonderful language seeking to hurt the institution of slavery a provision that may have spelled the end of the Democratic Party, and indeed the multiparty system of American politics:

> SEC. 3. And be it further enacted, that every person guilty of either of the offences described in this act shall be forever incapable and disqualified to hold any office under the United States.

This would mean any person who supported the South, who communicated with the Confederates, who believed in the Confederacy, who believed in states' rights or in the system of slavery.

If left unchallenged, it meant not only that Reed, the former ambassador to China, might never again serve in the government, given especially the swirling rumors of his impending arrest, but that with one stroke of the pen, Abraham Lincoln had effectively condoned giving his fellow Republicans a lifetime monopoly on the lucrative patronage of the federal government. If allowed to stand, no Democrat, no antiwar editor, no supporter of states' rights, could ever again enjoy a job in the federal government.

Not the young editor of the *Brooklyn Eagle,* not the antiwar writers being tarred and feathered by angry mobs, or publishers forced to close their family newspapers. Not the hundreds of men in the Buchanan administration who were more than likely gearing up for the upcoming presidential campaign to defeat Lincoln.

It can easily be argued that section three of the act sought to create a golden age of patronage control. With the Union restored, with the docile Lincoln presiding over a second term and more concerned with the many issues of unification, can one not imagine Seward and Weed taking unprecedented control of the patronage of New York, Forney and Hickman of the Philadelphia and Baltimore regions, and out west the Blair family? Cameron would get his share in Pennsylvania and so too men like Secretary Chase in Ohio and all would fight for control of the government positions in the Confederacy once victory was assured—and even before. Without fear of political patronage competition, no matter the turn of the administration, no matter whether a Democrat or Whig or another Republican won the Executive Mansion, the ports of the nation, the post offices, the clerkships, the plumb jobs and government printing contracts would be forever barred from any man who had lived in the Confederacy and any anti-war advocate in the North.

If the Confiscation Act was allowed to stand, the most effective manipulators of the greatest patronage administration of the nation's history could look forward to extraordinary riches and power for the rest of their lives. That is what must have grated most upon the likes of men like Reed and Biddle. That is what was at stake for many sitting in this tiny Philadelphia courtroom in 1863. Democrats longed for a political victory against Lincoln in the presidential election to come in 1864, and a return to the rewards of government jobs. This bill unchecked would remove any motivation for any but the most devoted party loyalist to vote for anyone but Lincoln.

From Reed's perspective, the stakes could not have been higher. Forney had already called for mob action should he win the case in court. More than likely the administration would seek to confiscate his house if they won—and never again would he serve in a government capacity. And, oh yes, the rights to publish whatever one believed would have been severely crimped.

The struggle in Washington for control of the levers of government had grown in many ways as brutal as those on the Civil War battlefields. The Republicans strove, as many a Democratic editor screamed in warning, to become the one party of the Union.

This was the situation as confronted by those who regarded themselves—or who were labeled—as part of the loyal opposition.

As the day wore on, George Biddle took over for Reed, moving from the timeline of events to sorting through the complicated network of government officials, tracing the chain of command from the bottom up.

The most distinguished government official named in the suit was William Millward, the United States marshal for the Eastern District. Millward started his career as a leather manufacturer before moving to government. He had served two nonconsecutive terms in the House of Representatives, first as a Whig from 1855–1857, then as a Republican from 1859 to March 1861. After Millward lost reelection for the second time in four years, President Lincoln appointed the thirty-nine-year-old former congressman as United States marshal in 1861.[14]

Millward took to his post with zeal, confiscating Democratic newspapers from trains in New York, raiding post offices in Philadelphia and barges and ships in ports throughout the East. After the infamous New York grand jury targeted Democratic newspapers in June 1861, Millward had the task of seizing papers from railroad stops and destroying papers found on the streets and in offices.

John Hodgson knew Millward well. After the reinstatement of the *Jeffersonian's* property after their circuit court victory, Hodgson was faced with a new strategy in the administration's attempt to censor his paper. The *Jeffersonian* was silent for a two-month period from the end of August to late October 1861, the time between its seizure and the return of its property from the United States government. West Chester's postmaster refused to deliver the paper, on direct order, he said, from the postmaster of the United States, Montgomery Blair.

> It appearing to this department that the *Jeffersonian,* a newspaper published at West Chester, Pennsylvania, and the *Christian Observer,* published at Philadelphia, Pennsylvania, are used for the purpose of overthrowing the government of the United States, and are giving aid and comfort to the enemies now at war with the United States, it is ordered that said papers be excluded from all the post offices and mails of the United States until further orders.[15]

"The above will explain to our patrons why they did not receive the *Jeffersonian Extra* of last week, which was deposited in the post office here, on Thursday, the seventeenth, in time to have been forwarded by the Philadelphia mail of that afternoon."

Apparently the government had put aside their embarrassing defense in the small Philadelphia courtroom, as another card remained to be played. The *Jeffersonian* reported more on this latest obstacle in the lead story of its return issue, pointing to familiar assailants.

> TO THE PATRIOTS OF THE *JEFFERSONIAN*
> Those of our patrons, and the public generally, who were advised of the result of the proceedings instituted in the district court of the United States for the suppression of the *Jeffersonian*—a result altogether in our favor, and clearly showing that there was no legal ground for assailing us—

will, doubtless, be surprised to learn that the postmaster general, influenced we presume by such patriots as John Hickman and Co., has directed the postmaster at West Chester, and perhaps at other points, not to permit the *Jeffersonian* through the mails. This is done, too, before the postmaster general or his prompters knew what would be the course of our paper, except that, as they had reason to infer, if would be Democratic and opposed to abolitionism.

Whether we would continue to discuss the merits of the Civil War in which our country is unfortunately involved, or whether we would, as is our disposition, avoid such discussion as heretofore pursued, they had no information.[16]

Hodgson was sure to highlight the wrongs, and assured his readers of such plots "towards the *Jeffersonian* and its proprietor; and we shall at once take steps to ascertain the truth of this impression. John Hickman and Co. may…endorse Frémont's abolition proclamation in Missouri…and it appears that they can induce the postmaster general to prohibit the mail circulation of a Democratic newspaper!"[17]

Locally, the man behind the arrests and the other problems faced by the *Jeffersonian* was none other than William Millward. Behind him was a loyal fleet of deputies and district attorneys, all products of the patronage system. In Philadelphia, his ally was George Coffey who, like Millward, received a ringing endorsement to the president from editor John Forney. Also like Millward, Coffey received his appointment directly from the president.[18]

George Coffey had been known to Lincoln since at least August 1860, when congressman and Republican national convention delegate William Kelley put one of his speeches in Lincoln's hands. "May I encroach upon your limited leisure enough to run your eye over it," asked Kelley. "Mr. C. is as modest as he is courageous, and I am anxious that he may know you have read the address which brought forth such tokens of disapprobation from his audience."[19]

By December, Coffey was comfortable enough with the president-elect that he sent Lincoln an endorsement for Simon Cameron's appointment to a cabinet post.[20]

Later that day, the defense called the district attorney, George Coffey, to testify. There had been no press coverage the day before, and there would not be any until closing arguments were completed, and the chief justice had given his charge to the jury the following day. All seemed to be holding their breath regarding the outcome. Would the Democrats be crushed once again? Or would the Republicans suffer one of their few defeats in the effort to shut down dissenting voices?

George Coffey, Philadelphia's federally appointed district attorney, was the pivotal testimony. William Reed knew the pressures of Coffey's job well, he himself having served as the city's district attorney decades before. On Coffey's testimony lay the burden of proof. Only he could answer, and provide evidence, as to who made the order to confiscate the *Jeffersonian*.

John Knox asked Coffey only one question about the *Jeffersonian's* seizure:

Knox: "State whether you authorized that order," he directed, handing Coffey a piece of paper, "and to whom you delivered it."

Coffey: "That is my signature. I think I gave the order to Mr. Jenkins."

For the government's defense, this simple question took matters out of the hands of the marshal and his deputies. Coffey sent a direct order to Millward's deputy, John Jenkins. If he was only following orders, then neither he, Deputy William Schuyler, nor William Millward could be held personally responsible for any activities that might be considered illegal.

That was all from the government, a disappointing crescendo to a year and a half of mounting frustration for the Hodgsons.

The full cross-examination was printed in a Philadelphia newspaper. Within Coffey's brief testimony was the evidence Reed and Biddle needed to show the lack of centralized control over government appointees, and the lengths to which local officials used the acts of Congress to sanction their own abuses against old enemies. In essence, they needed to establish a paper trail and a clear interpretation of the Confiscation Act.

> Cross examined by Mr. Biddle:
>
> Q: The order recites in it at the conclusion, "I, being authorized by the president of the United States."
>
> A: So I was.
>
> Mr. Knox: I object to all that.
>
> Mr. Biddle: I was merely calling his attention to the concluding sentence, and I did intend to ask him what particular authority he had for making that particular order.
>
> Mr. Knox: I object.
>
> Chief Justice Lowrie: Of course you have the right to stand upon Mr. Coffey's order alone, if you choose.
>
> Mr. Knox: But I have the right to take my objection upon this ground: that whatever appears upon the face of the warrant or order when issued by an officer of the United States, pointed out by the act of Congress, is conclusive as to the marshal, that it was by the authority of the president. It is not an open question.

> Mr. Biddle: We conceive that the plaintiff here has a right to redress, if his property has been unlawfully taken from him. I conceive, also, that when he is met by a defence of the nature that has been opened by Mr. Knox, that there must be some limitation to the proposition asserted by him, because if it is carried to the fair and logical results plainly deductible from it, it becomes a proposition monstrous and abhorrent, not only the laws and Constitution of the United States and the state of Pennsylvania, but to every system of jurisprudence.[21]

Chief Judge Lowrie "explained that he understood the proposition to be that the order was a justification to the mere ministerial officer, not that it would be a justification for others."[22]

Biddle was really imploring the judge and the jury to remember that two years after the bloody conflict began, after the loss of tens of thousands of lives, the wholesale closing of antiwar newspapers and the arrests of an entire class of antiwar Southern sympathizers, that the Constitution was still the core value of the Union, not some higher law as the Republicans were fond of saying.

> Mr. Biddle: If so, it is a matter of importance to know what authority the district attorney had. He assumes that the mere assertion of the authority is sufficient.
>
> Chief Justice Lowrie: My trouble is in my ignorance that I do not know that the president has the right to direct Mr. Coffey to take away any man's property.
>
> Mr. Knox: The act of August 1861 authorizes the seizure of property used in aiding the rebellion. The act directs the president to use the district attorneys for the purpose.

Mr. Reed: If you will look at the act of Congress, you will see that the president is to direct the seizure, and the district attorneys are afterwards to direct the condemnation.

Immediately, Knox interrupted his opposing colleague William Reed.

Mr. Knox: It does not say "after." The question is whether Mr. Coffey had authority or not. [23]

To this, Chief Justice Lowrie, a lifelong Democrat who was under great pressures from the Republican press to uphold the Confiscation Act, pushed the debate: "I see all sorts of questions looming up here, but I think they have the right to ask that question. I do not know what use will be made of it."

After the fires were extinguished, Reed assumed the questioning for the prosecution, starting again with Biddle's first question to the district attorney. The question, clearly, rested on the intention of the first Confiscation Act.

Did a property seizure require a direct written order from the president to set it in motion, or did local officials have the authority to act on his behalf at their own discretion? And if the order did not exist from the president, what were Coffey, Millward, and his deputies covering up? Were there adequate checks and balances to prevent any local official from seizing the property of an old enemy? Coffey attempted to keep the issue as simple as possible by insisting that he had acted under direct orders of Lincoln.

Mr. Coffey: There was a despatch [sic] sent by me to the president of the United States, and to that I received a reply; my recollection of the facts is, that I telegraphed to the president and asked for the authority; I believe that I telegraphed to the president and the secretary of war; on the same day I received a despatch [sic] in reply; I recollect only the substance of that reply, and it closed I think with—"your action is approved—be temperate and firm"; I think the answer came from the War Department on behalf of the president; I had taken no action before that, except to inquire into the course of the paper; in my despatch [sic] to the president, I spoke of course of the *Jeffersonian* and another newspaper now published in Richmond, the *Christian Observer;* I spoke of the *Jeffersonian* as publishing articles inflaming or disturbing the minds of the people; and that I desired to test whether the act of 1861 applied; there was no warrant before me, nor affidavit; the order was the first paper in the case.[24]

Strangely enough, orders leading to the seizure of other papers, the *New York Daily News* and others on the list created by the New York grand jury during the 1861 summer of rage, were clearly ordered by the War Department. There was also correspondence concerning the seizure of the *Christian Observer,* the paper that was sharing its presses with John Hodgson the week of the seizure, yet any correspondence relating to the *Jeffersonian* is not to be found.

Coffey did send Lincoln a telegram on August 22 informing the president that he used the Confiscation Act to seize all copies of the *New York Daily News* that were to be found in Philadelphia. Clearly, the president knew of Coffey's activities, and if he did not approve, Lincoln at least did not deter the activities. But the *Jeffersonian* was named nowhere in the correspondence.[25]

A similar order was given on September 5, 1861, Coffey receiving a note from then Secretary of War Simon Cameron under the shelter of the same justification for another seized paper. It gave discretion to the district attorney, which in Coffey's mind gave him license to seize any paper troubling to him, the administration, or perhaps just to his friends.

> SIR: You are hereby authorized to cause the seizure of the *Register* at Norristown, and the *Carbon Democrat,* at Mauch Chunk, if in your opinion there is sufficient ground for proceeding against them under the act of Congress approved 6th of August, 1861.
> SIMON CAMERON.
> Secretary of War.[26]

A few days later, Amasa Converse, the twenty-two-year editor and proprietor of the *Christian Observer,* wrote to Lincoln about the suppression of his paper, having been told by Marshal Millward that "he was acting under orders received from you through an official channel."

Furthermore, Converse pleaded directly to Abraham Lincoln, "I cannot believe that you would justify the proceeding if you knew the facts. This action must have been induced by misrepresentation. I have some reason to believe that I know the persons who have poisoned the mind of the government upon this subject, and to understand their motives." Unfortunately, Converse does not name his suspects.[27]

In his testimony concerning the *Jeffersonian,* Coffey further absolved the deputies.

> Mr. Reed: Had you seen the newspapers before the order of seizure?
>
> Coffey: Yes. I have some of them yet. I think they were sent to me by Mr. McVeagh, the district attorney of the county; I do not know in whose handwriting the body of the order is written, but the signature is mine,

and I am responsible for the seizure; I delayed the filing of the information on account of the visits of Mr. [William] Hodgson and his father to me; Mr. Hodgson requested that the property should be given up to him; we had conversation about it some dozen times, and it amounted to this: I told him that if he would agree not to oppose the war for the restoration of the Union of the thirty-four states, I certainly would not oppose the restoration of the paper. He declined to do that particular thing; he said he would die rather than give such a pledge to that.[28]

John Knox offered Coffey's signed order to Marshal Millward into evidence. Biddle objected. The judge stayed the order and the dispatch was accepted. The telegram contains all the ingredients of the defense claims. It ties together the Confiscation Act, the chain of command, and the order of the president.

According to the provisions of the Act of 6 August 1861, I hereby request you to seize upon all copies of the *Jeffersonian* newspaper published in the borough of West Chester, Chester County Pennsylvania, as well as all property of every kind whatsoever used in about the publication of said newspaper, that may be found in your bailiwick, for confiscation and condemnation, according to law—I being authorized by the president of the United States.

George A. Coffey, U.S. Attorney
Philadelphia, 23d August, 1861.[29]

The fact that there was an order from Coffey to Millward, argued Reed directly, was inconsequential. The merits of the case rested on orders from the president to Coffey.

George Coffey appeared to be playing the martyr. He was a man living on borrowed time who seemed to have chosen to play an important role as long as he could. Put up by John Forney and prominent congressmen for his position in early 1861, by October of that year, conveniently as the *Jeffersonian's* first court case came to trial, Forney was pushing equally as hard for his removal.

Coffey had since fallen into poor health, which to Forney would have provided adequate cover for his removal. In a letter to Lincoln, in which Forney gleefully reported that his paper "wields ten times more influence in Pennsylvania than it has ever before wielded," he reported Coffey's sudden illness and wrote, "Should Mr. Coffey not be able to attend to his active duties—which is now beyond questions—some provision might be made for him, by his successor."[30]

But Coffey had held on despite Forney's attempts to replace him. Forney provides physical reasons for Coffey's removal, but there may have been more sinister motives. Coffey's letter was written between the *Jeffersonian's* seizure and its circuit court appearance. Did Forney have something to hide? Was he protecting John Hickman? Or was it a series of unrelated coincidental events?

The jury would soon be asked to sift through the confusion, taking on the entire United States Congress and the president from the cramped courtroom in Philadelphia.

Chapter Thirteen

MERE TRESPASSERS

*"We caution Democrats about using the term nation. The United States
are not a nation, but a union. Jefferson, the Father of the Democratic
Party, never used the word nation or national—it was the Union, the
federal or general government, the Republic. It would be well for editors of
papers, speakers, writers, and public men to return to the old time-honored
terms. Nation means now a consolidated abolition, military despotism."* [1]

—John Hodgson, April 11, 1863

Thursday, February 5, 1863, broke bitterly cold in Philadelphia
with the thermometer registering eight degrees in some places.
The snow started early and soon a blanket covered the entire East
Coast all the way down to Washington. Strangely enough, by mid-
afternoon the weather turned warm, and by evening it was spitting
rain on the busy correspondents who clamored for the scoop inside
the Philadelphia courtroom. [2]

The treachery of weather must have been very much on the minds
of combatants on both sides, as just a few weeks earlier General Burnside

launched one of the most doomed maneuvers of the war. Burnside's Army of the Potomac and Robert E. Lee's Army of Northern Virginia had squared off for most of the winter. In early January, Burnside penned an order that said in part that "the auspicious moment seems to have arrived to strike a great and mortal blow to the rebellion, and to gain that decisive victory which is due to the country." The Union general's attack around Fredericksburg, in upper Maryland, was greeted with support from the press yet also with a storm seemingly direct from the heavens. The roads quickly turned to mud. The Union's wagon trains sunk, as did the men. Within a couple of days hundreds of mules had perished. Frustration ran so high that Union soldiers fought one another. Famously, at least one Confederate created a signboard proclaiming "Burnside Stuck in the Mud."[3]

Humiliation followed the difficult retreat for the Union solders. The men had thought they would march all the way to Richmond and had burned their camps. Lincoln immediately relieved Burnside, replacing him with General Hooker. The battle became known as the "Mud March," and it did little to lower the fears swirling around the people in Pennsylvania and Maryland that the bloody battles would soon come to their doorsteps.

No matter the weather or the fears from the front, life went on for those still at home. The men in Philadelphia who were not in uniform were engaged in business central to the war, whether finance, insurance, or manufacturing. The theaters in Boston and New York and in Philadelphia were open to good-sized audiences. Up in New York and, in fact, everywhere in the country, everyone was abuzz over the upcoming weekend marriage of the legendary circus performer and midget Tom Thumb to another midget, Lavinia Warren. Frank Leslie's *Illustrated Newspaper* devoted its cover to the twenty-nine-pound bride dressed in the latest bridal fashions. *Harper's Weekly* and most newspapers also fell over themselves covering the event.[4]

That Thursday night in Boston, the actor John Wilkes Booth performed in a production of the Irish Catholic playwright Richard Lalor Shiel's *The Apostate*. It was a performance he gave many times, and would perform on one occasion before Abraham and Mary Lincoln at Ford's Theater. The play, in which his character Duke Herzog Pescara spoke passionately about revenge, would also be the last role he would play on stage before that fateful evening at Ford's Theater in April 1865. During Hodgson's trial, preparations were underway to welcome Booth to Philadelphia, as within a month the charming and handsome actor would be appearing at the Arch Street Theater downtown.

Now into the second day, the well-versed and war-weary men on both sides of the courtroom had examined and cross-examined their witnesses over the question of whether the federal marshal's had the legal right to confiscate the Hodgson's antiwar newspaper. The irascible John Hodgson was getting his chance to help land a knock-out blow against the Lincoln administration and his bitter political enemies. Or face yet again another moment of public humiliation.

Political tensions remained high throughout the city.

On this very day, George Fahnstock wrote into his diary: "The opposition of the Democratic Party to the administration is daily becoming more apparent. Some indeed fear a revolution in the North. Dark hints are thrown out about arms being secretly collected in New York, to be used against the government in case any attempt is made to incarcerate a Democrat in Fort Lafayette."[5]

The attorneys, Reed and Biddle for the prosecution, Knox and Webster for the defense, had discussed the right of the United States government to seize the property of an operating newspaper. Whether that paper had aided the Southern cause was not at question, nor whether it operated with the intention of aiding the Southern cause.

The question was whether the president of the United States had filed a direct order to local officials to conduct the seizure, or whether the local officials had taken it upon themselves to act in his name. Ultimately, the case rested on the constitutionality of the Confiscation Act, a vague congressional bill that had yet to be tested since its passage in August 1861. For the first time, a jury would take it upon themselves, whether they wished it or not, to tip the scales of justice.

Following a full day of testimony, on the second day, Thursday, February 5, 1863, counsel offered their summations, taking the course of the entire day. No newspaper published their remarks. Nor did the court reporter who had recorded the testimony of the Hodgsons, Coffey, Millward, and others, make notes.

One can expect that the government traced the history of the Confiscation Act, and the trail of orders that ran from the officials in Pennsylvania to those in Washington.

For Hodgson's lawyers, the day would be devoted to questioning whether Lincoln had indeed authorized the seizure of the *Jeffersonian.*

Absent from testimony was discussion of the role of Congress in the Confiscation Act, particularly those involved in the passage of the bill. To the court, such details were inconsequential. The bill had been passed and signed by the president, and it was from the law as it was written that the case was being heard. Also nowhere in the case were accusations against those who had mobbed the *Jeffersonian* a mere week before its seizure. The roles of Congressman John Hickman, his editorial ally John Forney, and their suspected role in John Hodgson's fate were inadmissible. There was not evidence enough to introduce such attacks on well-known men.

Everyone in the courtroom was on their best behavior. There were no sarcastic articles and comments from the Republicans nor Democrats. The lawyers were polite to one another and to the judge. But the drama was building. How would Lowrie summarize this case to the jury?

Would the judge focus on the Confiscation Act or make some sort of mention of the elephant in the courtroom—freedom of speech. To do so might well anger some of the more radical Republicans and inspire yet another wave of mob actions, or even some sort of attack on the judge himself.

For Lowrie, the threat to his personal well-being was far from an abstract concern. Everyone in the courtroom understood that judges were not exempt from the political arrests afflicting Confederate sympathizers.

One recent case involved a Judge Andrew Duncan Duff of Illinois. He was arrested on August 15, 1862, just six months before Lowrie was to preside over the *Jeffersonian* trial. According to the officer who took the judge into custody, his guilt was in delivering a speech a month before in which he exposed "frauds perpetrated on the government, and that such exposition tended to discourage enlistments." Judge Duff was held for more than three months in the Old Capitol prison in downtown Washington, when he was suddenly discharged without trial. Before being released, he was forced to swear to an affidavit that the would not prosecute the persons who had caused his arrest.[6]

An even more troubling case was that of Judge Richard Bennett Carmichael of southern Maryland, not far from Annapolis. A highly Democratic recounting of his case admits that the judge was vocal in his opposition to the recent arrests in his county and said so to a grand jury charged to decide the issue of arbitrary arrests. Despite rumors of an impending arrest of the judge, nothing took place until spring.

In the midst of a trial, "he was set upon by a gang of ruffians from the city of Baltimore, dragged from the bench, and beaten and hacked, until he was brought senseless to the floor and drenched in his blood." The men had apparently been brought to the court under the control of the provost marshal, a special agent of the War

Department. After the beating, he was seen to by a doctor and then taken under arrest.[7]

Judge Carmichael was imprisoned for more than six months, including a stay at Fort Lafayette. He was released just four weeks before the Hodgson trial.

For Judge Lowrie, a Democratic judge trying a politically charged case, the stakes were high. An emotional charge to the jury might land him at Fort Lafayette. Or the courtroom doors might burst open at any moment and a Philadelphia gang leave him bloodied on the floor of his own court. More than likely, Lowrie had his own network of informants and knew the limits that would be permitted in his guidance to the twelve men now sitting before him. His safest course of action was to walk that fine line, staying true to his beliefs on the strength of the Constitution while at the same time expressing no personal animosity toward either the federal agents sitting in the courtroom or for the president.

Lowrie chose to speak directly to that which was on the minds of so many Americans. He put aside concerns for his own safety and tackled directly the Constitutional issues confronting the American democracy in a time of civil war.

The chief justice carefully read from his notes before a packed courtroom and the twelve men upon whose shoulders the case now rested. To them went the task of distilling the fever-pitch of emotions that had gripped Pennsylvania, and the entire country, for the past two years. Lowrie was explicit, calling out each of the issues of the case one by one. He knew the charge would fill columns in the morning papers, and that his words were for the entire American people, not just the cramped courtroom.

Lowrie began his instructions by directly confronting the wartime conflict between constitutional rights and an administration's fervor to rid itself of mortal enemies.

It is not at all strange that, in times of national crisis, and of national and popular disturbance and excitement, we find ourselves forced to revert to first principals in the discussion of cases, which, in ordinary times and rising among ordinary persons, could be disposed of with accuracy and dispatched by a simple justice of the peace. This case is one of that character.

We should not think of granting it anything but the utmost summary treatment, were it not that it grows of the very natural excitement that overspread the country in the breaking out of the present rebellion; and that the actors in it are important officers of the federal government who claim to have acted under the authority of a law of Congress and under the special authority of the president of the United States and in support of the Constitution and law, and of the safety and integrity of the Union.

Lowrie seemed to be agreeing with the government. It was a simple case: Congress passed a bill and the federal marshals implemented the intent of the bill. But Lowrie was not done, and he dug far deeper in his instructions to the jury.

The rebellion is the first extraordinary element in this case; but no one can pretend that our law was changed by the mere fact of the rebellion, so far as it relates to the rights that now claim to be vindicated by us. Not doubt that rebellion gave rise to an immense popular excitement that was quite natural and inevitable.

No doubt also this distrust would soon be visited upon those who, for any reason, should seriously question the most summary plans for suppressing the rebellion, for when people are excited they are sure to be impatient, and censorious of all plans that do not seem to them to promise the most speedy and summary success.

Never before had the antiwar Democrats heard the assaults against them described so politely. It was natural, argued the judge, that in a time of rebellion those disagreeing with the course of events should suffer. It was a peace offering to the men who made up the mobs and those who ordered them into the streets.

But now the judge came to his moment of choice and he left behind the safe territory of the government's defense. Lowrie must have fought to maintain his composure in telling the men of the jury that "none of these circumstances can at all change the Constitution or laws of the land."

Nor is the involvement of the president a legal exception.

> [The President] as well as we, are under the Constitution and laws of the United States and sworn to support, protect, and defend them, or take them as their rule of civil and official conduct, and they, and we, are to be judged by them in our civil and official conduct in all appropriate cases. The acts of the president and of his subordinates are, therefore without right unless they are authorized by some article of the Constitution or if the laws made under it are consistent with it.
>
> We can make no laws that can vest in him any new authority or that can protect those who obey his unauthorized orders. He would not claim that he could.

The judge was now fully committed, speaking on the emotions swirling across the country for the past two years.

And now it is proper for me to say that I see no sufficient evidence that the president of the United States authorized the seizure complained of there. I think it entirely improbable that he did. The district attorney thinks his dispatch came from someone in the War Department. This is no evidence of an order from the president and that element is therefore entirely out of the case.

And all these elements being removed, the case becomes the very common one in which it is alleged that a public officer has seized the goods of a citizen without proper warrant. It is common against both federal and state officers. We have had many of them. On an order issued by the district attorney the defendants, the marshal and his deputies, seized upon the office of the plaintiff's newspaper called the *Jeffersonian* and on all its contents for some supposed violation of laws, and afterwards the property was proceeded against for the forfeiture in the U.S. Court, and was soon abandoned by the district attorney.

What the law requires in order to justify such an act is written in the Constitution. Article four of the amendments, "The right of the people to be secure in their persons, houses, papers, and effects against unreasonable searches and seizures, shall not be violated, and no warrants shall issue but upon probable cause supported by oath or affirmation and particularly describing the place to be searched and the person or things to be seized."

We understand now the case we have before us. The defendants had no such warrant as required by the Constitution.

There is nothing in the Act of Congress of the sixth August 1861 that justifies it. It requires the president in certain cases to cause certain property to be seized, confiscated, and condemned but this means by due process of law. It is not to be done by the president himself but by due process of law by the proper functionaries and he is to see that they do their duty.

These defendants undertook to do this act without warrant and without any proper occasion shown to us, and therefore they are mere trespassers.

"Mere trespassers." So described a federal judge of the emotional response of patriotic men to the splitting in two of the Union. Those who took the law into their own hands and broke into the offices of newspaper offices were no different from common burglars.

His legal argument concluded, Lowrie turned to address the jury sitting just across from him. He spoke now obviously from the heart, in telling them that "the case is now in your hands, gentleman, and I am sure you will dispose of it in such as way that, long as you may live and I hope it may be long, you will never have reason to regret the part you have had in it. The damages you may give are of no sort of importance compared with the decision upon principals that has devolved upon me."[8]

The self-imposed restraint was broken. The town must have been abuzz with both the charge to the jury and expectantly awaiting the verdict for damages. John Forney rushed *The Press* to print, and that evening's edition provided a word for word accounting of the charge given by Justice Lowrie to the jury. There was no cry for mob action this time. Offered Forney without emotion, "After the charge had been delivered the jury retired, and the crowded courtroom was soon vacated."[9]

The talk that night—and the next morning—for many would focus on the charge to the jury. Chief Justice Lowrie had provided a stirring and balanced interpretation of the matter at hand. No one was to blame personally, he declared. Not the offending administration officials, for they were humans swept up in the excitement of the times. Not the president, who certainly did not authorize this break-in. But yet, infractions were committed, the Constitution was violated, and, therefore, justice must assert its calm voice in the midst of the swirling emotions of an uncertain time in our nation's history. "If the law of the land is the sober and abiding thought of the whole people…the strong ocean undercurrent of thought to which storms and tides and tempests do not reach," wrote the nervous judge. These words are perhaps the finest articulation of the need for an independent judicial system ever penned and then forgotten.[10]

What an evening it must have been for John Hodgson and William Reed and George Biddle and all the men who had suffered since the summer of rage two years before. Their fight was one of principal—not over territory, but of constitutional ideals. For the rights of free speech, many had endured months in jail and seen their careers destroyed.

An administration had knowingly stepped outside the Constitution. Its reasons may have been patriotic and noble and indeed history records it that way. Nonetheless, those caught on the wrong side refused to concede it proper for one institution, whether the Congress or administration, to trample over the judiciary.

Hodgson had been there before, waiting the results of a trial. But the stakes had never been so high. If the twelve men of the jury found for the government, then the Confiscation Act would mean the death knell for all Democrats. No Southern sympathizer would ever run a newspaper or write an editorial without taking on the risk of jail. So too the publisher carrying an opinion piece against the administration's path on the war.

A verdict in favor of the government would mean that rather than a summer of rage that seemed to have abated, the Union might confront a decade of imposed silence based on fear and intimidation.

Did the men of the jury understand the constitutional implications, or did they view this as a case of a loud-mouthed editor who got his comeuppance and now was wasting their time by crying for justice? These were the questions that must have been jumping into Hodgson's mind that night.

The jury immediately retreated to a private room to deliberate. Their task was to review two days of heated testimony from highly skilled lawyers. As the lawyers and their clients went out to eat and ponder the case, something startling was happening back at the courthouse. A verdict was almost immediately reached.

Unknown at the time to the Hodgsons and their lawyers, the men reached a unanimous conclusion within several hours, and the verdict sealed. The quick consensus may mean the men listened to Judge Lowrie's charge and decided in favor of the Hodgsons. Or it may mean that they voted in favor of their brothers and sons and fathers who had willingly joined the Union army for Old Abe and fought against the rebellion.

The next morning, Friday, February 6, 1863, eighteen months since the mobbing and then seizure of the *Jeffersonian,* and almost three years since Abraham Lincoln's inauguration, Chief Justice Walter H. Lowrie received the verdict the jury had sealed the night before.

Justice Lowrie calmly read the verdict to the packed courtroom. It was a surprise decision for many.

The jury of twelve men of "mixed politics" had decided to do their part in putting the summer of rage behind the Union. They had voted in favor of John and William Hodgson and their anti-Lincoln newspaper.

Lincoln's men had been found guilty of trespassing on private property. It was a vindication for the almost two years of struggle for John and William Hodgson. And a vindication for so many that had stood by them. For their efforts, the value of the "violence and outrage attending to it," was $512, the exact amount of lost revenue suffered during the government's seizure of his paper. It was a multiple victory: for the family business, of course. For the right to publish dissenting views, of course. But it was also a victory for something far more vital: that slow, cumbersome system of checks and balances. All the Democratic participants, whether Reed, Biddle, the Hodgsons, or even Justice Lowrie, exposed themselves to danger for little personal gain. They had achieved their greater calling and preserved a small piece of democracy for future generations.

Now the question stood as to whether someone would heed John Forney's earlier printed cry for mob action should the law not shut down the *Jeffersonian.*

Chapter Fourteen

REPERCUSSIONS

"Great allowance must be made for the eccentricities of the day. Sober second thought will probably regret many a harsh spoken sentence, and mutual challenges and suspicions of loyalty will give way to a more serious contemplation of the sober realities of the times."[1]

—John Hodgson, April 20, 1861

The *Jeffersonian*'s Pennsylvania supreme court victory was not about financial compensation: Democratic newspapers rejoiced, and the verdict breathed new life into Philadelphia's Democratic Party.

"Those who remembered the ferocious fanaticism of the year before—the appeals of Forney to the military and the mob to crush the refractory lawyers, listened with gratified astonishment to the bold but perfectly decorous language of those very lawyers," wrote the *New York World*. "Every man felt, as he listened to this appeal of liberty and law, that the day of lawless tyranny was drawing to a close. The counsel for the defense had the most fervent and elaborate appeals to passion and prejudice."[2]

Lost perhaps forever are the passionate appeals of the defense. The three government officials must have felt like scapegoats, obeying the laws of the land written by Congress and signed by the president and yet now found guilty of trespassing on the office of John Hodgson.

For the Democrats, it was a moment of rare victory too long in coming. Praise was heaped upon Biddle, Reed, and the estimable Chief Justice Walter Hoge Lowrie. "Honor, then we say, all honor to the Pennsylvania Chief Justice, and the Philadelphia jury. They have unbarred a gate of light upon a long darkened community…Honor to the Philadelphia lawyers who have quietly and resolutely done their duty."[3]

Loyal Democrats in Philadelphia praised Lowrie for making an "interesting point of progress in our political and judicial system."

> He has plainly told Mr. Lincoln and his officials what the law is, and that they are absolutely bound by it as any private citizen, however humble. And this is just what the administration in Washington and all its blind followers need to be told, plainly and bluntly at this time.… We are glad that there was one judicial office who was bold and conscientious enough to declare the truth, regardless of the consequences.…
>
> In him we find the sort of stuff these turbulent and revolutionary times demand.… He has taught us the value of a true man in high office…and the people should heed the lesson.[4]

Of course, Republicans rebuked the case. John Forney minimized its importance, amounting it "to little, as the plaintiff and his newspaper belonged to that insignificant class of persons and things which only attain importance by the mistaken zeal of good and loyal men."

Forney made the statement at the end of a lengthy column on the points of the case, which served, he wrote, "to amuse the leisure hours of Mr. Reed and Mr. Biddle, who seem to be the leagued defenders of the enemies of the Union."[5] On that point he was partially correct. But Forney, in the same issue, did offer praise for Judge Lowrie, writing that "our habitual respect for Mr. Justice Lowrie will prevent us from saying anything disrespectful about him or his court."

Nationally, the case can be said to have had little effect on the course of military events, or the administration's prosecution of acts to suppress insurrection at home. The Second Confiscation Act, passed in June 1862, had proven a formidable tool, and Lincoln's Emancipation Proclamation had changed the nature of the war and the nation forever by freeing slaves held in those states in secession. In between those acts, but just after announcing the forthcoming Emancipation Proclamation, Lincoln also issued the latest suspension of the writ of habeas corpus.

Up to the fall of 1862, the privilege of the writ of habeas corpus, which gave citizens the right to demand justification for their arrest, had been informally enacted, though some high profile cases had developed. Officially, the entire state of Florida was under the suspension, as were railroads, the telegraph lines, and other points in Missouri and between Washington, DC, and Bangor, Maine. But in September 1862, Lincoln issued a nationwide blanket suspension of the writ of habeas corpus "in respect to all persons arrested, or who are now, or hereafter during the rebellion shall be, imprisoned in any fort, camp, arsenal, military prison, or other place of confinement, by any military authority, or by sentence of any court martial or military commission." Ironically, even Lincoln's cabinet first learned of the suspension from the newspapers.[6]

And, of course, John Forney approved. "Your Emancipation Proclamation followed by that suspending the writ of habeus [sic] corpus against the sympathizers with secession has created profound satisfaction among your true friends," Forney wrote to Lincoln before meeting with him the following Monday, "but it has also multiplied your duties. We shall now be assailed front, flank, and rear by our enemies and if we would save the next national House of Representatives the power of the administration must be strongly felt in every congressional district in the free states."

Forney, of course, was delighted by Lincoln's maneuvers, and more importantly got the scoop. He could be candid with Lincoln and ask him for such things, for they were closer than ever. On December 1, Forney asked for an advanced copy of the president's Annual Message to Congress. He sent a messenger to Lincoln's personal secretary John Nicolay in the White House. "The Senate is filling with senators and I regret I cannot leave before the hour. I will do justice to the message in reading; and if you could let Mr. Cook, my friend, who bears this, have a copy it shall see no mortal eye but mine, and will be handed to you as you present it in Senate." Besides wanting to read the copy to better fulfill his role as secretary of the Senate, Forney was not shy about his true motive. "I hear that the *Star* is resolved to beat the *Chronicle* in getting it out. We'll see."[7]

The outcome of the case had important implications to constitutional law, and to the nation as a whole. The independence of the court, for the trial to have occurred at all amidst the political turmoil, gave satisfaction to a segment of society that had been mobbed, arrested, ridiculed, and insulted. Having suffered loss of jobs and income, they were now given some vindication for their belief in the freedom of the American press.

William B. Reed was a changed man after the verdict. He had grown militant over the course of the war and seemingly only more so after the court victory. He had helped to prevent a duplication of the Baltimore riots in Philadelphia, had at last come out of hiding, and had successfully vindicated the first amendment rights of John and William Hodgson. But Reed realized that neither the *Jeffersonian* and its limited circulation nor its victory had the ability to sway the mass of voters in Philadelphia. With the help of George Biddle, ex-congressman Charles Biddle, ex-New Jersey congressman James Wall, and others, Reed helped bring a new weapon to combat John Forney and the Republican newspapers in the state.

Launched in Philadelphia was a newspaper devoted solely to Democratic causes. This would have been impossible a year before. The *Age* published its first issue on March 25, 1863, taking up the cause of the radical element of the Democratic Party. Its editors and proprietors were A. J. Glossbrenner, Francis J. Grund, and William H. Welsh. Boileau's *Evening Journal* went out of business in the fall.

An extension of the city's Democratic Club, which hosted weekly speakers and had been the party's primary base during the war, the *Age* reprinted the speeches to complement its acidic editorial diatribes.[8] The two former advocates for the Hodgsons espoused differing views in the pages of the radical paper. Biddle wanted continuation of the war while Reed supported a truce even if this lead to permanent disunion.

It was a glorious time for the repressed Democrats. One writer goes so far as to gush that "from March until June two-thirds of the long speeches and reviews printed in the *Age* were by members of Philadelphia social elite and George Biddle, Charles and Edward Ingersoll, William Reed, and George Wharton, Richard Vaux, and Peter McCall poured forth a volume of oratory and writing which marked the greatest political resurgence of socially prominent leaders in the city's history."[9]

It was not all smooth sailing for the paper. On May 8, when the *Age* posted the news of the Union retreat at Chancellorsville and the arrest of Ohio congressman Clement Vallandigham outside of its offices, a group of men ripped the papers down and attacked an employee. Not content, they smashed the office windows and prepared to storm the building until the mayor thwarted their cause. It took several hours for the crowd to disburse.

The catalyst for the mob attack was John Forney, who that morning told readers to "unite the North by any means" and to "silence every tongue that does not speak with respect of the cause and the flag."[10] Forney had finally inspired a mob to immediate action.

The middle of 1863 represents one of the most highly charged moments for any major Union city during the course of the war. Tensions ran high as Washington tried to muster more troops. A Confederate attack on Pennsylvania was imminent. There was panic throughout Philadelphia as the reports came in regarding Lee's advance.

Ex-congressman James Wall of New Jersey, now a year since his arrest and only two months since the expiration of his term in the United States House of Representatives, told the Democratic Club that Lincoln should offer peace and that slavery should be made a permanent institution in an effort to appease their Southern brethren. Opponents could not restrain themselves. The speech was so radical that not even the *Age* reprinted it. Afterward, the police disbursed a large crowd outside of the lecture hall, and later had to protect Wall when a mob assembled outside of his hotel room.[11]

A few weeks later, Reed led a June 1 rally in Independence Square protesting the arrest of Vallandigham, the Ohio congressman recently arrested and banned to the Confederacy. Leader of the radical Democrats in Congress, and the man considered by all Republicans as the greatest threat in the Union's midst, Vallandigham had survived many attempts by his congressional colleagues to have him evicted from Washington for good. He and John Hickman had traded words in early 1862 on the House floor after a Baltimore paper accused

Vallandigham of conspiring with Southerners, leading Hickman to, as he said it, initiate the "the duty of this House to purge itself of unworthy members."[12]

Threats of a riot during the Independence Square rally caused an armed state militia regiment and federal troops to guard the protesters from Republicans who gathered to prevent the rally. Reed's position on the war, on the government, and on reconciliation with the South had been self-published in November 1862 "for my neighbours and personal friends," though it did not remain private. Called *A Statement and Vindication of Certain Political Opinions*, Reed writes as if not expecting to be free to speak much longer. It marked his entry from seclusion back into public politics, which he had avoided since early 1860. The work included an overview of his active life, and disclaimers for his activities, making it clear that his loyalties lie with the Constitution. "The home victims of passionate credulity will awaken to this reality by-and-by, and those who have stabbed the Constitution, and their apologists, will have no right to complain if the lawlessness they have initiated returns to plague its inventors in the form of gigantic repudiation."[13]

Having early in the war privately advocated secession, Reed now publicly called for appeasement and a truce, even if that meant a final separation from the Confederacy. "The traitor Vallandigham...has been sent South, and will be handed over to General Bragg," wrote a Philadelphian. "It is a pity that they do not send Wm. B. Reed, J. W. Wall, and a few score such from this city and New York. These rebel sympathizers are growing so bold as to talk openly of a military dictatorship, seizing the reins of government, and assassinating the president."[14]

Reed was somewhat despondent despite the momentum, appearing sucked dry by the lack of integrity offered by both parties. He wrote to Wall an extraordinarily personal and emotional letter in

August: "As I grow older and sadder, and I am fast doing both, my inclination and my capacity for better writing sensibly decay, and I am in danger of neglecting the common courtesies of life."

Thanking Wall for the "secret correspondence," Reed closed his four-page letter with a pessimistic view of the political climate. "Our cause is going vigorously, but I have taken no part yet," he wrote modestly. "I am not willing to speak unless I can speak the whole truth and yet, I know that in practicality is no virtue in a practiced politician."[15]

Reed's sadness may well have been due to the fact that his business was hurting. Few were willing to associate with his ever-bolder actions against the administration. His sadness may also have reflected the fact that the Democrats were losing the larger battle against Union. It was not a battle solely for the rebellion, but the larger issue over whether the Union would be forged into a single nation with a strong federal government or remain the loose association of states. Every day brought new power to Washington at the expense of the local government.

The same week that Reed was writing so pessimistically to Wall, the private secretary for Lincoln wrote, astonishingly, in praise of the riots in New York against the draft. John Hay, giving his true thoughts privately in his diary, praised the riots as helping defeat the doctrine of states' rights. "I thank God for the riot if as one of its results we set a great authoritative precedent of the absolute supremacy of the national power, military and civil, over the state."[16]

On this battlefield, which would continue long after the war was over, the Republicans were winning against their Jeffersonian Democrats. No single court victory would change the rising tide of federal power put into motion by Abraham Lincoln.

The activities of Reed, Biddle, and Wall were aimed at that summer's gubernatorial election. The coming of the Confederate army demoralized Republicans, and a successful invasion of Maryland by

Robert E. Lee would doom the reelection of Governor Andrew Curtin: that is, if the state was not an occupied territory run by a provisional Confederate government. A Philadelphia diarist considered the partisanship so dire that he could foresee another civil war in the North between Democrats and Republicans.[17]

With the prospects of a Confederate liberation, Democrats took to the streets. "Unhappily, so strong has grown the feeling of opposition to the present administration, that many men are pleased with the prospect of invasion, carnage, blood, and smoking ruins! They walk our streets today, radiant with joy, led on by W. B. Reed, Charles Ingersoll, Wharton, and a horde of worn out old Peace Democrats. Nothing would rejoice them more than our whole government laid to ashes."[18]

Business closed, homeowners locked their doors. The Democratic State Convention convened at Harrisburg, where Governor Curtin had assembled a militia of fifteen thousand troops to defend the capital, on Tuesday, June 16. The convention's primary platform was an end to the war, which soon spelled the end of their party's revitalization.[19]

On the eve of such activity, the men involved in the *Jeffersonian's* case were at the center of the state elections, and the case became an election topic for the Democratic Party. In June, former Pennsylvania chief justice George Woodward and current chief justice Walter Lowrie were put up at the Democratic convention in Harrisburg for the positions of governor and judge of the supreme court. Woodward had lost his first attempt in 1860, but now returned with renewed vigor. Within the resolutions adopted was the accusation that the president was arresting "citizens for the expression of honest opinions, and that he delegates this power to others, a large proportion of whom must, in the nature of things be incapable of wielding it honestly or wisely." Furthermore, that "those who attempt to suppress books and newspaper by violence are the enemies of a free government."[20]

Woodward and Lowrie, as would others, used the *Jeffersonian* as a campaign weapon.

Stumping for Woodward and Lowrie, Congressman J. Ross Snowden invoked Lowrie's verdict to a Philadelphia crowd in September 1863. A recent proclamation by Lincoln nationalizing the suspension of the writ of habeas corpus was being celebrated in Republican papers. Despite the president's continuing outrages against the people, Snowden quoted Judge Lowrie from earlier that year when he reminded the *Jeffersonian* jury and all in the courtroom that "all public functionaries in this land are under law, and that none from the highest to the lowest, are above it."[21]

But despite gaining considerable ground in early 1863, the death knell to Philadelphia Democrats was not politics, which they were winning. Their fate was determined on the battlefield. For three days beginning on July 1, 1863, Union and Confederate armies clashed in the Pennsylvania town of Gettysburg. On the third day, Confederate general George Pickett sent twelve thousand solders over an open field in a final attempt to assault and break the Union lines. In many ways, the results of the October elections in Pennsylvania also rested on the result. Pickett's men were mercilessly destroyed, and with it the vision of an America shared by William Reed, John Hodgson, and others also destroyed.

Philadelphia's Democratic Party never recovered after Gettysburg. Woodward lost the election by 15,825 votes to Republican incumbent Andrew Curtin. After twelve years on the supreme court of Pennsylvania, and six years as chief justice, Walter Lowrie lost his seat by one vote of the state Senate, and four votes in the House. Losing the election, his term ended in December 1863.[22]

Before leaving the bench, the supreme court had one more critical piece of business. Lowrie would attempt to undermine the Lincoln administration one last time, this time voting on the merits of the Conscription Act, which had been passed in March 1863, inaugurating the first draft of the war and resulting in the infamous New York Draft Riots in July. After review, the Pennsylvania supreme court ruled Lincoln's Conscription Act unconstitutional by a margin of three to two. But the judgment stood for only the briefest of time. In January 1864, with Lowrie now gone, again by a vote of three to two, the court reversed itself, and Lowrie's influence on the wartime bench disappeared.[23]

Many Democrats, even the most extreme of the party who despised Lincoln with their very being, by 1863 considered him a pawn being played by stronger forces in the Republican party. There was the patronage wing of the party, lead by the likes of Weed and Chase, and the radicals in Congress who with men like Benjamin Wade intensely disliked the president.

While stumping for Woodward and Lowrie in Philadelphia just prior to the state elections, Snowden concluded his remarks by citing Lowrie's verdict for the *Jeffersonian* and discussing the hope of a new country reestablished on constitutional law. Snowden, as had John Hodgson, thought that Lincoln had "not the power of ubiquity nor omniscience. He cannot know what his numerous subordinates, in different parts of our extended country, are doing in his name and by his authority."

Amazingly, throughout the bitter conflict of the previous two years between North and South, and between the South and itself, constitutional law had survived in its ultimate form. To conclude, Snowden echoed the statements of Lincoln two years prior when he addressed an emergency session of Congress on July 4, 1861. Said Snowden, "And above all, in the present crisis of our public affairs, we have the right of the ballot. Let us see to it that this right is exercised at the next election. It is a right sacred to freedom, and formidable to tyrants only. It is now our only hope for the future."[24]

Despite the many ways in which his writings were morally repulsive, John Hodgson was the saving grace for many a man during the Civil War. Like those dying in nearby battlefields, Hodgson was willing to defend his principles to the death. His perseverance proved a catalyst for men of political and social importance who could make his local battle a national fight for all of the principles the country once stood for. He was the voice that brought William Reed from retirement, George Biddle to professional fame, James Wall into the national debate, and exposed the hypocrisies of John Hickman and John Forney.

Hodgson's trial was indeed a test case, which, despite the tragedy of the war, represented everything good about the country. It was a victory for due process, an argument for the importance of elections, and a reminder that in the United States, revolution was not only four years away, but a process that occurred at the ballot box, not on the streets by force of mob.

The Democratic Party did not unseat the Republican governor in Pennsylvania, nor in Maryland, nor could they inspire the people to replace President Lincoln with General George McClellan in 1864. But what they—and we—did win was the ultimate victory of due process and the rights of those out of power. For that we should all remember their struggle with gratitude.

Epilogue

I t is said that little can be added to the examination of Abraham Lincoln. The body of literature suggests otherwise regarding the suppression of antiwar newspapers. When the issue is discussed in a secondary sort of manner, Abraham Lincoln has emerged unscathed by the verdict of most historians. Many ignore the issue, but those who do forgive him or excuse his actions.

Certainly he was familiar with the mob activity against the antiwar newspapers, with the activities of Seward, Cameron, Blair, and later Stanton, but was calculating enough to keep his distance. Lincoln was not unaware of what was taking place in his administration regarding the loyal opposition, as he received many letters from editors and citizens berating him for arrests and seizures, and met with the wives of some held in the federal jails. But the president chose not to get involved, which was likely what allowed marshals and district attorneys to enforce their own type of law in support of the Union cause.

Many, including Hodgson, came to blame Secretary of State Seward as being the architect of the summer of rage, and for the general chaos that allowed more corrupt politicians to settle old scores under the cover of war. Wrote Hodgson, "Seward was, we believe, the first member of the cabinet to order the arrest of citizens without warrant, and Weed sustained him in it."[25]

In the end, Lincoln achieved his goal at whatever the cost: the Union had been saved. And Hodgson might have realized that he had written incorrectly about the elasticity of the Constitution. Many of the freedoms taken away under the president did return as the threat of war subsided. On the other hand, history should well remember the only president in office during an American Civil War as having blinked when it came to having faith in the power of democracy to restore citizens' respect in our system of government.

And history can do worse than remember John Hodgson as a patriot who never feared that America suffered from too much democracy.

After the war, William Bradford Reed was retained to defend Confederate president Jefferson Davis, but Davis never went to trial. Reed continued to practice law in Philadelphia, and was a frequent contributor to several newspapers and journals. After salacious stories spread of the lawyer trying to cheat his clients out of money, Reed left Philadelphia for New York, where he wrote for the *New York World*. He continued to defend the embattled reputation of his grandfather, Revolutionary War hero General Joseph Reed. A defense of his own activities, it seemed, was useless. He was an estranged man who began again to publish anonymously even while in New York. While living there, writing for newspapers became his only source of income. Reed died in New York on February 18, 1876, "overcome by the disasters which beclouded the last years of his life."[26]

George Washington Biddle's best years were still before him. By the early 1870s he was one of the most prosperous lawyers in the city.[27] Despite rakish editorials alongside Reed in the *Philadelphia Age* throughout the remainder of the war, he went on to leave his Southern sympathies behind, becoming a member of the Pennsylvania Constitutional Convention in 1872–1873. Soon after, he represented the United States in a dispute with Great Britain over the Bering Sea. Later in his career, from 1880–1891, he served the prestigious position of chancellor of the Philadelphia Bar Association.[28]

John Forney's Philadelphia organ *The Press* gave the *Jeffersonian* case the greatest coverage of any newspaper. Of the verdict, Forney thought Judge Lowrie misguided, for when a writer provokes the wrath of a state "menaced with invasion," he wrote, surely it authorized "the persons whose safety he endangers, to take the law in their own hands, and to redress one wrong by another."[29]

Of everyone, John Forney reaped the most reward from the censorship of the *Jeffersonian* and other democratic newspapers. Forney's relationship with President Lincoln continued to blossom and his power in Washington and Philadelphia grew exponentially in the final years of the war. In May 1863, he provided Lincoln with a summary of his success. "I was compelled to leave Washington more than a week ago for the purpose of looking after the supply of new presses and engine required by the *Chronicle* in the office I'm erecting.... The *Chronicle* never was more powerfully and ably conducted, than during the last week as its circulation of twenty-five thousand daily proves."[30]

Forney remained an ardent supporter of Lincoln until his death in April 1865, but without his benefactor, the editor had a difficult time maintaining the empire he had created in Washington. In 1867,

Forney wrote a frustrated letter to Senator William Fessenden, angry that the Johnson administration was not supporting the *Chronicle*. Citing his paper as during the rebellion being a "faithful and fearless organ of the Republican party," Forney wanted Congress to transfer the publication of congressional activities from the *Globe* to the *Chronicle*. "All that Congress has to decide is to change its patronage from those who are indifferent or hostile to those who are earnestly and fervently its supporters."[31]

Nor did Forney ever seem to change his tactics. In April of 1868 during the impeachment trial of Andrew Johnson, the president bitterly told a reporter that "Forney had always been after some favor." Forney, according to President Johnson, had told him that the Lincoln administration had not rewarded his support with sufficient patronage, and the newspaper man asked for greater control over the congressional patronage.

In 1870, Forney sold the *Chronicle* and returned to Philadelphia. Over the next eleven years he founded a weekly magazine, called *Progress,* and wrote three books: *The Life and Military Career of Winfield Scott Hancock* (1880), *Anecdotes of Public Men* (2 volumes, 1873–1881), and *The New Nobility* (1881). Forney wrote until the very end, finishing his last two works just before his death in December 1881. Ironically, he had abandoned the Republican Party and died a Democrat.[32]

John Hickman declined renomination to the United States House of Representatives in late 1862, returning to West Chester to practice law. His final days in Washington fell a month after the Hodgsons were vindicated in the Philadelphia courtroom. In 1869, Hickman returned to government in the Pennsylvania House of Representatives. Hickman died in West Chester, his home for sixty-five years, in 1875. Hickman was never officially accused of coordinating the mob attack on the *Jeffersonian,* despite swirling rumors, and there is no written evidence tying him to either the mobbing or the seizure of the paper. The lack of any traditional paper trail from the Executive Mansion to the local Philadelphia government officials may suggest that Hodgson was right all along: Hickman and others were out to get him.

Despite their Pennsylvania supreme court victory, *The United States of America vs. the Jeffersonian Newspaper* did not end in Philadelphia. "So the case of Hodgson will be tried under the law of Congress known as the Indemnity Law, which provides for the trial of alleged trespasses by U.S. officers in the U.S. courts," it was reported in May 1863.[33]

Meanwhile, though being unimpeded physically, the Hodgsons continued to be newspaper fodder throughout the duration of the war. In May 1864, the *Village Record* accused the *Jeffersonian* of being the most "venomous enemy of the government" during the war and the most "sincere friend of the Rebel cause." A few months later, the Hodgsons "incited the basest scoundrels in the community to incendiarism." They, of course, returned every shot.[34]

Immediately after their victory in the Pennsylvania supreme court, an appeal was filed and granted on behalf of the defense. One and a half years later, in October 1864, the Hodgsons found themselves in a United States criminal court, once again defending their property. The case was argued under the Indemnity Law, which was created by Congress to try cases of alleged trespass in federal, not state, courts. The burden of proof, however, had not changed. Still at the center of debate was who had ordered the seizure. Like Lowrie before him, Judge Grier determined that "there was no justification for the seizure, that the district attorney had no power to issue a writ, ordering or requesting the seizure, and the marshal had no business to act in compliance with the request of that officer." All in all, the power to issue writs belong to the courts, he told the jury.

The jury deliberated overnight, and the following day again ruled in favor of the *Jeffersonian,* awarding damages in the amount of $501.[35]

According to the *Jeffersonian,* Chief Justice Grier admitted that there was "no evidence of malice but some evidence that the district attorney did this to satisfy some people out of doors." It was as close to a conspiracy on the part of John Hickman and John Forney as the Hodgsons ever proved.[36]

Through the end of the war, the *Jeffersonian* refused to tone down its columns. It was reported that the only newspaper in the state of Pennsylvania not to mourn the death of President Lincoln was the *Jeffersonian.* Hodgson displayed no flag, despite a general call made by the mayor of Philadelphia. Even the *Age* printed gracious words for the fallen president. Not Hodgson. His response was that when the *Age* hung a flag at half mast draped in black, it so incensed local abolitionists that they threatened to tear the office apart. "We were also threatened," wrote Hodgson.[37]

Yet still the Hodgson family emerges from the chaos of the war.

John Hodgson remained active in the Democratic Party, continuing his presence at the *Jeffersonian* almost until his death in 1877. He turned over formal control of the paper to his sons in 1865, but could not leave behind the business. Just before his death in 1877, he moved to Chester and started a new paper, the *Times.* He had out-lived all of his children except for William (Charles died in a train accident in 1876). Even a dry obituary captured well the image of the man, revealing that "Mr. Hodgson was essentially a newspaper man; one who lived the duties pertaining to a newspaper office. As a writer he was forcible and pointed, and his readers always understood the meaning of his articles."[38]

Aside from thousands of newspaper articles written over a thirty-five-year period with the *Jeffersonian* and his efforts to gain a verdict against the United States for the suppression of his paper, almost nothing is remembered of his life, and the test case for freedom of the press under Abraham Lincoln, no matter how repugnant the newspaper involved, soon became forgotten.

William Hodgson did equally as well—if not better—than his father.

A pamphlet published in 1942 by the *Daily Local News* sought to tell the story of the "House of Hodgson."

The lively tone of the brochure was all about celebrating a journalist family that had, at that point, survived more than one hundred years in the same area of the country. The brochure, of course, had nothing but good things to say. Readers in 1942 were introduced to vintage John Hodgson ("The Brave Pioneering Publisher") when it was written that "he was thirty-five-years-old when he founded the '*Jeff*,' and feared no one. And while his expressed views won the admiration of many, this more often created lifelong enemies." But the brochure does not really say why John Hodgson was brave. Nor whom his enemies were.

As indicated by the World War II era brochure, William Hodgson enjoyed a long and prosperous newspaper career in West Chester. The *Jeffersonian* remained in operation until it was succeeded by the *Daily Local News* in 1872, "the only daily in a Republican stronghold."[39] Hodgson was known for showing such generosity to his workers that one story says that when union organizers attempted to recruit at West Chester, several of Hodgsons employees told them to go home because they were already cared for. Near the end of his life he was featured in *The American Magazine,* where he was "shocked to find that he had been flaunted as a Santa Claus."[40] Hodgson died on October 18, 1917, in West Chester at the age of eighty-seven, a loyal Democrat to the end. His newspaper lineage continues today in suburban Philadelphia.

The editors, writers, and publishers who formed the loyal opposition to Lincoln have been forgotten by history. Associations devoted to freedom of the press, to journalists during the war, to newspapers published under duress, make no mention of the men and sometimes women who published what they believed.

In 1862 and 1863, a wave of books and periodicals by the editors and writers who had been jailed for their beliefs were published, mostly in Baltimore and Philadelphia, but within a few years the story was largely swept away. Men like James Wall and Judge Lowrie, had they supported the administration in the face of the same personal danger would be well studied today by historians. And W. B. Reed would certainly have a place in our proud history of defending the most unpopular of causes.

The role of the media had changed as dramatically as the landscape of the country during the nineteenth century. The mutually beneficial relationship between editor and politician remains, but the nature of the press, namely its accountability to the public, is the ultimate outcome. Yet still the powers of the president to censor the press, especially in times of national crisis, will continue to draw fiery debate from those opposed to the administration in power, just as it did during the infancy of America's press.

Of all the final comments of that turbulent era when newspaper freedoms became a battleground, the most succinct and honest was given by the son of John Hodgson, writing in his final published piece.

In his last will and testament, William Hodgson gave what many of his father's era, including Abraham Lincoln, might have taken as very good advice. Regarding his successful *Daily Local News,* the veteran by now of two eras of American journalism wrote:

> I desire that the paper shall continue to be non-partisan and non-sectarian, and strongly advise and desire that no employee of the corporation shall be actively engaged in politics or hold public office.

William Hodgson had seen as a young man the bitter consequences of the unhealthy marriage between publishers and politicians that reached its zenith with the Lincoln administration and wanted no part of that ever to return to his family's newspaper business.

Good advice, indeed.

THE FULL TEXT OF JUDGE LOWRIE'S CHARGE TO THE JURY

It is not at all strange that, in times of national crisis, and of national and popular disturbance and excitement, we find ourselves forced to revert to first principals in the discussion of cases, which, in ordinary times and rising among ordinary persons, could be disposed of with accuracy and dispatched by a simple justice of the peace. This case is one of that character.

We should not think of granting it anything but the utmost summary treatment, were it not that it grows of the very natural excitement that overspread the country in the breaking out of the present rebellion; and that the actors in it are important officers of the federal government who claim to have acted under the authority of a law of Congress and under the special authority of the president of the United States and in support of the Constitution and law, and of the safety and integrity of the Union.

These circumstances are quite unusual in an action of trespass for taking the property of a citizen and they seem to us to justify the parties in expecting for the case a more than ordinary degree of consideration.

So far as this case is ordinary it serves only an ordinary consideration: but so far as it involves circumstances that are unusual and extraordinary it serves something more. Let us consider how far these extraordinary circumstances affect the case or the law that is to be applied to it:

The rebellion is the first extraordinary element in this case; but no one can pretend that our law was changed by the mere fact of the rebellion, so far as it relates to the rights that now claim to be vindicated by us. No doubt that rebellion gave rise to an immense popular excitement that was quite natural and inevitable; we should be more or less than men if it had not arisen. No doubt also that excitement gave rise to great popular mistrust and suspicion towards all who seemed to oppose or discourage its great purpose of crushing the rebellion; it also was quite natural and inevitable.

A very earnest loyalty is quite liable to run to an extreme that is a strain upon the law. No doubt also this distrust would soon be visited upon those who, for any reason, should seriously question the most summary plans for suppressing the rebellion, for when people are exited they are sure to be impatient, and censorious of all plans that do not seem to them to promise the most speedy and summary success. We are not, in such circumstances, prepared to submit to the control of the law of the land and to those perpetual concessions to general opinion that are essential to harmonious social action, and, our distrust and suspicions are very apt to breed discord among us, and we ought to expect this and to know how to meet it consistently with social order. But we do not. By a natural law of such occasion, suspicions, slanders, oppressions, and violence are sure to arise and many things are said and done which the law of the land forbids, and which, under other circumstances, sound morality would condemn, though a liberal charity might overlook them.

But none of these circumstances can at all change the Constitution or laws of the land. The very purpose of law is to set a rule that shall remain fixed and immovable among the disturbances of society and that shall be the standard for judging them. Law does change in adaptation to the growth of a people: but if it adapted itself to all their excitement it would cease to be law.

The next important element in this case is the alleged fact that the act complained of was authorized by the president of the United States and was executed by important federal officers. But this element loses all its legal importance when we consider that all public functionaries in this land are under law and that none, from the highest to the lowest, are above it.

They, as well as we, are under the Constitution and laws of the United States and sworn to support, protect, and defend them, or take them as their rule of civil and official conduct, and they, and we, are to be judged by them in our civil and official conduct in all appropriate cases. The acts of the president and of his subordinates are, therefore without right unless they are authorized by some article of the Constitution or if the laws made under it are consistent with it.

We can make no laws that can vest in him any new authority or that can protect those who obey his unauthorized orders. He would not claim that he could.

Let us concede the maxim that circumstance alters cases and even the law that governs cases. But let us not be misled by it. In a certain sense, the law of self-defense changes according to the violence and nature of the attack or the danger, that is, the law allows self-defense and allows that it shall be so conducted that it shall be adequate to the emergency according to the best judgment of the person attacked; and thus it sanctions acts that, under other circumstances, it would condemn.

But then it never leaves it to any one to judge finally for himself, where the right of self-defense arises or when the danger is such that the attack of self-defense may begin. The law of the land alone can settle that. He who enforces rights without the aid of law, must both prove that he has such rights by law and that they are exposed to a danger that cannot safely await the regular forms of legal process.

A man who is caught committing theft, burglary, murder, and such like may be arrested by any one without legal process, because of the emergency: but then he must be placed in the regular road to a speedy trial, and to justify the arrest, the crime charged must be proved.

We shall have some use of these thoughts hereafter, but the use I want to make of them now is this. The federal and state constitutions place the government under just such restrictions as these. It tells the government how it shall proceed in defending society, and the social organism against all the forms of violence, disorder, and damages to which society is exposed. It puts all its functionaries under law so that they shall not invade the order of society by taking their own forms and modes of protecting it.

When they act without laws, they must justify themselves before the law by proving an emergency that demands their act. If it be not so then, they are above law.

If they may irresponsibly declare the existence of the emergency and also the acts which it demands of them, then as to them we have neither Constitution nor laws. Our Constitution was framed when the remembrance of the excitements, suspicions, divisions, disloyalty, and reasons for the Revolution were yet fresh in the minds of our statesman. And under the lights of all its experience, and they left no gap in it to be supplied by the fears or suspicions of excited times. It is still a sufficient rule of practice for our government, and it, better than anything else, embodies the settled and somber thought of this people. When we depart from it we expose ourselves to the rule of force, and to incalculable divisions of opinion, of counsel, and of action.

And now it is proper for me to say that I see no sufficient evidence that the president of the United States authorized the seizure complained of there. I think it entirely improbable that he did. The district attorney thinks his dispatch came from someone in the War Department. This is no evidence of an order from the president and that element is therefore entirely out of the case.

And all these elements being removed, the case becomes the very common one in which it is alleged that a public officer has seized the goods of a citizen without proper warrant. It is common against both federal and state officers. We have had many of them. On an order issued by the district Attorney the defendants, the marshall and his deputies, seized upon the office of the plaintiff's newspaper called the *Jeffersonian* and on all its contents for some supposed violation of laws, and afterwards the property was proceeded against for the forfeiture in the U.S. court, and was soon abandoned by the district attorney.

What the law requires in order to justify such an act is written in the Constitution. Article IV of the amendments, "The right of the people to be secure in their persons, houses, papers, and effects against unreasonable searches and seizures, shall not be violated, and no warrants shall issue but upon probable cause supported by oath or affirmation and particularly describing the place to be searched and the person or things to be seized." A similar law is written in all of our state constitutions and it is implied the written expression of the unwritten or customary law of the people, known to everybody descended through a long line of ancestry and of popular disturbances and recognized by everybody in times when a quiet reason holds the control for the passions.

Another law is to be connected with this one in order that it maybe be seen how such warrants are to be issued. It also is written in the Constitution, where it rests all judicial powers in the courts established by law, and requires that no man shall be deprived of life, liberty, or property, except by due process of laws. This makes the courts the only authority, whence any process can issue for the trial of rights or wrongs. Warrants properly issued by them are a shield to the officer who executes them. Warrants issued by others have no further authority.

When a great conflagration or a violent mob is ranging, there is no time for warrants, and the necessary work must be done without them. But then it is always done under responsibility to law through-out the court of justice. If the occasion and the law of the land justify what is done then the want of a warrant is excused.

We understand now the case we have before us. The defendants had no such warrant as required by the Constitution.

There is nothing in the Act of Congress of the 6th August 1861 that justifies it. It requires the president in certain cases to cause certain property to be seized, confiscated and condemned but this means by due process of law. It is not to be done by the president himself but by due process of law by the proper functionaries and he is to see that they do their duty.

These defendants undertook to do this act without warrant and without any proper occasion shown to us, and therefore they are mere trespassers. They are trespassers from the beginning to the end, and the first step in the matter being unjustified, no subsequent and unsuccessful proceedings under the act of 1861 can shelter them from liability for compensation. They would have been liable for malicious prosecution without probable cause, if the act had been under a warrant apparently valid. The plaintiff is entitled to full compensation for all that he has lost by their act.

Is the plaintiff entitled to exemplary damages? Yes! In so far as their act was inspired by mere wantonness. But exemplary or punitive damages are usually allowed, rather for the moral, than the legal, wrong that accompanies such acts. For the legal wrong, compensation is the measure of redress. For the moral wrong, the recklessness of the act, the personal malice, with which it is done, the violence and outrage attending it, for this you are authorized to allow exemplary damages, such as are reasonable under all the circumstances.

You must judge how far the defendants are guilty of any moral wrong beyond the legal wrong in the act complained of. It was not done on their notion or to gratify any selfish motive of theirs but under the apparent authority of their official superiors. Moreover, they did it partly under the influence of a widespread popular excitement, which was not chargeable to them.

We are all liable to such influences and very few of us, none of us, I should rather say, are able to resist them.

We should not be social beings at all if we should resist them all. We naturally should not be worthy of society if we did not. And yet we are entitled to rise above common opinion if we can: and when we do, we cannot better show that we have done so than by still expecting the common opinions of society.

In so far as the defendants acted under the influence of the widespread popular excitement, and not from mere personal motives, they are entitled to the benefit of it in mitigation of the exemplary damages you may be disposed to allow; not however to affect the plaintiffs right to full compensation for the actual loss sustained by him.

All that I have now said is in the exact line of the Constitution and statutes of the land, and of all the decision under them and under the principles of the common law (many of which you have heard and read) and a little while ago it would have been recognized by every body as the plain law of the land. I am not sure that it will do so now if the passions of men make the law.

But if the law of the land is the sober and abiding thought of the whole people, that lives through all disorders and excitements and judges them all, the strong ocean undercurrent of thought to which storms and tides and tempests do not reach—then what I have said is the law still. I know of no other law for this case. This is the law, and the plaintiff is entitled to damages—compensation if the defendants acted in good faith and under a mere mistake of authority and exemplary, if there was any bad faith intended in their act.

The case is now in your hands, gentleman, and I am sure you will dispose of it in such a way that, long as you may live and I hope it may be long, you will never have reason to regret the part you have had in it.

The damages you may give are of no sort of importance compared with the decision upon principles that has devolved upon me.

ABOUT THE AUTHORS

Jeffrey Manber has written extensively on America's role in shaping technology policy and on relations with Russia. He became immersed in the social and political issues surrounding the Lincoln administration more than ten years ago. Taking advantage of his proximity to the Library of Congress, he spent evenings reading the forgotten antiwar newspapers of the Union. After the attacks of September 11, the debate surrounding the elasticity of the Constitution during the Civil War took on a startling relevance. Now dividing his time equally between London and Virginia with his wife, Dana, he speaks and writes on the paradoxes of America's role in the world today.

A graduate of Monmouth College (IL) and Eastern Illinois University, Neil Dahlstrom is the co-author of *The John Deere Story: A Biography of Plowmakers John and Charles Deere.* He has worked in archives in both Virginia and Illinois, and has conducted extensive research into Civil War prisons and civilian life during the war. He is currently reference archivist at the Deere & Company corporate archives. He lives with his wife, Karen, in Moline, Illinois.

BIBLIOGRAPHY

Manuscript Repositories/Collections

Burlington County Historical Society, Burlington, New Jersey

Chester County Archives and Records Services, West Chester, Pennsylvania

Chester County Historical Society, West Chester, Pennsylvania

Historical Society of Pennsylvania, Philadelphia, Pennsylvania

    George W. Fahnstock Diary

Library of Congress, Washington, DC

    John Wein Forney papers, 1841–76

    William Henry Seward papers, 1831–71

    Edwin McMasters Stanton papers, 1831–70

    James Gordon Bennett papers, 1845–1931

    Simon Cameron papers, 1738–1889

    Edward Bates papers, 1859–66

    John Adams Dix papers, 1863–1873

    Abraham Lincoln papers, 1833–1916

New York Public Library

    Thomas Kinsella Scrapbook

The Rosenbach Museum & Library, Philadelphia, Pennsylvania

University of Delaware, Wilmington, Delaware

Biddle Family papers (MS 327)

Unpublished Sources in Private Possession

A. J. Juckett letters, Lynn K. Juckett, Battle Creek, MI

William Bradford Reed Manuscript, untitled, Jeffrey Manber

Articles

Abrams, Ray H. "The Jeffersonian, Copperhead Newspaper," *Pennsylvania Magazine of History and Biography,* vol. 57, 1933.

Luthin, Reinhard H. "A Discordant Chapter in Lincoln's Administration: The Davis Blair Controversy," *Maryland Historical Magazine,* March 1944.

Matthews, Sidney T. "Control of the Baltimore Press during the Civil War," *Maryland Historical Magazine,* Vol. XXXVI, June 1941.

Robinson, Elwin Burns. "The Press: President Lincoln's Philadelphia Organ," *The Philadelphia Magazine of History and Biography,* LXV, 1941.

Schankman, Arnold. "William B. Reed During the Civil War," *Pennsylvania History.*

Sears, Stephen W. "The First News Blackout." *Civil War Chronicles,* Winter 1994.

Seiter, John Reid. "Union City: Philadelphia and the Battle of Gettysburg," *Gettysburg Magazine,* 21, July 1999.

St. John, Gerard. "This is My Bar," *The Philadelphia Lawyer,* Winter 2002, Vol. 64, No. 4.

Wainwright, Nicholas. "Loyal Opposition in Philadelphia," *Journal of Pennsylvania History and Biography,* July 1964.

Reference Sources

American Annual Cyclopedia and Register of Important Events (New York: D. Appleton & Company, Inc., 1862–1866).

Biographical Dictionary of the United States Congress, 1774–1989, Bicentennial Edition (Washington, DC: United States Government Printing, 1988).

Bowman, John S., general editor. *Encyclopedia of the Civil War* (Greenwich, Connecticut: Brompton Books, 1992).

Hay, John and Nicolay. *Abraham Lincoln: Complete Works,* 2 volumes (New York: The Century Company, 1902).

Howell, George P. *Centennial Newspaper Exhibit, 1876. A Complete List of American Newspapers.* A Statement of the Industries, Characteristics, Population and Location of Towns in Which They are Published; Also, A Descriptive Account of the Great Newspapers of the Day (New York: Howell & Company, 1876).

Johnson, Allen and Dumas Malone, editors. *Dictionary of American Biography* (New York: Charles Scribner's Sons, 1931).

Kunhardt, Jr., Philip B, Philip B. Kunhardt, II, and Peter W. Kunhardt. *Lincoln: An Illustrated Biography* (New York: Portland House, 1992).

Lee, Richard M. *Mr. Lincoln's City: An Illustrated Guide to the Civil War Sites of Washington* (McLean, VA: EPM Publications, Inc., 1981).

Lincoln, Abraham. *The Collected Works of Abraham Lincoln,* Roy Basler, ed. (New Brunswick, NJ: Rutgers University Press, 1953).

Long, E.B., with Barbara Long. *The Civil War Day by Day* (Garden City, NY: Doubleday & Company, 1971).

Miers, Earl Schenck, editor-in-chief. *Lincoln Day By Day: A Chronology: 1809–1865* (Washington: Lincoln Sesquicentennial Commission, 1960).

Neely, Jr., Mark E. *The Abraham Lincoln Encyclopedia* (New York: Da Capo, 1982).

The War of the Rebellion: A Compilation of the Official Records of the Union and Confederate Armies (Washington: United States Government Printing Office, 1901).

Books

Andrews, J. Cutler. *The North Reports the Civil War* (Pittsburgh, PA: University of Pittsburgh Press, 1985).

Andrews, J. Cutler. *The South Reports the Civil War* (New Jersey: Princeton University Press, 1970).

Baldasty, Gerald J. *The Commercialization of News in the Nineteenth Century* (Madison, WI: University of Wisconsin Press,, 1992).

Beale, Howard K., editor. *The Diary of Edward Bates, 1859–1866* (Washington, DC: United States Government Printing Office, 1933).

Blue, Frederick J. *Salmon P. Chase: A Life in Politics* (Kent, OH: The Kent State University Press, 1987).

Burlingame, Michael, and John R. Turner Ettlinger, editors. *Inside Lincoln's White House: The Complete Civil War Diary of John Hay* (Carbondale and Edwardsville, IL: Southern Illinois University Press, 1997).

Burt, Nathaniel. *The Perennial Philadelphians: The Anatomy of an American Aristocracy* (Boston: Little, Brown and Company, 1963).

Carter, Hodding. *Their Words Were Bullets: The Southern Press in War, Reconstruction, and Peace* (Athens, GA: University of Georgia Press, 1969).

Chittenden, L[ucius] E. *Recollections of President Lincoln* (New York: Harper & Brothers, 1891).

Dix, Morgan. *Memoirs of John Adams Dix* (New York: Hasper & Brothers, 1888).

Donald, David, editor. *Inside Lincoln's Cabinet: The Civil War Diaries of Salmon P. Chase* (New York: Longmans, Green and Co., 1954).

Donald, David, editor. *Liberty and Union* (Boston: Little, Brown and Company, 1978).

Donald, David. *Lincoln* (New York: Simon & Schuster, 1995).

Dusinberre, William. *Civil War Issues in Philadelphia, 1856–1865* (University of Pennsylvania Press: 1965).

Gallman, J. Matthew. *Mastering Wartime: A Social History of Philadelphia During the Civil War* (Philadelphia: University of Pennsylvania Press, 2000).

Greeley, Horace. *The American Conflict: A History of the Great Rebellion in the United States of America, 1860–1864* (Hartford: O.D. Case & Company, 1867).

Hale, William Harlan. *Horace Greeley: Voice of the People* (New York: Harper and Brothers, 1950).

Handlin, Oscar and Lilian. *Liberty in America: 1600 to the Present* (New York: Harper & Row, 1986).

Harper, Douglas R. *West Chester to 1865: That Elegant & Notorious Place* (West Chester, PA: Chester County Historical Society, 1999).

Harper, Robert S. *Lincoln and the Press* (New York: MacGraw-Hill Book Company, Inc., 1951).

Harris, Brayton. *Blue and Gray in Black and White* (Dulles, VA: Brassey's, Inc., 1999).

Hendrick, Burton. *Inside Lincoln's Cabinet* (Boston: Little, Brown and Company, 1946).

History of the Hodgson Family: 1665–1892 (Coatesville, PA: Union Print, 1892).

Holzer, Harold. *Lincoln at Cooper Union: The Speech that Made Abraham Lincoln President* (New York: Simon & Schuster, 2004).

Howard, McHenry, ed. *James Robertson, Jr. Recollections of a Maryland Confederate Soldier and Staff Officer Under Johnston, Jackson and Lee* (Dayton, OH: Morningside Bookshop, 1975).

Huntzicker, William E. *The Popular Press, 1833–1865* (Westport, CT: Greenwood Press, 1999).

Isely, Jeter Allen. *Horace Greeley and the Republican Party, 1853–1861: A Study of The New York Tribune* (Princeton, NJ: Princeton University Press, 1947).

Johnson, Allen and Dumas Malone. *Dictionary of American Biography* (New York: Charles Scribner's Sons, 1931).

MacElree, Wilmer W. *Sidelights on the Bench and Bar of Chester County* (West Chester, PA: 1918).

Maihafer, Harry J. *War of Words: Abraham Lincoln and the Civil War Press* (Washington: Brassey's Inc.: 2001).

McCormack, Thomas J., ed. *Memoirs of Gustave Koerner, 1809–1896: Life Sketches Written at the Suggestion of His Children,* 2 volumes (Cedar Rapids, IA: The Torch Press, 1909).

McPherson, Edward. *The Political History of the United States of America During the Great Rebellion, 1860–1865* (New York: Da Capo Press, 1972).

Marshall, John A. *American Bastille: A History of the Illegal Arrests and Imprisonment of American Citizens During the Late Civil War* (Philadelphia, PA: Thomas W.

Hartley, 1876).

Miller, William Lee. *Lincoln's Virtues: An Ethical Biography* (New York: Alfred A. Knopf, 2002).

Mitgang, Herbert, editor. *Abraham Lincoln: A Press Portrait, His Life and Times from the Original Newspaper Documents of the Union, the Confederacy, and Europe* (Chicago: Quadrangle Books, 1971).

Neeley, Jr., Mark E. *The Fate of Liberty: Abraham Lincoln and Civil Liberties* (New York: Oxford University Press, 1991).

Neeley, Jr., Mark E. *The Union Divided: Party Conflict in the Civil War North* (Cambridge, MA: Harvard University Press, 2002).

Onarato, Michael Paul. *The Mission of William B. Reed, United States Minister to China, 18571858* (Washington, DC: Dissertation, Graduate School of Georgetown University, June 1959).

Paludan, Phillip Shaw. *A People's Contest: The Union and Civil War, 1861–1865* (New York: Harper & Row, 1988).

Paludan, Phillip Shaw. *The Presidency of Abraham Lincoln* (Lawrence, KS: University Press of Kansas, 1994).

Randall, J.G. *Constitutional Problems Under Lincoln* (Urbana, IL: University of Illinois Press, 1951).

Randall, J.G. *Lincoln the President* (New York: Dodd, Mead & Company, 1952).

Rehnquist, William H. *All The Laws But One: Civil Liberties in Wartime* (New York: Vintage Books, 2000).

Scharf, J. Thomas. *History of Baltimore City and County* (Baltimore: Regional Publishing Company, 1971).

Shultz, William J., and M.R. Caine. *Financial Development of the United States* (New York: Prentice Hall, Inc., 1937).

Schooler, Alice Kent. *Livable West Chester: An Architectural Overview* (West Chester, PA: Chester County Historical Society, 1985).

Sheeds, Scott Sumpter, and Daniel Carroll Toomey. *Baltimore During the Civil War* (Linthicum, MD: Toomey Press, 1997).

Sidali, Silvana R. *From Property to Person: Slavery and the Confiscation Acts, 1861–1862* (Baton Rouge: Louisiana State University Press, 2005).

Smith, Jeffrey. *War and Press Freedom: The Problem of Prerogative Power* (New York: Oxford University Press, 1999).

Speer, Lonnie R. *Portals to Hell: Military Prisons During the Civil War* (Mechanicsburg, PA: Stackpole Books, 1997).

Stevens, Sylvester K. *Pennsylvania: Birthplace of a Nation* (New York: Random House, 1967).

Tebbel, John, and Sarah Miles Watts. *The Press and the Presidency: From George Washington to Ronald Reagan* (New York: Oxford University Press, 1985).

Thomas, Benjamin P. *Abraham Lincoln: A Biography* (New York: Alfred A. Knopf, 1952).

Urban, John W. *In Defense of the Union; or Through Shot and Shell and Prison Pen* (Monarch Book Company, 1887).

Van Deusen, Glyndon G. *Thurlow Weed: Wizard of the Lobby* (Boston: Little, Brown and Company, 1947).

Van Deusen, Glyndon G. *William Henry Seward: Lincoln's Secretary of State, the Negotiator of the Alaska Purchase* (New York: Oxford University Press, 1967).

Volo, Dorothy Denneen, and James M. Volo. *Daily Life in Civil War America* (Westport, CT: Greenwood Press, 1988).

Weed, Harriet A., editor. *Autobiography of Thurlow Weed* (Boston: Houghton, Mifflin and Company, 1884).

Weisberger, Bernard A. *Reporters for the Union: How the Robust and Opinionated War Correspondent, Soldiering with the Civil War Armies, Got His News—and Became a New American Character* (Boston: Little, Brown and Company, 1953).

Welles, Gideon. *Lincoln and Seward: Remarks upon the Memorial Address of Chas. Francis Adams, on the Late Wm. H. Seward* (New York: Sheldon & Company, 1874).

Williams, T. Harry. *Lincoln and His Generals* (New York: Gramercy Books, 1952).

Woodward, Major E. M. *History of Burlington County, New Jersey, with Biographical Sketches of Many of Its Pioneers and Prominent Men* (Philadelphia: Everts & Peck, 1883). Reprinted in 1980 by the Burlington County Historical Society; "The Burlington Story," Volume Thirteen, Number 3, 1983.

Primary Sources

Biddle, Charles. "Speech of the Hon. Charles J. Biddle of Pennsylvania, Delivered in the House of Representatives," June 2, 1862.

Biddle, George Washington. "Speech of George W. Biddle before the Democratic Central Club, Philadelphia, Saturday Evening," April 4, 1863 (recorded in the *Jeffersonian*, April 18, 1863).

Biddle, George Washington. "An Inquiry into the Proper Mode of Trial, The Annual Address Delivered before the American Bar Association," August 20, 1885.

Biddle, George Washington. "Some Remarks from the Law of Libel," January 1, 1887.

Brown, George William. *Baltimore and the Nineteenth of April, 1861: A Study of the War* (N. Murray, Publication Agent, Johns Hopkins University: Baltimore, 1887).

Cromwell, Sidney. *Political Opinions in 1776 and 1863: A Letter to a Victim of Arbitrary Arrests and "American Bastilles"* (New York: Anson D.F. Randolph, 1863).

Dickinson, Daniel. "The Union: An Address by the Hon. Daniel S. Dickinson, Delivered before the Literary Societies of Amherst College, July 10, 1861" (New York: James G. Gregory, 1861).

Everett, Edward. "Success of our Republic: An Oration by Hon. Edward Everett, Delivered in Boston, Mass., July 4, 1860," The Pulpit and Rostrum (New York: H.H. Lloyd & Co., 1860).

Forney, John. "Forty Years of American Journalism: Retirement of Mr. J. W. Forney from the Philadelphia *Press*, His Editorial, Farewell, and the Response of His Successor, 1877."

Forney, John. *Anecdotes of Public Men* (New York: Harper & Brothers, 1873).

Gilchrist, William. "Two Months at Fort La Fayette by a Prisoner" (New York: Printed for the Author, 1862).

Hickman, John. "A Caustic Review of Mr. Buchanan's Administration by a Pennsylvania Democrat: Speech of Hon. John Hickman, of Pennsylvania," Delivered in the U.S. House of Representatives, December 12, 1859.

Hickman, John. "Democracy—The Old and the New: Speech of Hon. John Hickman, of Penn., On the Battle Ground of Brandywine," September 11, 1860.

Hickman, John. "Great Speech of John Hickman in the Independent Democratic Convention at Harrisburg, on the 13th inst." April 27, 1859.

Hickman, John. "Popular Sovereignty—The Will of the Majority Against the Rule of a Minority: Speech of Hon. John Hickman, of Penn.," Delivered in the U.S. House of Representatives, January 28, 1858.

Hickman, John. "Speech of Hon. John Hickman, of Penn.," Delivered in the U.S. House of Representatives, May 1, 1860.

Hickman, John. "Who Have Violated Compromises: Speech of Hon. John Hickman, of Pennsylvania," Delivered in the U.S. House of Representatives, December 12, 1859.

"Horace Greeley decently Dissected, in a Letter on Horace Greeley, Addressed by A. Oakley Hall to Joseph Hoxie, Esq." (New York: Ross & Tousey, 1862).

Howard, Frank Key. *Fourteen Months in American Bastilles* (Baltimore: Kelly, Hedian & Piet, 1863).

Howard, McHenry. "Recollections of a Maryland Confederate Soldier and Staff Officer," William & Wilkins Co., 1914.

McClure, A. K. "Fusion in Pennsylvania, by Col. A.K. McClure, Chairman of the Peoples' State Committee," Philadelphia, October 6, 1860.

McClure, A. K. "The Life and Services of Andrew G. Curtin: An Address Delivered in the House of Representatives at Harrisburg, PA, January 20, 1895" (PA: Clarence M. Busch, 1895).

"Proceedings at the Mass Meeting of Loyal Citizens, on Union Square, New York, 15ᵗʰ Day of July, 1862" (Published by Order of the Committee of Arrangements under the Supervision of John Austin Stevens, Jr., Secretary; New York: George F. Nesbitt & Co., Printers, 1862).

Reed, William Bradford. "A Paper Containing A Statement and Vindication of Certain Political Opinions," Philadelphia, 1862. (Attributed to William Bradford Reed.)

Reed, William Bradford and Charles Ingersoll. "The Diplomatic Year: Being A Review of Mr. Seward's Foreign Correspondence of 1862 by a Northern Man," Philadelphia, 1868. (Attributed to William Bradford Reed and Ingersoll.)

Reed, William Bradford. "The Last Appeal," 1860.

Reed, William Bradford, and Manton Marble, editor. *Memories of Familiar Books, with a Memoir of the Author* (New York: E. J. Hale & Son, 1876).

Reed, William Bradford. *President Reed of Pennsylvania: A Reply to George Bancroft and others* (Philadelphia: H. Challen, 1867).

Reed, William Bradford. "The Presidential Question. Speech of William B. Reed, delivered before the National Democratic Association," Philadelphia, September 4, 1860.

Reed, William Bradford. "Speech of William B. Reed, of Pennsylvania, delivered before the Democratic Central Club at Philadelphia, March 29, 1863."

Russell, William Howard. "My Diary North and South" (New York, 1863).

Sangston, Laurence. *The Bastilles of the North: By a Member of the Maryland Legislature* (Baltimore: Kelly, Hedian & Piet, 1863).

Snowden, J. Ross. "Speech of J. Ross Snowden, delivered at Philadelphia, Thursday, September 17, 1863" (Philadelphia: Age, 1863).

"To the Inhabitants of the Great and Growing City of Philadelphia" (Philadelphia, 1851), in the Printed Ephemera Collection, Portfolio 156, Folder 8, at the Library of Congress.

"Trial of Abraham Lincoln by the Great Statesmen of the Republic. A Council of the Past on the Tyranny of the President" (New York: Office of the Metropolitan Record, 1863).

"United States vs. William Hodgson," Eastern District of Pennsylvania Circuit Court, October 7, 1861.

Wall, James. "Address Delivered by Hon. James W. Wall, at Newark, N.J., July 4th, 1863" (Newark, NJ: Daily Journal Print, 1863).

Wall, James. "Address of the Hon. James W. Wall, of New Jersey before the Montgomery County Agricultural Society," October 4, 1860.

Wall, James. "Government Interference with the Press: Letter to Mr. Blair by James W. Wall, His Reception and Speech at Burlington on Friday Evening, September 27th, 1861."

Wall, James. "Speech of Hon. James W. Wall of New Jersey on the Indemnification Bill; Delivered in the Senate of the United States, March 2, 1863" (Washington, 1863).

Wall, James. "Speech of Hon. James W. Wall of New Jersey on the Missouri Emancipation Bill, delivered in the United States Senate," February 7, 1863.

Wall, James. "The Constitution: Originating in Compromise, It Can Only be Preserved by Adhering to Its Spirit, and Observing its Every Obligation. An Address delivered by James W. Wall, Esq., at the City Hall of Burlington," February 20, 1862.

"William Hodgson vs. William Millward," et al., Eastern District of Pennsylvania Supreme Court, February 3–5, 1863.

Wood, Benjamin. "The State of the Union: Speech of Benjamin Wood of New York in the House of Representatives," May 16, 1862.

Newspapers

National Vedette

Connecticut

New Haven Gazette (New Haven)

Advertiser and Farmer (Bridgeport)

Illinois

Chicago Tribune (Chicago)

Iowa

Daily Davenport Democrat (Davenport)

Maine

Democrat (Bangor)

Whig and Courier (Bangor)

Maryland

Daily Exchange (Baltimore)

Daily Republican (Baltimore)

Baltimore American (Baltimore)

Baltimore American and Daily Advertiser (Baltimore)

Baltimore Post (Baltimore)

The South (Baltimore)

New York

Albany State Register

New York Daily News

New York Herald

New-York Times

New York Tribune

Brooklyn Daily Eagle

Ohio

Circleville Watchman (Cincinnati)

Pennsylvania

American Republican (West Chester)

Chester County Times (West Chester)

Daily Evening Journal (Philadelphia)

Daily Local News (West Chester), formerly the *Jeffersonian*

Doylestown Democrat (Doylestown)

Easton Sentinel (Easton)

Jeffersonian (West Chester)

Pennsylvanian (Philadelphia)

Public Ledger (Philadelphia)

Village Record (West Chester)

Evening Bulletin (Philadelphia)

Inquirer (Philadelphia)

Age (Philadelphia)

Westmoreland County Democrat (Greenburg)

The Press (Philadelphia)

Washington, DC

Congressional Globe

Washington Chronicle

NOTES

CHAPTER ONE: THE NEWSPAPER PRESIDENT

1. William Harlan Hale, *Horace Greeley: Voice of the People,* 256.
2. *Jeffersonian,* November 3, 1860.
3. Rice, Thorndike, editor, *Reminiscences of Abraham Lincoln by Distinguished Men of His Time,* Seventh edition (New York: The North American Review, 1888), 436.
4. George Washington to Mathew Carey, June 25, 1788 (The Papers of George Washington, University of Virginia); George Washington to Edmund Randolph, August 26, 1792 (The Papers of George Washington, University of Virginia).
5. *Sangamo Journal,* March 1832.
6. Harry Maihafer, *War of Words: Abraham Lincoln and the Civil War Press* (New York: Brassey's Inc., 2001), 7–8.
7. Robert Harper, *Lincoln and the Press* (New York: McGraw, Hill Book Company, 1951), 19–20.
8. Harold Holzer, *Lincoln at Cooper Union: The Speech that Made Abraham Lincoln President* (New York: Simon & Schuster, 2004), 44–45; *Collected Works of Abraham Lincoln,* III, 347, 373, 515. Lincoln inadvertently left his collection of speeches in a hotel in Columbus, Ohio, and word got out of his intentions. Local publishers Follett, Foster & Co. heard of Lincoln's idea and finally arranged to publish the debates.
9. Norman B. Judd to Abraham Lincoln, May 13, 1859 (The Abraham Lincoln Papers at the Library of Congress, Series 1. General Correspondence. 1833–1916).
10. Maihafer, *War of Words,* 13; Benjamin Thomas speculates that Judd financed the deal and advanced the $400 to Lincoln; Benjamin Thomas, *Abraham Lincoln: A Biography* (Alfred Knopf: New York, 1952), 196.
11. Burton J. Hendrick, *Lincoln's War Cabinet,* 19.
12. It is often cited that Lincoln allowed the use of his name as presidential fodder in order to enhance his Senatorial chances. Certainly some of his actions suggest that like any shrewd

modern-day politician, he read well the possibility for the Democratic Party to split on a national level and understood the many powerful enemies that Seward had gathered in his long political career. The year 1860 was a wide open one—yet few realized it as early as Abraham Lincoln.

13. Maihafer, *War of Words*, 13, 26; *Memoirs of Gustave Koerner, 1809–1896* (The Torch Press: Cedar Rapids, IA, 1909), 108–111. Gustav Koerner was an attorney, former Lieutenant Governor, and Illinois Supreme Court judge. He and Lincoln had even argued a case together, and when Lincoln gave up his law practice after being nominated by the Republican Party to run for president, Koerner took over his most important active case, the city of St. Louis against the Ohio and Mississippi Railroad Company. When Koerner took over Lincoln's newspaper, he leaned on the president to take care of his former editor, which Lincoln did by appointing Theodore Canisius as Consul to Vienna at an annual salary of $1,000. Koerner would also be one of the twelve pallbearers at Lincoln's funeral (Koerner, 443); For the appointment of Canisius, Gustave Koerner to Abraham Lincoln, June 13, 1861 (The Abraham Lincoln Papers at the Library of Congress, Series 1. General Correspondence. 1833–1916) and Abraham Lincoln to William Seward, June 29, 1861 (The Abraham Lincoln Papers at the Library of Congress, Series 1. General Correspondence. 1833–1916).

14. Maihafer, *War of Words*, 14.

15. Philip B. Kunhardt Jr., Philip B. Kunhardt III, and Peter W. Kunhardt, *Lincoln: An Illustrated Biography* (New York: Alfred A. Knopf: 1992), 77.

16. Harper, *West Chester to 1865: That Strange & Notorious Place* (West Chester, PA: Chester County Historical Society, 1999), 696; Lincoln spoke at Cooper Union on February 27, 1860.

17. *Chester County Times*, February 11, 1860.

18. Maihafer, *War of Words*, 15–16; Holzer, *Lincoln at Cooper Union*, 149.

19. Holzer, *Lincoln at Cooper Union* (New York: Simon & Schuster, 2004), 88–98.

20. For example, the *Lancaster Examiner & Journal* offered a slate of Salmon Chase for president and Lincoln for vice president, reprinted in *Daily Illinois State Journal*, October 18, 1859.

21. The impact of Matthew Brady's portrait of Lincoln is in Holzer, *Lincoln at Cooper Union*, 88–100.

22. John M. Taylor, *William Henry Seward: Lincoln's Right Hand* (New York: HarperCollins, 1991), 73.

23. Hendrick, *Lincoln's War Cabinet*, 19. Seward was a fascinating politician worthy of the many historical examinations of his career. At one moment he was among the more enlightened of men in public office during the Civil War, supporting the rights of immigrants and opposed to slavery in any form. At the same time, he maintained a life-long association with one of the most powerful political machines led by Thurlow Weed. It was paradoxically an association he did not hide, nor never sought to apologize for; yet there is no hint that he ever gained personally from Weed's firm control over New York's patronage.

24. Maihafer, *War of Words*, 18–19.

25. Benjamin Thomas, *Abraham Lincoln: A Biography*, 210.

26. Thomas, *Abraham Lincoln*, 210–212.

27. Thomas, *Abraham Lincoln*, 213.

28. Thomas, *Abraham Lincoln*, 213; Cartter was appointed Minister of Bolivia and chief justice of the supreme court of Washington, DC, in 1863, Harper, *Lincoln and the Press*, 53.

29. Hale, *Horace Greeley*, 223–24.

30. Allan Nevins and Milton Halsey Thomas, editors, *The Diary of George Templeton Strong: The Civil War, 1860–1865* vol. 3 (New York: Macmillan Company, 1952), entry for May 19, 1860.

31. Maihafer, *War of Words*, 25–26, 33.

32. Bernard A. Weisberger, *Reporters for the Union: How the Robust and Opinionated War Correspondent, Soldiering with the Civil War Armies, Got His News—and Became a New American Character* (Boston: Little, Brown and Company, 1953), 6.

33. Harper, *Lincoln and the Press*, 97.

34. Andrews, J. Cutler. *The North Reports the Civil War* (Pittsburgh, PA: University of Pittsburgh Press, 1985).

35. Editor Thomas Kinsella claimed that the *Brooklyn Eagle* had the largest circulation of any evening paper in the country, Harper, *Lincoln and the Press*, 122.

36. Thomas, *Abraham Lincoln*, 232.

37. Neeley, *The Fate of Liberty*, 19.

38. Hale, *Horace Greeley*, 232.

39. The *Missouri Democrat* was an organ of the Republican Party, having followed its founder, the Blair family, when they jumped to the newly formed party.

40. Hendrick, *Lincoln's War Cabinet*, 85.

41. Gideon Welles, *Diary of Gideon Welles, Secretary of the Navy under Lincoln and Johnson* (New York: W. W. Norton & Company, Inc., 1960), entry for August 25, 1864, 121.

42. *New York Herald*, August 5, 1861.

43. L. E. Chittenden, *Recollections of President Lincoln* (New York: Harper & Brothers, 1891).

44. Salmon P. Chase, ed. David Donald, *Inside Lincoln's Cabinet*, 12.

45. *Philadelphia Inquirer*, August 22, 1861.

46. "The Sedition Act of July 14, 1878," *The Laws of the United States of America,* printed by Richard Folwell, Philadelphia, 1796–1798.

47. *Philadelphia Inquirer*, August 23, 1861.

48. John W. Urban, *In Defense of the Union; or Through Shot and Shell and Prison Pen* (Monarch Book Company, 1887), 30.

CHAPTER TWO: THAT TORY HODGSON

1. *Jeffersonian*, December 28, 1861.

2. Michael Burlingame, and John R. Turner Ettlinger, editors. *Inside Lincoln's White House: The Complete Civil War Diary of John Hay* (Carbondale and Edwardsville, IL: Southern Illinois University Press, 1997), entry for April 20, 1861.

3. Scott Sheads and Daniel Carroll Toomey. *Baltimore During the Civil War* (Lithicum, Maryland: Toomey Press, 1997), 4–7.

4. *Jeffersonian*, November 3, 1860.

5. Ray H. Abrams, "*The Jeffersonian*, Copperhead Newspaper," *Pennsylvania Magazine of History and Biography*, vol. 57, 1933, 265.

6. Kunhardt, Jr., Kunhardt III and Kunhardt. *Lincoln*, 130–133.

7. *Jeffersonian*, January 12, 1861.

8. Ray H. Abrams, "*The Jeffersonian*, Copperhead Newspaper," *Pennsylvania Magazine of History and Biography*, vol. 57, 1933, 261.

9. Burton, J. Hendrick, *Lincoln's War Cabinet,* 132–134. Good discussion of the fallout; so upset was the New York public at the thought of a compromise on the issue of slavery that there was public discussion of taking away the public contract for government printing, which had long been the source of Weed's strength.

10. *Jeffersonian,* November 24, 1860.

11. *Jeffersonian,* November 3, 1860.

12. *The House of Hodgson: Ownership for a Century,* 6 (CCHS).

13. Douglas Harper, *West Chester to 1865: That Elegant & Notorious Place,* 288.

14. *American Republican,* May 2, 1843.

15. *Jeffersonian,* July 27, 1861.

16. Harper, *West Chester to 1865,* 487.

17. Harper, *West Chester to 1865,* 457.

18. William Dusinberre, *Civil War Issue in Philadelphia, 1861–1865* (Philadelphia: University of Pennsylvania, 1965), 13.

19. 1860 United States Federal Census. West Chester, Chester, Pennsylvania, June 30, 1860, M653–1094, page 748, National Archives and Records Administration. Living with Hodgson was Eliza Hodgson (sister), William Hodgson, Ann Hodgson, Mary E. Hodgson, Fannie D. Hodgson, Charles Stowe, Alban Ottey, Isaac Evans, Benjamin M. Mills, Harry Baker, and Elizabeth Mailand.

20. Robert Harper, *Lincoln and the Press* (New York: McGraw-Hill Book Co., Inc., 1951), 87.

21. *Jeffersonian,* February 23, 1861.

22. Abraham Lincoln, "First Inaugural Address," March 4, 1861, Basler, CW, IV, 262–271.

23. L. E. Chittenden, *Recollections of President Lincoln,* 103.

24. *Jeffersonian,* March 9, 1861.

25. Abraham Lincoln to William H. Seward, April 1, 1861 (Reply to Seward's "Some Thoughts for the President's Consideration"). Library of Congress, Abraham Lincoln Papers, Series 1. General Correspondence. 1833–1916.

26. *Jeffersonian,* April 13, 1861.

27. *Jeffersonian,* April 20, 1861.

28. *Jeffersonian,* April 20, 1861; *Daily [Davenport, IA] Democrat and News,* April 15, 1861.

29. *American Annual Cyclopaedia* 1861 (New York: D. Appleton & Company, 1862).

30. *Daily [Davenport, IA] Democrat and News,* April 15, 1861.

31. Harper, *Lincoln and the Press,* 319.

32. John Forney, *Anecdotes of Public Men,* 225; A more personal reason may also have tempered Douglas's views of the man who had defeated him for the presidency. Years before, both he and Lincoln had courted a young woman for marriage. Lincoln had won that "contest" as well and married Mary Lincoln, the object of Douglas's desires.

33. William Harlan Hale, *Horace Greely: Voice of the People.* (New York: Harper and Brothers, 1950) 242.

34. *Baltimore Daily Exchange,* April 15, 1861.

35. Charles Shippan to his mother, April 16, 1861, CCHS.

CHAPTER THREE: PUBLISHING AND POLITICS

1. *Jeffersonian,* December 28, 1861.

2. *Black and White in Blue and Gray.*

3. *Jeffersonian,* September 25, 1858.
4. William Harlan Hale, *Horace Greeley: Voice of the People,* 148–149, 153.
5. The investigation into the use of patronage by the Buchanan administration to influence the creation of an antislavery government in Kansas was led by congressman John Covode of Pennsylvania. Although John Forney was a primary figure in the investigation due to his close ties with President James Buchanan, he was eventually absolved of any wrongdoing.
6. The Government Printing Office was established by Congressional Joint Resolution 25, June 23, 1860.
7. For appointments, Gustave Koerner to Abraham Lincoln, June 13, 1861 (The Abraham Lincoln Papers at the Library of Congress, Series 1. General Correspondence. 1833–1916).
8. *Brooklyn Eagle,* August 22, 1861.
9. *Brooklyn Eagle,* August 22, 1861; Harper, *Lincoln and the Press,* 76; *Cincinnati Commercial,* April 2, 1861. The minister to Rome was Rufus King, *Milwaukee Sentinel.* The minister to Portugal was Rufus Hosmer, *Michigan Republican.* The minister to Turkey was James Watson Webb, *New York Courier and Enquirer.*
10. Mark Neeley, Jr., *The Fate of Liberty,* 33–35.
11. *Reporters For the Union,* 229.
12. Harry Maihafer, *War of Words: Abraham Lincoln and the Civil War Press,* 1. Maihafer cites the 1860 census as estimating 2,500 periodicals and 373 daily newspapers in 1860.
13. *New-York Times,* August 1861.
14. *Jeffersonian & Democratic Herald* (later the *Jeffersonian*), April 7, 1855.
15. "Party vs. Country" in *The New-York Times,* August 8, 1861; "The Popular Demand" in the *Chicago Tribune,* August 16, 1861.
16. *Christian Observer,* August 23, 1861.
17. *The Press,* August 22, 1861.
18. *The Press,* August 22, 1861.
19. *The Press,* August 6, 1861.
20. Stephen W. Sears, "The First News Blackout." *Civil War Chronicles* Winter 1994, 16–23; Harry Maihafer, *War of Words,* 1.
21. J. Cutler Andrews, *The North Reports the Civil War* (University of Pittsburgh Press: Pittsburgh, PA, 1985), 8.
22. Cutler, *The North Reports the Civil War,* 8 (Adams S. Hill to Darwin Ware, November 23, 1857, according to Cutler, the letter was in the possession of Arthur Hill, Esq., Boston, MA).
23. Cutler, *The North Reports the Civil War,* 7.
24. *Jeffersonian & Democratic Herald,* November 17, 1855.
25. *New York Herald,* 1835.
26. *Jeffersonian & Democratic Herald,* November 17, 1855.
27. *Jeffersonian & Democratic Herald,* November 17, 1855.
28. *Jeffersonian & Democratic Herald,* November 17, 1855.
29. *New-York Times,* August 16, 1861.
30. *New-York Times,* August 16, 1861.
31. Chittenden, *Recollections of President Lincoln.*
32. Harris, Brayton, *Blue and Gray in Black and White,* 64.
33. Richard Lee, *Mr. Lincoln's City: An Illustrated Guide to the Civil War Sites of Washington* (McLean, VA: EPM Publications, Inc, 1981).

34. *The Press,* quoted in the *New-York Times,* August 1, 1861.

35. *Brooklyn Eagle,* August 9, 1861.

CHAPTER FOUR: THE FIRST BATTLEGROUND

1. *Jeffersonian,* December 28, 1861.

2. *Baltimore American & Daily Advertizer,* April 1861; Events can be found in Scott Sheads and Daniel Carroll Toomey. *Baltimore During the Civil War* (Lithicum, MD: Toomey Press, 1997).

3. Scott Sumpter Sheads and Daniel Carroll Toomey, *Baltimore During the Civil War.*

4. Michael Burlingame and John R. Turner Ettlinger, editors, *Inside Lincoln's White House: The Complete Civil War Diary of John Hay* (Carbondale and Edwardsville, IL: Southern Illinois University Press, 1997).

5. General Winfield Scott to Major George Cadwalader, May 16, 1861. OR II, 1, p.571–572.

6. *Ex Parte Merryman.* Congress would not grant the suspension of the writ of habeas corpus as a special wartime act until March 3, 1863 (Habeas Corpus Act of Congress, March 3, 1863).

7. William Rehnquist, *All the Laws But One,* 32.

8. Rehnquist, *All the Laws But One,* 38.

9. Sheads and Toomey, *Baltimore During the Civil War,* 4–7

10. Sheads and Toomey, *Baltimore During the Civil War,* 67.

11. Memoirs of John Adams Dix, Volume II p. 24.

12. Baltimore *South,* April 22, 1861.

13. Sheads and Toomy, *Baltimore During the Civil War;* George William Brown *Baltimore and the Nineteenth of April, 1861: A Study of the War* (Baltimore: N. Murray, Publication Agent, Johns Hopkins University, 1887).

14. McHenry Howard, ed., and James Robertson, Jr., *Recollections of a Maryland Confederate Soldier and Staff Officer Under Johnston, Jackson and Lee* (Dayton, OH: Morningside Bookshop, 1975), iii-iv.

15. Sheads and Toomy, *Baltimore During the Civil Wa*r, 30; Benjamin Butler, *Butler's Book* (A.M. Thymer Co., 1892), 228–229.

16. McHenry Howard, youngest son of Charles Howard, fled south on June 1, 1861; Sheads and Toomy, *Baltimore During the Civil Wa*r, 30, 35–38.

17. Abraham Lincoln, "Special Message to Congress," in Basler, *Collected Works,* IV, 421–440.

18. Lincoln, "Special Message to Congress," in Basler, *Collected Works,* IV, 421–440.

19. Lincoln, "Special Message to Congress," in Basler, *Collected Works,* IV, 421–440.

20. Silvana Sidali, *From Property to Person: Slavery and the Confiscation Acts, 1861–1862* (Baton Rouge, LA: Louisiana State University Press, 2005) 59.

21. Abraham Lincoln, "Address in Independence Hall," Philadelphia, Pennsylvania, February 22, 1861, in Basler, *Collected Works,* IV, 240.

22. Horace Greeley, *The American Conflict,* 563; House Resolution was moved by Democrat John McClerland of Springfield, Illinois for the persecution of the war passed by a vote of 121 to 5.

23. The most comprehensive review of the complex congressional debates surrounding the Confiscation Act is Siddali, *From Property to Person: Slavery and the Confiscation Acts, 1861–1862* (Baton Rouge, LA: Louisiana State University Press, 2005).

CHAPTER FIVE: THE LOYAL OPPOSITION

1. *Jeffersonian,* July 13, 1861.
2. *Daily Local News,* August 31, 1878.
3. Wilmer W. MacElree, *Sidelights on the Bench and Bar of Chester County* (West Chester, 1918), 293.
4. *Jeffersonian,* October 7, 1854.
5. *Village Record,* October 17, 1854.
6. Harper, *West Chester to 1865: That Strange & Notorious Place,* 640–642.
7. *Jeffersonian,* quoted in Harper, *West Chester to 1865,* 641–642.
8. *Great Speech of Hon. John Hickman in the Independent Democratic Convention at Harrisburg, on the 13th Inst.* [1859].
9. Joseph Lewis to Josephine Lewis, October 12, 1858. CCHS.
10. *New York Tribune,* February 20, 1860, February 14, 1860. The *Tribune* added to the report of its Washington correspondent, "We say that hunting in couples, after the [Henry] Edmundson and Keitt fashion, is assassination in spirit, in purpose and, will be held and stigmatized as such by all decent men."
11. Silvana Siddali, *From Property to Person: Slavery and the Confiscation Acts, 1861–1862,* 63–64.
12. Holzer, *Lincoln at Cooper Union,* 71.
13. Allen Johnson and Malone Dumas, *Dictionary of American Biography* (New York: Charles Scribner's Sons, 1931), 526.
14. Andrews, J. Cutler. *The North Reports the War.* (Pittsburgh: University of Pittsburgh Press, 1985); *Forty Years of American Journalism: Retirement of Mr. J. W. Forney from the Philadelphia "Press," His Editorial, Farewell, and the Response of His Successor,* 1877.
15. *Jeffersonian,* July 13, 1861.
16. *Jeffersonian,* July 13, 1861.
17. Siddali, *From Property to Person, 1861–1862,* 62–63. The passage of the First Confiscation Act became one of the defining bills of the Special Session of the Thirty-seventh Congress. As the primary issue of the bill was over whether slaves would be identified as property liable to confiscation, the Senate and House Judiciary committees worked diligently to define the language of the bill before it reached the floor of each house. As the chairman of the House Judiciary, John Hickman played a major role in what became the final bill.
18. *Congressional Globe,* 37th Congress, 1st session, 74.
19. *Congressional Globe,* 37th Congress, 1st Session, 74 (1861).
20. *Congressional Globe,* 37th Congress, 1st Session, 74 (1861).
21. Horace Greeley, *The American Conflict,* 562.
22. Greeley, *The American Conflict,* 563.
23. O.R., II, 2, 790–801.
24. *Congressional Globe,* 37th Congress, 1st Session, 72 (1861)
25. *Congressional Globe,* 37th Congress, 1st Session, 72, (1861); Journal of the Senate, July 15, 1861, 42. Part Four of the First Confiscation Act was from the Confiscation Act (S. 26) offered by Illinois Senator Lyman Trumbull, chairman of the Senate Judiciary Committee.
26. *Congressional Globe,* 37th Congress, 1st Session, 72, (1816); Journal of the Senate, July 15, 1861, 42.
27. *New-York Times,* August 7, 1861 "An Act to Confiscation Property Used for Insurrectionary Purposes," *U.S. Statues at Large, Treatises, and Proclamations of the United States of Amer-*

ica, vol. 12 (Boston, 1863), 319; Blaine, James G., *Twenty Years of Congress: From Lincoln to Garfield.* 2 vols. (Norwich, CT: Henry Bill Publishing, 1886), vol. 1, 343.

28. "An Act to Confiscation Property Used for Insurrectionary Purposes," *U.S. Statues at Large, Treatises, and Proclamations of the United States of America,* vol. 12 (Boston, 1863), 319.

29. John Forney, *Anecdotes of Public Men,* 222.

CHAPTER SIX: SUMMER OF RAGE

1. "Address Before the Young Men's Lyceum, of Springfield, Illinois," January 27, 1838, Basler, Roy P. CW, I, 113.

2. *Jeffersonian,* March 7, 1863.

3. *Jeffersonian,* July 6, 1861.

4. Robert Harper, *Lincoln and the Press.*

5. *Jeffersonian,* July 6, 1861.

6. *Jeffersonian,* July 6, 1861.

7. *The Daily Exchange,* August 8, 1861.

8. The *Bridgeport Farmer* was mobbed on August 24, 1861, shortly after a "Peace Meeting" in nearby Stepney, which was presided over by showman P. T. Barnum, at least until secessionists threatened to shoot him.; Brayton Harris, *Blue & Gray in Black & White,* 99.

9. *New Haven Register,* reprinted in the *Jeffersonian,* July 6, 1861.

10. Mark Neeley, *The Fate of Liberty,* 19–23.

11. Lawrence Sangston (attributed). *The Bastilles of the North by a Member of the Maryland Legislature* (Kelly, Hedian & Piet, 1863) 43.

12. *American Republican,* reprinted in the *Jeffersonian,* July 29, 1861.

13. *The Daily Exchange,* August 10, 1861.

14. *Chicago Tribune,* August 14, 1861.

15. *The Daily Exchange,* August 15, 1861.

16. *Chicago Tribune,* August 14, 1861.

17. *Whig and Courier,* August 1861.

18. *The Daily Exchange,* August 19, 1861.

19. *Brooklyn Daily Eagle,* August 13, 1861.

20. Russell, *My Diary North and South,* 57.

21. *History of the [London] Times, 1841–1884* (Written, Printed and Published at the office of the Times, 1939), 368.

22. *History of the [London] Times, 1841–1884,* 374.

23. *History of the [London] Times, 1841–1884,* 371.

24. *American Annual Cyclopaedia,* 1862, Vol. 1, 329; Robert Harper, *Lincoln and the Press,* 113–114.

25. Harper, *Lincoln and the Press,* 114–115.

26. Thomas Kinsella Scrapbook, New York Public Library.

27. *Brooklyn Eagle,* August 13, 1861.

28. *Brooklyn Eagle,* August 13, 1861.

29. Thomas Kinsella Scrapbook, New York Public Library. The scrapbook also indicates that Kinsella later had a career in Brooklyn politics and finally served in the United States Congress in 1871 during which time he supported Horace Greeley in the *Tribune's* editor's political quest for the presidency.

30. Thomas Kinsella Scrapbook, New York Public Library.

31. Harper, *Lincoln and the Press*, 190.
32. *Philadelphia Inquirer,* August 21, 1861.
33. *Circleville Watchman,* September 1861, in O.R. II, 56, Samuel Hill to Simon Cameron with attachment.
34. London *Daily News,* September 5, 1861.
35. *New York Ledger,* reprinted in *The Press,* August 22, 1861.
36. *Philadelphia Inquirer,* August 21, 1861.
37. *The Press,* August 23, 1861.
38. *New-York Times,* August 20, 1861.
39. *The Press,* August 22, 1861.
40. *Daily Exchange,* August 24, 1861.
41. *Daily Exchange,* August 21, 1861.
42. *Philadelphia Inquirer,* August 22, 1861.
43. *The Press,* August 23, 1861.
44. Toronto *Globe,* reprinted in the *New-York Times* of August 19th, 1861.
45. London *Daily News,* September 5, 1861.
46. *Philadelphia Inquirer,* August 21, 1861.
47. London *Daily News* September 5, 1861.

CHAPTER SEVEN: THE JEFFERSONIAN IS MOBBED

1. Abraham Lincoln, "Address to the New Jersey General Assembly," February 21, 1861, Basler, CW, IV, 236–237.
2. Douglas Harper, *West Chester to 1865: That Elegant & Notorious Place,* 713.
3. Harper, *West Chester to 1865,* 714.
4. *Jeffersonian,* April 20, 1861.
5. *Jeffersonian,* April 20, 1861.
6. "To the Inhabitants of the Great and Growing City of Philadelphia" (Philadelphia, 1851), in the Printed Ephemera Collection, Portfolio 156, Folder 8, at the Library of Congress.
7. Historic American Buildings Survey (HABS), Volume 20, West Chester 1–4. (Chester County Historical Society); Harper, Douglas, *West Chester to 1865: That Elegant & Notorious Place* (West Chester, PA: Chester County Historical Society, 1999).
8. *Chester County Times,* February 23, 1861.
9. *Philadelphia Inquirer,* August 21, 1861; *Village Record,* August 24, 1861; *Philadelphia Bulletin,* reprinted in the *American Republican,* October 22, 1861.
10. *Evening Bulletin,* reprinted in *The Press,* August 21, 1861.
11. "To the Inhabitants of the Great and Growing City of Philadelphia (Philadelphia, 1851), in the Printed Ephemera Collection, Portfolio 156, Folder 8, at the Library of Congress.
12. *Jeffersonian,* January 17, 1863.
13. *Evening Bulletin,* reprinted in *The Press,* August 21, 1861.
14. *Village Record,* May 10, 1864.
15. *Village Record,* June 23, 1864.
16. *Jeffersonian,* November 3, 1860.
17. *Jeffersonian,* May 25, 1861.
18. *Village Record,* August 24, 1861.
19. *Village Record,* August 24, 1861.

20. *Philadelphia Inquirer,* August 21, 1861.

21. *Philadelphia Bulletin,* reprinted in the *American Republican,* October 22, 1861.

22. "To the Inhabitants of the Great and Growing City of Philadelphia" (Philadelphia, 1851), in the Printed Ephemera Collection, Portfolio 156, Folder 8, at the Library of Congress.

23. *Philadelphia Journal,* reprinted in *Daily Exchange,* August 24, 1861.

24. *Daily Exchange,* August 24, 1861.

25. *Jeffersonian,* October 26, 1861.

CHAPTER EIGHT: SUFFERING FOR LIBERTIES

1. *Jeffersonian,* January 17, 1863.

2. *Bastilles of the North,* 1863, published by Kelly, Hedian & Piet, 27.

3. *Bastilles of the North,* 1863, published by Kelly, Hedian & Piet, preface.

4. A careful study of statistics is in Mark E. Neely, Jr., *The Fate of Liberty: Abraham Lincoln and Civil Liberties* (New York: Oxford University Press, 1991), 124–133.

5. *Danville Intelligencer,* reprinted in the *Jeffersonian,* December 28, 1861.

6. "Message of President Abraham Lincoln at the First, or Extra Session of the 37th Congress, July 4, 1861," Basler, CW, IV, 421–441.

7. On appointment of Dix see Abraham Lincoln to Simon Cameron, July 29, 1861, Basler, CW, IV, 463; Nominations of John Dix, Benjamin Butler and Nathaniel Banks were sent to the Senate for confirmation at the rank of Major General on July 29, 1861.

8. *The Memoirs of John Adams Dix* (two volumes, New York: Harper & Brothers, 1883); *New-York Times,* April 21, 22, 23, 1879; Guilder, Leonard, ed., *Who Was Who in America, 1607–1896* (1963).

9. John S. Bowman, general editor. *Encyclopedia of the Civil War* (Greenwich, Connecticut: Brompton Books, 1992).

10. John Dix to Henry Halleck, September 15, 1862 (Dix Memoir, II, p. 36).

11. Major-General John A. Dix to Colonel E.D. Townsend, July 24, 1861 (Dix, V. 2, p. 25).

12. Scott Sumpter Sheads and Daniel Carroll Toomey. *Baltimore During the Civil War,* 42–43.

13. Major-General John A. Dix to Montgomery Blair, August 31, 1861 (Dix, V. 2, p. 30).

14. Major-General John A. Dix to Montgomery Blair, August 31, 1861 (Dix, V. 2, p. 30).

15. *Daily Exchange,* August 21, 1861.

16. J. Thomas Scharf, *History of Baltimore City and County* (Baltimore: Regional Publishing Company, 1971).

17. *Daily Exchange,* July 15, 1861

18. Frederick Schley to William Seward, September 12, 1861. O.R. II, 2, 679–80.

19. Simon Cameron to Nathaniel Banks, O.R. II, 1, 678–679.

20. McClellan to Cameron, September 11, 1861, O.R. II, 2, 793.

21. Simon Cameron to John Dix, September 11, 1861, OR.

22. John Dix to Simon Cameron, September 11, 1861, O.R. II, 2, 793.

23. Baltimore *Daily Exchange,* September 11, 1861.

24. Endorsement of Montgomery Blair to George McClellan, to a letter from John Dix to Blair, August 31, 1861. O.R. II, 2, 590–91.

25. O.R. II, 2, 672.

26. O.R. II, 2, 791–93.

27. Allan Pinkerton to William Seward, September 23, 1861, O.R. II, 2, 795.

28. Nathanial P. Banks to Lieutenant-Colonel Thomas Ruger, September 16, 1861, O.R. II, 2, 681.

29. Laurence Sangston, *The Bastilles of the North By a Member of the Maryland Legislature,* 5.

30. Frank Key Howard, *Fourteen Months in American Bastilles* (Baltimore: Kelly, Hedian & Piet, 1863).

31. Baltimore *American,* September 21, 1861.

32. Seward to Dix, September 20, 1861, O.R., II, 2, 780.

33. W. W. Glenn to John Dix, October 3, 1861, O.R., II, 2, 781. Glenn was released on December 2, 1861.

34. Frank Key Howard to Lydia Howard, October 14, 1861, O.R., II, 2, 781–2.

35. Lieutenant Charles O. Wood to Lieutenant Colonel Martin Burke, October 22, 1861, O.R., II, 2, 782.

36. Lieutenant Colonel Martin Burke to Lieutenant Charles O. Wood, October 23, 1861, O.R., II, 2, 782.

37. Frank Key Howard to Lieutenant Colonel Martin Burke, October 23, 1861, O.R., II, 2, 783.

38. The College of New Jersey was later named Princeton University.

39. Major E. M. Woodward, *History of Burlington County, New Jersey, with Biographical Sketches of Many of Its Pioneers and Prominent Men* (Philadelphia: Everts & Peck, 1883). Reprinted in 1980 by the Burlington County Historical Society; "The Burlington Story," Volume Thirteen, Number 3, 1983.

40. *Crisis,* September 29, 1861.

41. American Annual Cyclopeaedia (1862), Vol I, 329.

42. *Chicago Tribune,* August 27, 1861.

43. American Annual Cyclopeaedia (1862), Vol I, 480.

44. O.R., II, 2, 772, James Wall to Simon Cameron, September 11, 1861.

45. *New York Herald,* September 12, 1861.

46. O.R., II, 2, 773, Samuel R. Comfort, Henry L.R. Vandyke, M. MacDonald and A. MacDonald to William Seward, September 12, 1861.

47. O.R. II, 2, 774, Letter to Simon Cameron, signed "Union Now and Forever," September 20, 1861.

48. O.R., II, 2, 773, James Wall to Simon Cameron, September 18, 1861; James Wall to Captain Burling (Fort Lafayette) September 18, 1861.

49. O.R. II, 2, 775–776, William Seward to Charles S. Olden, September 23, 1861.

50. O.R. II, 2, 774.

51. Sangston, *The Bastilles of the North By a Member of the Maryland Legislature,* 38–39.

52. O.R, II, 2, 777.

53. James Marshall, *American Bastile.*

54. O.R., II, 2, James W. Wall to William Bradford Reed, undated, 778.

55. *Baltimore American,* September 21, 1861. Upon his release, Howard published "Fourteen Months in an American Bastille."

56. Sangston, *The Bastilles of the North By a Member of the Maryland Legislature,* 43.

CHAPTER NINE: THE COST OF THEIR CONVICTIONS

1. *Jeffersonian,* December 28, 1861.

2. *Jeffersonian,* August 8, 1848.

3. *Jeffersonian,* August 8, 1848.

4. *Jeffersonian,* August 8, 1848.

5. Mark Neeley, Jr., *The Union Divided,* 38–39; John Reid Seitter, "Union City: Philadelphia and the Battle of Gettysburg."

6. Mark Neeley, Jr., *Fate of Liberty,* 19–24.

7. *New York Herald* reprinted in the *Crisis,* January 29, 1862.

8. *Crisis,* January 29, 1862.

9. *Jeffersonian,* January 12, 1862.

10. *Crisis,* January 29, 1862.

11. *Diary of Gideon Welles*

12. Interestingly, in ordering Frémont to back off from liberating slaves of Southern owners, Lincoln personally sent the general a copy of the August 6th Confiscation Act and ordered him to conform to key sections. Letter to General Frémont, September 2, 1861.

13. Basler, *CW,* V, 388–389 (August 22, 1862). William Harlan Hale, *Horace Greeley: Voice of the People,* 261–262.

14. William E. Huntzicker, *The Popular Press* (Westport, CT: Greenwood Press, 1999).

15. Dusinberre, *Civil War Issue in Philadelphia, 1861–1865,* 148, 181.

16. *Crisis,* January 29, 1862.

17. A. J. Juckett to "Dear Friend," February 6, 1863, Juckett Family Letters.

18. Jeffrey Smith, *War and Press Freedom: The Problem of Prerogative Power* (New York: Oxford University Press, 1999), 121.

19. Smith, *War and Press Freedom,* 168.

20. Fahnstock Diary, January 29, 1863.

21. Fahnstock Diary, January 31, 1863.

22. London *Daily News,* February 5, 1863.

CHAPTER TEN: "HAVE WE A GOVERNMENT?"

1. *Jeffersonian,* April 20, 1861.

2. *Jeffersonian,* November 26, 1861.

3. *Jeffersonian,* October 26, 1861.

4. *Jeffersonian,* December 28, 1861.

5. *Jeffersonian,* December 28, 1861.

6. *Jeffersonian,* November 2, 1861.

7. *Jeffersonian,* November 26, 1861.

8. The Pierce Butler affair is in O.R., II, 2, 505–509.

9. In *Lincoln and the Press,* Robert Harper calls the New York *World* the "spokesman for all Lincoln hating newspapers." On June 1, 1863, General Ambrose Burnside issued General Order No. 84, which suppressed the *Chicago Times* and prohibited the delivery of the *World* to the Ohio Department. Harper, *Lincoln and the Press,* 235, 258.

10. Manton Marble, editor, *Memories of Familiar Books, with a Memoir of the Author* (New York: E.J. Hale & Son, 1876); Onarato, Michael Paul, *The Mission of William B. Reed, United States Minister to China, 1857–1858* (Washington, DC: Dissertation, Graduate School of Georgetown University, June 1959). Diaries kept by Reed during his trips are in the Library of Congress, mm790374999.

11. William Bradford Reed, *A Paper Containing a Statement and Vindication of Certain Political Opinions* (Philadelphia: John A Campbell, 1862).

12. *Speech of the Hon. William B. Reed, on The Presidential Questions. Delivered Before the National Democratic Association* (Philadelphia, September 4, 1860).

13. *Speech of the Hon. William B. Reed, on The Presidential Questions. Delivered Before the National Democratic Association* (Philadelphia, September 4, 1860).

14. Reed, *A Paper Containing A Statement and Vindication of Certain Political Opinions.*

15. Reed, *A Paper Containing A Statement and Vindication of Certain Political Opinions.*

16. The Reed-Bancroft feud is chronicled in William Bradford Reed, *President Reed of Pennsylvania: A Reply to George Bancroft and Others* (Philadelphia: H. Challen, 1867).

17. An unfinished narrative of the life of Benedict Arnold written by William Bradford Reed is owned by the author.

18. Dusinberre, *Civil War Issues in Philadelphia, 1861–1865,* 135.

19. Gerard J. St. John, "This is My Bar," *The Philadelphia Lawyer,* Winter 2002, Vol. 64, No. 4. Battery A included George Washington Biddle, William Henry Rawle, Charles Morgan, Clement Penrose, C. Stuart Patterson, Charles Chauncy, Henry D. Landis, John Graver Johnson, and future Chief Justice James Mitchell.

20. The book, coauthored by George Biddle, was a two-volume general reference book, *General Index to the English Common Law.* It was on Lincoln's bookshelf according to Catalog Number 117 from the Lincoln Book Shop in Chicago, Illinois.

21. *The Press,* as reprinted in the *Jeffersonian,* October 26, 1861.

22. *Anecdotes of Public Men,* 55.

23. Gerard J. St. John, "This is My Bar," *The Philadelphia Lawyer,* Winter 2002, Vol. 64, No. 4.

24. St. John, "This is My Bar," *The Philadelphia Lawyer,* Winter 2002, Vol. 64, No. 4.

25. Senator Walter Lowrie served from December 1819 to March 1825.

26. *Jeffersonian,* October 26, 1861.

27. *Jeffersonian,* January 17, 1863.

28. Arnold Schankman, "William B. Reed and the Civil War," 464.

29. "Loyal Opposition in Philadelphia," *Journal of Pennsylvania History and Biography,* July 1964, 300.

30. Abraham Lincoln, "Special Message to Congress," in Basler, *Collected Works,* IV, 421–440.

CHAPTER ELEVEN: THE GOVERNMENT CONSPIRACY

1. *Jeffersonian,* December 28, 1861.

2. Abraham Lincoln, "Draft of Address for Sanitary Fair at Baltimore," ca. April 18, 184, Basler, CW, VII, 303.

3. Radical Congressman Benjamin Wade of Ohio despised Mrs. Lincoln for her fondness of social graces such as French and holding of parties. "Are the President and Mrs. Lincoln aware that there is a civil war?" He wrote in declining to attend a White House function. Lincoln's War Cabinet, page 278

4. "Sitting Presidents and Vice Presidents Who Have Testified Before Congressional Committees," Senate Historical Office and the Senate Library, 2004; *Jeffersonian,* February 15, 1862.

5. *Jeffersonian,* February 15, 1862.

6. *Great Speech of Hon. John Hickman in the Independent Democratic Convention at Harrisburg, on the 13th Inst.* [1859].

7. Nathan Geer, editor of the Peoria *Transcript* reported to Lincoln in April 1860, Washington, New York, and Hartford "have set you up for President and Hickman of Penn. For vice…"

Nathan Geer to Abraham Lincoln, April 1860, The Abraham Lincoln Papers at the Library of Congress, Series 1. General Correspondence. 1833–1916.

8. *Jeffersonian,* July 2, 1859, including reprint of John Hickman to "Patrick Mullin, Michael O'Connell, and others of my dear Irish and German fellow-citizens," June 25, 1859.

9. *Jeffersonian,* July 2, 1859, including reprint of John Hickman to "Patrick Mullin, Michael O'Connell, and others of my dear Irish and German fellow-citizens," June 25, 1859.

10. *Jeffersonian,* April 12, 1856.

11. *National Vedette,* reprinted in the *Jeffersonian,* June 11, 1859.

12. *National Vedette,* reprinted in the *Jeffersonian,* June 11, 1859.

13. Abraham Lincoln, "Speech at Columbus, Ohio, September 16, 1859," CW, III, 408.

14. Abraham Lincoln, "Notes for Speeches at Columbus and Cincinnati, Ohio," September 16, 17, 1859. CW, III, 425–462.

15. *Pennsylvanian,* 1860.

16. Joseph Medill to Abraham Lincoln, December 18, 1860, (The Abraham Lincoln Papers at the Library of Congress, Series 1. General Correspondence. 1833–1916).

17. John Hickman to John Forney, May 2, 1861, Papers of John W. Forney, LOC, mm78021113.

18. John W. Forney, *Anecdotes of Public Men,* 75–76.

19. Forney, *Anecdotes of Public Men,* 166.

20. Forney, *Anecdotes of Public Men,* 342.

21. Orville H. Browning to Abraham Lincoln, July 1861 (The Abraham Lincoln Papers at the Library of Congress, Series 1. General Correspondence. 1833–1916).

22. John Forney's influence, and his pride in that influence, is best recounted in his book *Anecdotes of Public Men,* a compilation of biographies he first published in installments in *The Press.*

23. Hearings of the Covode Smelling Committee, United States Senate, 1860, reported in the *Jeffersonian,* June 16, 1860.

24. The Letters of John Hay, August 1, 1863.

25. Robert Harper, *Lincoln and the Press,* 180.

26. *Jeffersonian,* July 13, 1861.

27. *William Hodgson vs. William Millward, et al.,* Eastern District of Pennsylvania Supreme Court, February 3–5, 1863.

CHAPTER TWELVE: *HODGSON VS. THE UNITED STATES OF AMERICA*

1. Abraham Lincoln to Albert G. Hodges [Draft], April 4, 1864 (The Abraham Lincoln Papers at the Library of Congress, Series 1. General Correspondence. 1833–1916).

2. *The Press,* February 6, 1863.

3. *Jeffersonian,* February 7, 1863

4. *William Hodgson vs. William Millward, et al.,* Eastern District of Pennsylvania Supreme Court, February 3–5, 1863.

5. *William Hodgson vs. William Millward, et al.,* Eastern District of Pennsylvania Supreme Court, February 3–5, 1863.

6. *An Act to suppress Insurrection, to punish Treason and Rebellion, to seize and confiscate the Property of Rebels, and for other Purposes,* July 17, 1862, U.S., *Statutes at Large, Treaties, and Proclamations of the United States of America,* vol. 12 (Boston, 1863), pp. 589–92.

7. *William Hodgson vs. William Millward, et al.,* Eastern District of Pennsylvania Supreme Court, February 3–5, 1863.

8. *William Hodgson vs. William Millward, et al.,* Eastern District of Pennsylvania Supreme Court, February 3–5, 1863.

9. *William Hodgson vs. William Millward, et al.,* Eastern District of Pennsylvania Supreme Court, February 3–5, 1863.

10. *William Hodgson vs. William Millward, et al.,* Eastern District of Pennsylvania Supreme Court, February 3–5, 1863.

11. *William Hodgson vs. William Millward, et al.,* Eastern District of Pennsylvania Supreme Court, February 3–5, 1863.

12. See Arnold Schankman, "William B. Reed and the Civil War," for discussion on the tragedy of Reed and many of the topical testimonials written at the time of his death. Most politely allude to Reed's difficulty in earning a living during the War, and his subsequent career as a writer far removed from politics, and Schankman mentions that—like many of the antiwar editors and publishers—he is surprisingly forgotten by historians today. Also relevant is an unpublished book by Reed that is highly complimentary toward Benedict Arnold—not as a traitor to his country, but rather as one misunderstood. Certainly one can argue that Reed felt equally misunderstood.

13. Reed had a history of working without pay. From 1850–1856 he served without pay as Professor of American history and English literature at the University of Pennsylvania. Arnold Schankman, "William B. Reed and the Civil War," 455.

14. *Biographical Dictionary of the United States Congress, 1774–1989,* Bicentennial Edition (Washington, DC: United States Government Printing, 1988).

15. *Village Record,* October 22, 1861.

16. *Jeffersonian,* October 26, 1861.

17. *Jeffersonian,* October 26, 1861.

18. Abraham Lincoln, Memorandum on Cameron Recommendations, December 31, 1860 (The Abraham Lincoln Papers at the Library of Congress, Series 1. General Correspondence. 1833–1916); Abraham Lincoln, Tally of Philadelphia Patronage Endorsements, April 1861 (The Abraham Lincoln Papers at the Library of Congress, Series 1. General Correspondence. 1833–1916).

19. William D. Kelley to Abraham Lincoln, August 7, 1860 (The Abraham Lincoln Papers at the Library of Congress, Series 1. General Correspondence. 1833–1916).

20. George Coffey to Abraham Lincoln, December 17, 1860 (The Abraham Lincoln Papers at the Library of Congress, Series 1. General Correspondence. 1833–1916).

21. *Village Record,* February 10, 1863.

22. *Village Record,* February 10, 1863.

23. *Village Record,* February 10, 1863.

24. *Village Record,* February 10, 1863.

25. George Coffey to Abraham Lincoln, August 22, 1861 (The Abraham Lincoln Papers at the Library of Congress, Series 1. General Correspondence. 1833–1916).

26. Simon Cameron to George A. Coffey, September 5, 1861, *O.R.* II, 2, p. 19.

27. Amasa Converse to Abraham Lincoln, August 28, 1861 (The Abraham Lincoln Papers at the Library of Congress, Series 1. General Correspondence. 1833–1916).

28. *Village Record,* February 10, 1863.

29. *Village Record,* February 10, 1863.

30. John Forney to Abraham Lincoln, October 4, 1861 (The Abraham Lincoln Papers at the Library of Congress, Series 1. General Correspondence. 1833–1916).

CHAPTER THIRTEEN: MERE TRESPASSERS

1. *Jeffersonian,* April 11, 1863.

2. George W. Fahnstock., Diary, entry for February 5, 1863, Historical Society of Pennsylvania.

3. General Order No. 7, General Ambrose Burnside, Army of the Potomac, January 20, 1863, O.R. I, XXI, 127; Williams, T. Harry. *Lincoln and His Generals,* 194202.

4. *Harper's Weekly,* January 31, 1863.

5. Fahnstock, Diary, February 4, 1863, Historical Society of Pennsylvania.

6. John Marshall, *American Bastile,* 293–302.

7. Marshall, *American Bastile,* 437.

8. *The Press,* February 5, 1861.

9. *The Press,* February 5, 1863.

10. *The Press,* February 5, 1861. Italics added by the authors.

CHAPTER FOURTEEN: REPERCUSSIONS

1. *Jeffersonian,* April 20, 1861.

2. It is possible that James Wall contributed this column.

3. New York *World,* reprinted in the *Jeffersonian,* February 21, 1863.

4. *Mercury* (Philadelphia), reprinted in the *Jeffersonian,* February 14, 1863.

5. *The Press,* February 6, 1863.

6. Proclamation Suspending the Writ of Habeas Corpus, September 24, 1862, Basler, CW, V, 436.; Neely, *The Fate of Liberty,* 51.

7. John Forney to John G. Nicolay, December 1, 1862 (The Abraham Lincoln Papers at the Library of Congress, Series 1, General Correspondence. 1833–1916).

8. William Dusineberre, in "Civil War Issues in Philadelphia," states that this group "poured forth a volume of oratory and writing which marked the greatest political resurgence of socially prominent leaders in the city's history," 157–158.

9. Dusineberre, *Civil War Issues in Philadelphia:* 1861–1865, 59.

10. *Age,* May 8, 1863; *The Press,* May 8, 1863; William Dusineberre, in "Civil War Issues in Philadelphia," 158.

11. William Dusineberre, in "Civil War Issues in Philadelphia," 159; *Age,* May 9 and 11, 1863; *North American,* May 9 and 11, 1863; *Inquirer,* May 9 and 11, 1863; *Dispatch,* May 10, 1863.

12. *Reply of Hon. Clement L. Vallandigham, of Ohio, to Mr. Hickman, of Pennsylvania, on Democratic Loyalty to the Union; in the House of Representatives, February 19, 1862* (Washington: Congressional Globe Office, 1862). Vallandigham was accused of encouraging secession in the Baltimore *South.*

13. William Bradford Reed, *A Paper Containing a Statement and Vindication of Certain Political Opinions,* 26.

14. William Dusineberre, in "Civil War Issues in Philadelphia," 157–162. Seitter, John Reid, "Union City: Philadelphia and the Battle of Gettysburg," *Gettysburg Magazine,* No. 21; Fahnstock, George W., Diary, Historical Society of Pennsylvania, May 22, 1863; James

Wall served out his short term in the United States Congress from January 14 to March 3, 1863 where he spoke most defiantly on the defense of the Constitution. Like previous attempts, he lost his bid for reelection and resumed his law practice in Burlington, New Jersey, and continued to write for a number of newspapers. In 1864 he published "Speeches for the Times by Hon. James. W. Wall, of New Jersey," a collection of pre-war and wartime orations. In 1869 he moved to Elizabeth, New Jersey, where he died on June 9, 1872, at the age of 52.

15. William B. Reed to James Wall, August 15, 1863, Historical Society of Pennsylvania.

16. Letters of John Hay, August 14th, 1863

17. George W. Fahnstock, Diary, June 4, 1863, Historical Society of Pennsylvania.

18. Fahnstock, Diary, June 15, 1863, Historical Society of Pennsylvania.

19. John Reid Seitter, "Union City: Philadelphia and the Battle of Gettysburg," *Gettysburg Magazine*, No. 21; Charles Ingersoll said in a speech that "the people should vote Democratic if they wanted the war ended." Irwin Greenberg, "Charles Ingersoll: The Aristocrat as a Copperhead," *Pennsylvania Magazine of History and Biography,* 197.

20. *Appletons Annual Cyclopedia,* 1863, page 739. The Democratic Convention was held on June 17, 1863.

21. "Speech of Hon. J. Ross Snowden, delivered at Philadelphia, Thursday, September 17, 1863 (Philadelphia: Printed at the *Age* Office, 430 Chestnut St., 1863)."

22. *Appletons Annual Cyclopedia,* 1863, page 740. George Woodward lost to Andrew Curtin 269,496 to 254,171 votes. Walter Lowrie lost 17 to 16 in the Senate, and 52 to 48 in the House. Judges were directly elected by the state legislature at this time. Lowrie afterward practiced law in Pittsburgh before again taking the bench in western Pennsylvania, where he remained until his death in 1876.

23. Nicholas B. Wainwright, "Loyal Opposition in Philadelphia," Journal of Pennsylvania History and Biography, July 1964, 308.

24. "Speech of Hon. J. Ross Snowden, Delivered at Philadelphia, Thursday, September 17, 1863" (Philadelphia: Printed at the *Age* Office, 430 Chestnut St.).

25. *Jeffersonian,* March 7th, 1863.

26. William Bradford Reed, *Memories of Familiar Books, With a Memoir of the Author,* edited by Manton Marble (New York: E. J. Hale & Son, Publishers, 1876 (quotation from the edited memoir, p. xi).

27. Gerard St. John, "This is My Bar," *The Philadelphia Lawyer,* Winter 2002, Vol. 64, No. 4.

28. "Legends of the Philadelphia Bar," *The Philadelphia Lawyer,* Winter 2002, Vol. 64, No. 4. Biddle died in 1892.

29. *The Press,* February 6, 1863.

30. John Forney to Abraham Lincoln, May 12, 1863 (The Abraham Lincoln Papers at the Library of Congress, Series 1, General Correspondence. 1833–1916).

31. John W. Forney to William Fessenden, February 8, 1867, Library of Congress, Papers of John W. Forney, mm78021113.

32. Allen Johnson and Dumas Malone, ed. *Dictionary of American Biography, Volume VI* (New York: Charles Scribner's Sons, 1931), p. 526–27.

33. *Village Record,* May 5, 1863.

34. *Village Record,* May 10, 1864, November 15, 1864.

35. *Philadelphia Bulletin,* reprinted in the *Village Record,* October 29, 1864.

36. *Jeffersonian,* October 29, 1864.

37. *Jeffersonian,* May 6, 1865.

38. *Daily Local News,* March 12, 1881.

39. *The American Magazine,* 460–462 (CCHS).

40. *The House of Hodgson, Ownership for a Century* (CCHS).

INDEX